Aristotle's Economic Thought

Aristotle's Economic Thought

SCOTT MEIKLE

CLARENDON PRESS · OXFORD
1995

*This book has been printed digitally and produced in a standard specification
in order to ensure its continuing availability*

OXFORD
UNIVERSITY PRESS

Great Clarendon Street, Oxford OX2 6DP

Oxford University Press is a department of the University of Oxford.
It furthers the University's objective of excellence in research, scholarship,
and education by publishing worldwide in

Oxford New York

Auckland Bangkok Buenos Aires Cape Town Chennai
Dar es Salaam Delhi Hong Kong Istanbul Karachi Kolkata
Kuala Lumpur Madrid Melbourne Mexico City Mumbai Nairobi
São Paulo Shanghai Singapore Taipei Tokyo Toronto

with an associated company in Berlin

Oxford is a registered trade mark of Oxford University Press
in the UK and in certain other countries

Published in the United States
by Oxford University Press Inc., New York

© Scott Meikle 1995

The moral rights of the author have been asserted
Database right Oxford University Press (maker)

Reprinted 2002

ISBN 0-19-815225-6

To Kirsten

ACKNOWLEDGEMENTS

It is a pleasure to thank my friends and colleagues Pat Shaw and Chris Martin for reading large parts of the manuscript, and for much critical discussion. To Hillel Ticktin and Geoff Kay I owe a special debt for having introduced me to the murky depths of exchange value.

Some of the material has appeared in print before. I am grateful to the *Journal of Hellenic Studies, Polis,* the *Classical Quarterly, Phronesis,* and Basil Blackwell, for permission to make use of it here.

Lindsay Judson's article 'Aristotle on Fair Exchange' deals in part with an earlier article of mine on the same subject, which appeared in the *Journal of Hellenic Studies* in 1991, and which reappears in a slightly altered form as Chapter 7 of the present book. Judson's article also presents arguments addressing issues that are fundamental to the interpretation of Aristotle offered here, but it unfortunately reached me too late to be taken account of.

Translations are always from Ross, Rackham, Barker, or Irwin. On the few occasions when another translator has been used, this has been indicated in the text.

I acknowledge the granting of one term of study leave towards preparing the book by the Department of Personnel Services (Academic) of Glasgow University.

S.M.

Glasgow
1994

CONTENTS

ABBREVIATIONS

The works of Aristotle are abbreviated as follows:

Cat.	*Categories*
De Gen. An.	*De Generatione Animalium*
De Part. An.	*De Partibus Animalium*
EE	*Eudemian Ethics*
HA	*Historia Animalium*
Met.	*Metaphysics*
MM	*Magna Moralia*
NE	*Nicomachean Ethics*
Pol.	*Politics*
Rhet.	*Rhetoric*
S. El.	*De Sophisticis Elenchis*

INTRODUCTION

The influence of Aristotle's economic writing has been incalculably great, yet it amounts to fewer than half a dozen pages of the *Nicomachean Ethics* and the *Politics* in the Bekker text. It was the backbone of medieval thinking about commercial behaviour and matters that we would call 'economic'.[1] It still provides the foundation for Catholic social teaching, and it was an important influence in Islamic economic thought. It is usually held to be the first analytical contribution to economics, and histories of economic thought usually begin with it.[2] Aristotle's theory of money substantially informed treatments of the subject into the twentieth century, and most schools of modern economic thought have had claims of Aristotelian paternity made on their behalf, including Jevonian utility theory, mathematical economics, neo-classical economics, and Marxism.

The main texts are *NE*, 5. 5 and *Pol.*, 1. 8–10. The interpretation of them is now in a chaotic state. Even the object of Aristotle's inquiries is disputed. It has been seen as economic analysis, as entirely ethical and having nothing to do with economic analysis, and as snobbish political prejudice against traders and money-makers. The chapters are usually thought to lack intellectual cohesion, and to amount to little more than an expression of aristocratic anti-business attitudes. Few parts of the Aristotelian corpus are held in lower esteem, and they are seldom included in selected editions of Aristotle's works.[3]

The chaos has appeared only in the past 120 years or so. Over centuries of commentary the texts did not prove so troublesome. The ancient commentaries did not make such heavy

---

[1] On its role in medieval thought about commerce and money, see O. Langholm, *Wealth and Money in the Aristotelian Tradition: A Study in Scholastic Economic Sources* (Oslo, 1983).

[2] Plato is usually high on the list of honourable mentions, but he gets less attention because he is less systematic and analytical.

[3] See e.g. J. L. Ackrill (ed.), *A New Aristotle Reader* (Oxford, 1987).

weather of them, and neither did Aquinas, whose analysis of
NE 5. 5 is superior to most modern work.[4] The texts have not
been badly mangled in the transmission, the substance of the
chapters is not especially obscure, and the logic of the argument is not particularly difficult to unravel. Since the chaos is
of recent origin, perhaps its source lies nearer home, in some
feature of modern thought which was absent from the thought
of earlier times. If so, the obvious suspicion is that it will have
something to do with the modern subject of economics, which
has loomed so large in recent interpretation.

There has been a difficulty peculiar to our own time in coming to understand the nature of ancient society. It began to
show itself forcefully in the last quarter of the nineteenth century, just when economics made its first serious impact on the
study of antiquity.[5] Since then, the discussion of the social
nature of antiquity has generated a division between 'modernists' and 'primitivists', and the question at issue between
them has been the usefulness or otherwise of trying to comprehend antiquity in terms drawn from modern economic theory. The 'modernist' view is that the ancient economy is to be
understood as an early and restricted version of what we are
familiar with today, not as something different in kind, and
that it is to be studied by bringing to bear the same economic
concepts we use to study the economy of our own time.
Against this, Finley and others (the 'primitivists') have argued
that ancient 'economic' activity was indeed different in kind,
and that the use of modern economic concepts is fatal to our
attempts to understand it.

A powerful political agenda has lain just beneath the surface
of the dispute. Meyer made this quite clear from the beginning. He declared, with no attempt at concealment, that
'Athens in the fifth and fourth centuries stands as much under

[4] Aquinas, *Commentary on the Nicomachean Ethics*, trans. C. I. Litzinger (Chicago, 1964), i. 417–28, esp. 423 ff.

[5] An introductory account can be found in M. M. Austin and P. Vidal-Naquet, *Economic and Social History of Ancient Greece: An Introduction* (London, 1977), pt. 1, ch. 1. See also Éduard Will's account of the debate up until the Second World War in 'Trois quarts de siècle de recherches sur l'économie grecque antique', *Annales*, 9 (1954), 7–22.

the sign [*unter dem Zeichen*] of capitalism as England has stood since the eighteenth century and Germany since the nineteenth century.'[6] Such forthrightness is uncommon today, but if the terms of engagement have become less frank, the agenda is essentially unchanged.

The dispute extended to Greek 'economic' literature, and battle lines were drawn over the question of whether there is anything in Hesiod, Lysias, Xenophon, Aristophanes, Plato, Aristotle, the pseudo-Aristotelian *Oeconomica*, and the rest, that can properly be called 'economic' on any reasonable definition of the term. Aristotle's chapters are by far the most analytical and searching of the ancient 'economic' sources; indeed there is nothing else like them in Greek literature, and their interpretation has naturally been at the heart of this aspect of the dispute.

The most striking fact about surviving Greek literature dealing with what today we would call 'economics' is how little there is of it. Laistner's collection of the main texts, question-beggingly entitled *Greek Economics*, makes only a slim volume.[7] What there is of it, apart from Aristotle's contributions, is not in any sense theoretical or analytical, and more than one modern commentator has used such terms as 'banal' and 'commonplace' to describe it. Both sides of the dispute have had to have some explanation of these peculiarities.

On the modernist side it is claimed that it is hard to believe that the Greeks bothered less than we do about providing for life's needs and luxuries, and if that is what the study of economics is all about, as it is on some definitions, then it is surprising that the Greeks should have done as little of it as the primitivists claim. The Greeks were curious and inventive in just about everything else, so it is a mystery that they should

---

[6] E. Meyer, cited in H. Bolkestein, *Economic Life in Greece's Golden Age*, ed. E. J. Jonkers (Leiden, 1958), 148–9. When Meyer was writing, the SPD (Sozial-demokratische Partei Deutschlands—German social-democratic party), led by Kautsky, Bernstein, and Liebknecht, was growing vigorously and causing alarm. Bolkestein noted that Meyer's opinion, and its pretty clear underlying message that civilization is to be identified with the system of market economy or capitalism, was endorsed by many scholars, especially in Germany.

[7] M. L. W. Laistner, *Greek Economics* (London, 1923).

have been so apparently wanting in this one field, and this field of all fields. It is equally mysterious that economics, alone among the disciplines of modern thought, should appear to find so little foundation in the Greek heritage, which has been so profoundly influential almost everywhere else. The paucity and peculiarities of ancient economic literature, on this view, are not as great as they may seem, and they are to be explained by the restricted scale and undeveloped form of ancient economic activity, not to its being in any way different in kind.

On the primitivist side it is argued that there is one fundamental fact that makes all the difference: the Greeks did not have a market economy. Without that they could not have done any economic thinking, because market economy and economic thought are necessarily, and not accidentally, connected. The paucity of ancient economic thought, on this view, is even greater than it appears, because even those texts that have the strongest 'economic' flavour—Aristotle's—are really entirely ethical in character rather than 'economic' in any sense.

So Aristotle's 'economic' thought, in addition to its own intrinsic interest, has come to have a crucial position in this wider dispute about the character of antiquity. If even Aristotle's work is not 'economic', then no Greek writing is. Furthermore, Aristotle's reputation as the father of economics is at stake.

Finley begins his book *The Ancient Economy* with some observations about the *Short Introduction to Moral Philosophy* published in 1742 by Francis Hutcheson, Professor of Philosophy in the University of Glasgow and the teacher of Adam Smith. Book 3 of this work is entitled 'The Principles of Oeconomics and Politics', and it opens with three chapters on marriage and divorce, the duties of parents, children, masters, and servants, but it is otherwise exclusively devoted to politics. It is in Book 2, entitled 'Elements of the Law of Nature', that we find an account of property, succession, contracts, the value of goods and coin, and the laws of war. Finley comments that 'these were evidently not part of "oeconomics" ... Hutcheson was neither careless nor perverse: he stood at

the end of a tradition stretching back more than 2000 years
. . . The book that became the model for the tradition still represented by Hutcheson was the *Oikonomikos* written by the Athenian Xenophon before the middle of the fourth century BC.' This was a work of practical advice to the gentleman landowner about the sound management of an estate, its slaves, household, and land. Finley concludes: 'There was no road from the "oeconomics" of Francis Hutcheson to the *Wealth of Nations* of Adam Smith, published twenty-four years later.'[8]

If that is so, then questions about our own time are thrown into relief. If the Greeks thought only in terms of ethics, or *politikê* and *ethikê*, then they had only ethics as a source of reasons for public decision-making. In modern society based on market economy, swathes of the most important kinds of decisions have been removed from the field of ethics altogether, and transferred into the province of economics. The relation between economics and ethics is a contested matter, but opinion has swung decisively, certainly among economists in this century, towards the view that the relation is minimal or non-existent, and that economics is an independent science.

By the fourth century BC, Athens had developed the production and circulation of commodities, or exchange values, to a significant degree. Primitivists need not find this hard to swallow; anti-modernist reservations should be about the scale and significance of market relations, not about their existence.[9] I shall argue that Aristotle has a body of thought directed specifically at analysing that development. In the past century, an intense dispute has raged around the analysis of exchange value, between the friends and foes of market economy. Such fundamental strife seldom leaves classical studies unaffected, and this strife has been the underlying cause of the chaos in the interpretation of Aristotle.

[8] M. I. Finley, *The Ancient Economy* (Berkeley, 1973), 17–20.
[9] See M. I. Finley, 'Aristotle and Economic Analysis', in *Studies in Ancient Society* (London, 1974), 38 (orig. pub. in *Past & Present*, 47 (1970)) who does not dispute the production of commodities. The topic is discussed in Ch. 8.

Exchange Value: *Nicomachean Ethics,* 5. 5

☞ 1 ☜

Nicomachean Ethics, 5. 5 in recent decades has been read both as ethics and as economic analysis. On the ethical reading, most fully defended by Finley, the aim of the chapter is to arrive at a formula for fair exchange which accommodates Greek sensibilities about the inequality and status of the contracting parties. On the economic reading, the chapter is variously thought to be an attempt to explain the formation of market price, as Schumpeter thought; to show the substance of economic value to be utility, as Kauder and Soudek thought; or to show it to be labour, as Gordon, Ross, Hardie and others thought.

The text cannot bear much of the responsibility for this chaos of interpretation, because its argument is fairly straightforward. The *Nicomachean Ethics* is thought by scholars to be a reliable text, and most of whatever is wrong with it now was probably wrong with it in the third century BC. Book 5 itself is one of the three common books shared with the *Eudemian Ethics.* They are accepted Aristotelian doctrine, and the usual view nowadays is that both works are Aristotle's. Kenny has argued that the common books originally belonged to the *Eudemian Ethics* rather than the *Nicomachean Ethics,* and that the *Eudemian* has a good claim to be a late and definitive statement of Aristotle's ethical position.[1]

There are problems with the text, of course, and two of them should be mentioned now. The ordering of Aristotle's

[1] See A. J. P. Kenny, *The Aristotelian Ethics: A Study of the Relationship between the Eudemian and Nicomachean Ethics of Aristotle* (Oxford, 1978).

sentences is jumbled. But the dislocations do not obliterate the objectives of Aristotle's inquiry, or the strategy and detail of his argument. It is difficult to believe that the dislocations are the main cause of the interpretative chaos, because worse textual problems in Aristotle are overcome as a matter of routine.

The second problem is the interpretation of the ratio which Aristotle wants to govern the fair exchange of products, 'as builder to shoemaker, so many shoes to a house'. This is a notoriously intractable problem, and much of the interpretation of the chapter seems to depend on the solution to it. The low esteem in which the chapter is held by most commentators, who think it is too muddled to amount to much, is due partly to the confusion that has surrounded this ratio. In fact nothing important depends on it. The problems presented by the ratio have to do with Aristotle's discussion of justice, *dikaiosunê*, in the earlier chapters of Book 5, not with the substance of chapter 5 itself. It is a distinct problem, and discussion of it will be deferred until Chapter 7. The difficulty occasioned by the ratio is not a cause of the interpretative chaos but a part of it.

Today *NE* 5. 5 is not regarded as one of Aristotle's outstanding successes, and it has attracted a number of very unflattering appreciations. Finley's verdict is representative: 'that this is not one of Aristotle's more transparent discussions is painfully apparent'.[2] Soudek thought that it 'belongs to the obscurest parts of his writings', and refers to it as 'this dark passage in the *Ethics*'. Bonar refers to it as 'this much tortured passage', and so more or less does Langholm.[3] I think it can be shown that these views are exaggerated, and that Aristotle's work has been absurdly undervalued. It will also become clear, I hope, that the main reason for this is to be found in the economic beliefs which scholars have brought to the study of Aristotle.

---

[2] Finley, 'Aristotle and Economic Analysis', 33.

[3] J. Soudek, 'Aristotle's Theory of Exchange: An Inquiry into the Origin of Economic Analysis', *Proceedings of the American Philosophical Society*, 96 (1952) (reprinted in M. Blaug (ed.), *Aristotle (384–322 BC)* (Aldershot, 1991), 11–41), 45. J. Bonar, *Philosophy and Political Economy* (London, 1909), 40. Langholm, *Wealth and Money*, 48.

①value
②exchange
value

Aristotle divides what we would call 'economic value' into two parts, use value and exchange value, and exchange value becomes the uniting theme of *NE* 5. 5 and *Pol.* 1. 8–10. The distinction is the foundation of economic thought, and Aristotle was the first to draw it:

> with every article of property there is a double way of using it; both uses are related to the article itself, but not related to it in the same manner—one is peculiar to the thing and the other is not peculiar to it. Take for example, a shoe—there is its wear as a shoe and there is its use as an article of exchange; for both are ways of using a shoe, inasmuch as even he that exchanges a shoe for money or food with the customer that wants a shoe uses it as a shoe, though not for the use peculiar to a shoe, since shoes have not come into existence for the purpose of exchange. (*Pol.* 1. 9, 1257ᵃ6–13).

Sir Erich Roll writes that 'In these words, Aristotle laid the foundation of the distinction between use-value and exchange-value, which has remained a part of economic thought to the present day.'[4] Aristotle carries the distinction through much more rigorously than economists do today, and indeed, from the perspective of the Aristotelian tradition in philosophy, modern economics elides the distinction. It is pivotal in all Aristotle's economic thought. Just as he gives two definitions of value itself, so he is led to give two definitions rather than one of the fundamental economic concepts of wealth and exchange. Each of these concepts is given a use-value definition, and a contrasting exchange-value definition. The doubling-up of these definitions will be looked at again early in Chapter 3, and in Chapter 5 it will be seen that Aristotle gets into difficulty over the nature of money just because he is anxious to sustain a use-value definition of it, as well as an exchange-value definition, even though his own analysis suggests the conclusion that its nature is purely that of exchange value.

It will be useful to say something about both sorts of value at this point. The artefacts of human labour are intended to serve particular purposes. An artefact is designed and made to

---

[4] E. Roll, *A History of Economic Thought* (London, [1938] 1961) 34–5.

have just those qualities which make it useful for a particular purpose, and it is said to have value in use, or to be a use value, in virtue of that fact. But they can be exchanged as well as used, and if they become subjects of systematic commerce they acquire a second kind of value, value in exchange or exchange value. It is necessary to distinguish between occasional exchange, barter, or swops, and exchange that takes place within a system of exchange or a market. In the latter, but not in the former, things of one kind are systematically exchangeable with things of every other kind in definite and non-random proportions, according to a 'going rate'. Expressed in money, this going rate is price. The term 'exchange' will be reserved here for exchange that is systematic, and 'exchange-able' will be used to mean capable of systematic exchange.

def. of exchange

Use value is simply a matter of the natural properties of the artefact or product. Objects such as hammers, grain, loaves, or houses, are useful for particular purposes, and they are designed and made in order to meet particular needs: 'everyone who makes something makes it for some end or purpose. What is made is not itself the final end, only what is done is that' (*NE* 6. 1139ᵇ1 f.).

Exchange value, however, is not so straightforward. A given sum of money represents certain amounts of every kind of thing that is made. To use Aristotle's own examples, 5 minae = 1 house = 5 beds = so much food = so many shoes. These things are manifestly by nature incommensurable with one another, and so are the indefinitely wide variety of other things that can and do stand in these equations. The problem is to explain how they may be brought into equations at all. The relation of equality can hold between two things only if those things are commensurable in the first place. Objects which exchange in this way are things of different kinds, and being of different kinds they are by nature incommensurable, though they may be commensurable in some other way which does not have to do simply with their natural constitutions. It becomes Aristotle's main problem in the chapter to explain how this can be possible.

Book 5 of the *Ethics* deals with justice or fairness. Various

distinctions are made in the first two chapters, the third deals
with distributive justice, and the fourth with corrective justice.
The fifth, which concerns us here, deals with fairness in
exchange, and it opens with a brief criticism of the
Pythagorean view that justice in general is reciprocity.
Aristotle rejects this view as fitting neither corrective nor distributive justice. The purpose of this polemical preamble is
made clear immediately: the notion of reciprocity (*antipeponthos*) may not be adequate to account for corrective and distributive justice, 'but in associations for exchange justice in the
form of reciprocity is the bond that maintains the association'
(1132ᵇ31 f.). In other words, in the subject of the new chapter,
voluntary transactions for the exchange of goods, the appropriate form of justice is precisely a form of reciprocity.

At this point Aristotle takes the first step towards defining
the particular form of reciprocity that is appropriate in the context of exchange. He says it is 'reciprocity . . . on the basis of
proportion, not on the basis of equality' (τὸ ἀντιπεπονθὸς κατ'
ἀναλογίαν καὶ μὴ κατ' ἰσότητα, 1132ᵇ32–3). The reciprocity
must be of proportions of things, not the 'simple reciprocity'
of Rhadamanthys, which would mean giving one thing for one
thing (1132ᵇ25). It would not be fair for a builder and a shoemaker to exchange one house for one shoe, because a house is
too great or too much (*kreîtton*) to give for a shoe (1133ᵃ13).
So they must exchange in proportions, so many shoes to a
house.

Kreîtton usually means 'better than' or 'superior to'. To
translate it in this way here, however, could be misleading if it
suggests, as it has to some commentators, that Aristotle might,
at least in part, be concerned with the quality of products, or
even with the position of their producers in a hierarchy of status and inequality. There is little to be said for the view that
Aristotle has social inequality in mind anywhere in *NE* 5. 5,
though most modern commentators have assumed that he did
(the issue will be discussed in Chapter 7). The idea that
Aristotle has the quality of products in mind gains what cred-
ibility it has entirely from the misleading translation of *kreîtton*. Ross's translation of *kreîtton* at 1133ᵃ13 as 'better than' is

10

often accepted, as it is by Hardie, and Rowe offers the variation 'superior to'.[5] Von Leyden claims that the 'equalizing' of products in exchange includes quality as well as quantity.[6] There is no justification for the suggestion that Aristotle is thinking of differences of quality between products, either in the immediate context or elsewhere in the chapter. Aristotle's problems throughout are concerned exclusively with quantities. Differences of quality between products are never discussed, and no hint of them arises except in these mistranslations of *kreîtton*. Aristotle is making the assumption, quite reasonable in the context, that goods are of exchangeable quality and not inferior or defective things of their kind. In a comparable context in the *Magna Moralia*, which is undoubtedly a work of Aristotle's school, though not usually considered to be from Aristotle's own hand, the word *kreîtton* does not occur. Instead we find derivatives of *axios*, so that an expression like 'more value than' would be suitable at *MM* 1194ª18 and 25. It is better in this context to translate *kreîtton eînai* as 'to be too much' or 'to be worth more', because the context is the unfairness of exchanging one house for one shoe. Rackham has 'worth more than', and Dirlmeier 'hochwertiger ... als'.

Aristotle resumes (after a brief digression on the spirit of the Charites which will be discussed in Chapter 8 (3)) by asking how 'reciprocity of proportion' ($\tau\grave{o}$ $\mathring{a}\nu\tau\iota\pi\epsilon\pi o\nu\theta\grave{o}s$ $\kappa\alpha\tau$' $\mathring{a}\nu\alpha\lambda o\gamma\acute{\iota}\alpha\nu$) is to be achieved. His answer is that it is done by establishing 'equality of proportion' ($\tau\grave{o}$ $\kappa\alpha\tau\grave{a}$ $\tau\grave{\eta}\nu$ $\mathring{a}\nu\alpha\lambda o\gamma\acute{\iota}\alpha\nu$ $\mathring{\iota}\sigma o\nu$, *NE* 5, 1133ª10–11); that is, the proportions of shoes and houses to be exchanged should be equalized (*isasthênai*, 1133ª18, 1133ᵇ15–16). If that is done first, he says, and the exchange transacted on that basis, then the previous requirement of 'reciprocity of proportion' will have been met (1133ª10–12). So the development of his argument has now put him in this position: further progress in explaining what

[5] W. F. R. Hardie, *Aristotle's Ethical Theory* (Oxford, 1968), 196. C. J. Rowe, *The Eudemian and Nicomachean Ethics: A Study in the Development of Aristotle's Thought* (Proceedings of the Cambridge Philological Society Supp. 3; Cambridge, 1971), 101.

[6] W. von Leyden, *Aristotle on Equality and Justice* (London, 1985), 14.

Exchange Value: Nicomachean Ethics

fair exchange as 'reciprocity of proportion' (τὸ ἀντιπεπονθὸς κατ᾽ ἀναλογίαν) means now depends on explaining the meaning of 'equality of proportion' between products (τὸ κατὰ τὴν ἀναλογίαν ἴσον). How can it be possible, to use Aristotle's example at 1133ᵇ23 ff., that '5 beds = 1 house'?

This problem is soon seen to rest on another which is logically prior: if a certain quantity of one product is to have the relation of equality to a certain quantity of another, then the two kinds of product must be 'comparable in a way' (sumblêta pôs, 1133ᵃ19). This vague relation is more closely defined in due course as 'commensurability' (summetria, 1133ᵇ16, 18, 19, 22).

Aristotle knew that his theory of fair exchange is only as good as the solution he produces to this problem of commensurability. If he cannot say exactly how such diverse products can be commensurable, then he cannot say that a relation of equality can hold between proportions of them, and so his theory of fairness in exchange would collapse, and he knew it: 'If there were no exchange there would be no association, and there can be no exchange without equality, and no equality without commensurability' (οὔτ᾽ ἀλλαγὴ ἰσότητος μὴ οὔσης, οὔτ ἰσότης μὴ οὔσης συμμετρίας, 1133ᵇ17–18). Two-thirds of the chapter still remain, and they are devoted entirely to the problem of explaining how this commensurability is possible. Nothing more is said about fair exchange.

Aristotle is clear that the problem is inherent in the very nature of exchange. It arises because 'one man is a carpenter, another a farmer, another a shoemaker, and so on' (Pol. 3, 1280ᵇ20 f.).[7] He suggests that if like were exchanged for like—medical services for medical services for instance—there would be no problem. But the things exchanged are, of course, always different things: 'For it is not two doctors that associate for exchange, but a doctor and a farmer, or in general people who are different and unequal; but these must be equated. This is

---

[7] It is not anachronistic to attribute an understanding of the division of labour to Aristotle. It was understood before his time, and Plato makes clear in the discussion with Adeimantus in Rep. 2 that it was a commonplace to suggest that the polis came into being in the first place just to achieve the greater abundance of material goods that the division of labour makes possible, 369b–371e.

12

Exchange Value: Nicomachean Ethics

why all things that are exchanged must be somehow comparable' (*sumblêta pôs*, *NE* 5, 1133ª16–19) or 'commensurable' (*summetra*). This commensurability of things that are different by nature, which is logically presupposed by proportions of them being equated, is the core of the problem which exchange presents to economics, though it is one which economists have rarely confronted head-on.

It is necessary to bear in mind the positions in metaphysics from which Aristotle is writing. His metaphysics is not prominent on the surface as he develops his argument in the chapter, but as is usually the case in his inquiries, it underlies his thought and governs its direction. The problem of the commensurability of goods in exchange presents itself acutely for Aristotle because of his theory of substance and categories. Things that exist are of two kinds. There are individual entities like a human, a house, a loaf, a sheep, or a bed, which are substances. And there are features that are not substances: qualities, quantities, and relations, like white or just, long or heavy, north or large, which though they exist, exist in a different way; not as substances do, but as attributes or modifications of substances.[8] These categories are the irreducible orders of being, and a quality, say, can no more be reduced to a quantity or a relation, than the number 9 can be reduced to a horse. Aristotle's philosophy is not conducive to overlooking or eliding differences of kind between things or attributes.

His problem is occasioned by the fact that a relation of equality or inequality can exist between things only if they are commensurable. When things are commensurable, they are so in respect of some property they share, and if that property is measurable, they may be said to be equal or unequal in respect of it. Two things cannot simply be said to be be 'equal' without qualification. They can be, and be said to be, equal in length, for example, provided they are both extended in space. But the possibility of a relation of equality holding between

---

[8] For an account of these Aristotelian ideas, which are central to the argument of this chapter, see Michael Frede, 'Categories in Aristotle', in his *Essays in Ancient Philosophy* (Oxford, 1987) (orig. pub. in D. O'Meara (ed.), *Studies in Aristotle* (Washington, 1981), 1–24).

them rests on the fact that they are already commensurable in both being spatially extended. A sound cannot be said to be equal to a sausage, because there is no property in respect of which the two things are commensurable. What is a measurable property in one, intensity or length, is not a property possessed by the other, so they are not commensurable and cannot be equated.[9]

The most various things are equated in exchange; things that are measured in respect of quite different properties, and on quite different kinds of scales: weight, length, area, duration, and so forth.[10] Yet, in spite of these manifold differences, they are equated in exchange. So the problem is to discover the property they must all share, in virtue of which they are commensurable, as they must be since they are equated.

Aristotle's first problem is to determine the order of being into which this commensurating property falls. Consider the category of quality. Things can be compared in quality, and when they are, they may be said to be like or unlike: 'it is in virtue of qualities only that things are called *similar* and *dis-*

---

[9] Böhm-Bawerk criticizes Marx for having followed Aristotle in thinking that an equality is involved in the relation of commodities: 'Marx had found in old Aristotle the idea that "exchange cannot exist without equality, and equality cannot exist without commensurability" ', and he complains that 'this appears to me to be very old-fashioned', *Karl Marx and the Close of his System*, ed. P. M. Sweezey (London, 1975), 68. Carver has suggested that Aristotle's equations of commodities 'are not equations in the strict mathematical sense, in his view, but useful expressions for a rough commensurability in terms of demand', *Marx's Social Theory* (Oxford, 1982), 88. The text tells heavily against this suggestion. If Aristotle intended '5 beds = 1 house' to be an equation of demands, then perhaps the '=' might not be strict equality. But I shall argue in this chapter and the next that Aristotle does not think that commodities become commensurable in virtue of demand, and so if the belief that he did is the reason for thinking that Aristotle intended the equality to be rough rather than strict the suggestion falls. It is difficult to see much in the idea that the equation of commodities is rough rather than strict. Relationships like '5 beds = 1 house', and '1 house = 5 minae', have the logical properties of equality, reflexivity, symmetry, and transitivity, and the relation of equality is defined in terms of those properties. Russell writes that 'All kinds of equality have in common the three properties of being reflexive, symmetrical and transitive, i.e., a term which has this relation at all has this relation to itself; if A has the relation to B, B has it to A; if A has it to B, and B has it to C, A has it to C', *The Principles of Mathematics*[2] (London, 1903), 159.

[10] Among Aristotle's own examples there are even some that seem not to have measurable properties at all, like medical services, *NE* 5, 1133ª17. These present peculiarly difficult problems, but Aristotle does not discuss them.

14

similar; a thing is not similar to another in virtue of anything but that in virtue of which it is qualified. So it would be distinctive of quality that a thing is called similar or dissimilar in virtue of it', (*Cat.* 11ᵃ16–19). The proposition '5 beds = 1 house', however, does not assert a likeness or unlikeness between beds and houses. So whatever it is in virtue of which they are commensurable cannot be a quality.

The relation Aristotle has identified between proportions of houses, food, and shoes, is one of equality, and he writes of quantity in the *Categories* that 'most distinctive of a quantity is its being called both equal and unequal . . . For example, a body is called both equal and unequal, and a number is called both equal and unequal, and so is a time . . . But anything else—whatever is not a quantity—is certainly not, it would seem, called equal and unequal. For example, a condition is certainly not called equal and unequal, but, rather, similar; and white is certainly not equal and unequal, but similar. Thus most distinctive of a quantity would be its being called both equal and unequal' (*Cat.* 6ᵃ26–36).

Beds and houses are qualitatively different things, and in respect of some qualities they may be said to be similar, and in others dissimilar. But proportions of houses, food, and shoes, cannot occur in equations like '5 beds = 1 house' as proportions of things considered qualitatively, because then they could only be said to be similar or dissimilar, not equal or unequal. Since the expression '5 beds = 1 house' asserts a relation of equality, then beds and house cannot occur here as qualified entities, but only as quantities of something qualitatively the same. They are quantities of some one thing, and that thing will be identical with that in virtue of which they are commensurable (supposing there is only one). Aristotle's problem is to discover what they can be quantities of; this is what the problem of commensurability amounts to. Things are incommensurable as substances or use values. They are commensurable as exchange values, so the problem is to find what kind of quantity exchange value is.[11]

---

[11] This was the interpretation Marx gave of *NE* 5. 5; see *Capital*, i (London, 1976), 151. Marx was the first modern author, subsequent to the appearance of political

Exchange Value: Nicomachean Ethics

(It is worth adding here that, since beds, houses, and so on, are described and discriminated as use values by reference to their qualities, it follows that the commensurability cannot derive from their existence as use values, because it is not a matter of quality. This consideration has a bearing on the question of whether Aristotle is, as he has often been claimed to be, the forefather of the utility theory of value; this will be returned to in later chapters. It is also worth noting that Aristotle nowhere considers exchange value under the category of relation, as economists since Bailey in 1825 frequently have. The metaphysical reasons why it would be impossible for Aristotle to do this are discussed in Chapter 6 (1) below.)

What Aristotle has in mind can be illustrated by a price list in which things for sale are drawn up in a left-hand column, and their prices opposite them in a right-hand column. The left-hand column is a list of useful things, each qualitatively different from the others: a mattress, a knife, so much bread. These are things that have by design particular qualities in virtue of which they are useful for particular purposes and meet particular needs, and they are inherently different. In the right-hand column there are simply numbers, 1, 5, 100, 11, each representing so much exchange value expressed in money. In the left-hand column there are a number of particular natures; in the right-hand column there is a single 'nature', qualitatively undifferentiated, and the entries in the column simply denote different amounts of it.

The metaphysical import of the argument is that use value

economy as an apparently independent science, to offer an interpretation of Aristotle's economic thought. His debt to Aristotle's analysis of exchange and money is even more evident in *A Contribution to the Critique of Political Economy* (London, 1971), 27, 42, 50, 68, 117, 137, 155. Marx's own treatment of use value and exchange value follows the logic of Aristotle's analysis; he employs the same metaphysical apparatus, which distinguishes between categories of quality, quantity, and relation, and his analysis is founded on those distinctions. This reflects a general debt Marx owes to Aristotelian metaphysics, which pervades his work as a whole, and sets him apart from most other modern writers in the social sciences, whose metaphysical debt is usually owing to Hume and the Enlightenment. This matter is discussed briefly in the final chapter. An illuminating discussion of the relation between Aristotle and Marx is to be found in W. J. Booth, *Households: On the Moral Architecture of the Economy* (New York, 1993), pt. 3.

and exchange value fall into different logical categories. 'Use value' as a collective term collects substances as substances, that is, as the things they are by nature, and so use value is necessarily qualitatively differentiated and heterogeneous. Exchange value, when it exists, inheres in those same substances, but since the term denotes a quantity it cannot collect them in the same way, as substances. It must do so without regard to differences between them as substances. A quantity is undifferentiated, homogeneous, and lacks species. A difference of logical category is the most basic difference possible, and it is irreducible. Yet these two different characters, use value and exchange value, both exist in the same collection of articles or products. Consequently, a product which is the subject of exchange must be the bearer of two quite distinct natures which are conjoined, as it were, in a hypostatic union.

   For Aristotle, strictly, only a substance can have a nature. So, strictly, exchange value cannot have a nature because it is not a substance. But it does have what Aristotle calls a 'the what it is', or 'the what it is of the thing' (*ti esti*), which is what he is trying to track down. When we speak of the *ti esti* of exchange value, we attribute *per se* being to it, as we attribute *per se* being to justice when we say what justice is, or that there is such a thing as justice. This *per se* being is identical with the accidental being we attribute to something when we say that it is just, or that it is an exchange value.[12] It seems fair, because of this, to regard it as no more than a matter of terminology to speak of exchange value having a nature. Whatever kind of feature of things something may be, whether quality, quantity, or relation, it will be subject to analysis of the kind that Aristotle gives to substances, that is, analysis in terms of form and matter, the four causes, and so forth. Exchange value is susceptible to such metaphysical analysis just as place is in Book 4 of the *Physics,* and abstract mathematical objects in *Metaphysics M* and *N.*

   Aristotle's problem is to identify 'the what it is' of exchange value, and in the *Ethics* he makes little further progress with

---

[12] See Frede, 'Categories in Aristotle', in his *Essays in Ancient Philosophy*, 41–4.

it, beyond considering and ruling out a number of possible solutions. But in the *Politics* Book 1, he adds further clarification to the distinction between the natures of use value and exchange value, in the course of analysing the different forms of exchange, and the effects that the pursuit of exchange value as an end has on the behaviour of people in the polis. The metaphysical gulf Aristotle establishes between use value and exchange value makes it quite impossible, consistently with his metaphysics, to achieve the object of the neo-classical theory of Jevons, Gossen, Walras, and Menger. That object was, in Schumpeter's words, to show 'what A. Smith, Ricardo, and Marx had believed to be impossible, namely, that exchange value can be explained in terms of use value'.[13] To achieve such a merger, it is necessary to reject the Aristotelian metaphysics of substance and attribute. Hume, among other anglophone authors of the early modern period, did this. He denounced substance as 'an unintelligible chimaera', made no distinctions between categories of predicates, and avoided logic altogether except to give judgement on what kind of knowledge it can be according to the canons of empiricist epistemology.[14] Economists have shown a marked predilection for Humean metaphysics.

From *NE* 5, 1133ª19 onwards Aristotle tries different ways of explaining the commensurability of commodities, first trying money, and then need (*chreia*), as the commensurating element. The details of these attempts will be looked at in the next section, but first it is necessary to take some bearings. These subsequent efforts of Aristotle's seem more recognizably economic, because they centre on the more obviously economic notions of money and demand (really need, *chreia*, but this is often misconstrued as an economic notion because of its persistent mistranslation as 'demand'). For that reason, commentators on *NE* 5. 5 in search of Aristotle's economic thought, have focused their attention almost entirely on these passages, often with a view to deciding which modern school

---

[13] J. Schumpeter, *History of Economic Analysis* (Oxford, 1954), 911–12.
[14] D. Hume, *A Treatise of Human Nature*, ed. L. A. Selby-Bigge (Oxford, 1946), 222.

of economics they most closely resemble. This has meant that Aristotle's metaphysical analysis of the problem of what we would call 'economic value', which we have so far been examining in this chapter, has been largely overlooked. This in turn has meant that the passages in which Aristotle tries to find solutions to the problem have generally been misconstrued, because the problem has not been grasped accurately enough, in spite of Aristotle's care in formulating it. Insensitivity to the metaphysics, especially the logic of categories, has played a part in this.

This failure to observe the role of metaphysics in Aristotle's economic thought has had serious consequences for understanding the more overtly economic discussions in the *Politics*, 1. 8–10. These chapters have a strong 'economic' flavour, because their subject-matter is trade, wealth, exchange, money, and interest. They have commanded the lion's share of attention, understandably, from Aristotle's economic commentators. But subject-matter is not always a good guide in judging the nature of an inquiry, and in this case it is a misleading one. Insufficient attention to the metaphysics of Aristotle's discussion has been a major cause of errors of interpretation, and due attention to it creates serious doubts that Aristotle's inquiries can be considered 'economic' in any sense at all. The object of Aristotle's inquiry is to discover the nature of a property, exchange value, and an inquiry with that kind of aim is a metaphysical inquiry. The fact that the property inquired into has its home in economics does not make the inquiry itself an economic one. The category distinction Aristotle has established between use value and exchange value is fundamental to his analysis of wealth, exchange, and money in the *Politics*; this will become clear in Chapters 3, 4, and 5. That distinction of category is established in his formulation of the metaphysical problem about the nature of the commensurability of goods in exchange, or exchange value, and if the metaphysics is overlooked, the category distinction can be missed, as it usually has been. Without it, the distinctive character of Aristotle's economic thought, and the analytical strength and coherence of its insights, will be lost altogether. His position may or may not ultimately be defensible, but before that can be decided, it has to be established exactly what his position is.

The casual attitude commonly taken towards the metaphysics underlying Aristotle's discussion is made more serious by the fact that its consequences play neatly into what is already a strong disposition in modern thought to see no very significant distinction between use value and exchange value. On the contrary, neo-classical economics is founded on the view that in the notion of utility there is a conceptual connection between them. Following the decline of classical political economy in the first half of the nineteenth century, the economic thought that followed it became occupied with attempts to throw a bridge across what, until then, had been seen as an unbridgeable gap between use value and exchange value. This had already become evident in the first half of the century in the work of Bailey and Mill, even before the appearance of neo-classical economics. Interpreters of Aristotle since then, with only a single exception, have succumbed in one degree or another to the temptation to assimilate Aristotle to the view which became orthodox in the wake of these bridging operations. The temptation is a strong one and, without sufficient attention to the metaphysics of Aristotle's inquiries, it is all too likely to prove irresistible. Spengler is one of the few commentators to have noticed that in Aristotle's account the relation between use value and exchange value is not one of untroubled harmony. Without reflecting on it further, Spengler assumes this to be a weakness: Aristotle had been 'unable to reconcile his observations concerning exchange value with those pertaining to what later came to be called "value in use" '.[15] But this was not due to an incapacity on Aristotle's part; he had reasons for thinking an ultimate reconciliation to be beyond anybody's capacities, because it followed from his analysis that it was logically impossible. Spengler is making the assumption that the metaphysical basis of the neo-classical reconciliation of use value and exchange value is metaphysically watertight, and that Aristotle had

---

[15] J. J. Spengler, 'Aristotle on Economic Imputation and Related Matters', *Southern Economic Journal* (1955), 371–89.

simply failed to discover what Bailey, Jevons, and Menger suceeded in discovering.

⌐ 2 ⌐

The development of Aristotle's thought from *NE* 5, 1133ª19 is fertile yet contradictory. He repeatedly changes direction as he tries, now in one way and now in another, to explain commensurability, and in the end he gives up the task as epistemically impossible. In the process, he introduces two themes which appear and reappear, interweaving with each other and with observations that contradict them. The first of these is the idea that money, just because it is a common measure of everything, makes products commensurable, and thus makes it possible to equalize them. The second is the idea that it is need (*chreia*) which makes things commensurable.

His first thought is that money was introduced in the first place precisely because 'all things exchanged must be able to be compared in some way'. He says that 'It is to meet this requirement that men have introduced money . . . for it is a measure of all things . . . how many shoes are equal to a house or to a given quantity of food' (1133ª19–22); 'it is necessary for everything to be expressed in money' (1133ᵇ14–15).[16] The idea is that the existence of a common standard of measurement itself constitutes commensurability, and makes the equalization of goods possible. The same thought reappears later at

[16] The sentence is διὸ δεῖ πάντα τετιμῆσθαι, 1133ᵇ14–15, and it is sometimes translated in ways that obscure the thought. Rackham has 'Hence the proper thing is for all commodities to have their prices fixed', and Ross has 'This is why all goods must have a price set on them.' Both versions are reminiscent of Burnet's view: 'τετιμῆσθαι, "to have a price put on them", not, we may be sure, by "the higgling of the market". Aristotle no doubt is thinking of a tariff prescribed by the magistrates', *The Ethics of Aristotle* (London, 1900), 229 n. Burnet in turn may have in mind Grant's suggestion that 'the process of equalisation' is done 'by "demand" or the higgling of the market', *The Ethics of Aristotle* (2 vols.; London, 1874), ii. 120 n. Against all this Finley is justified in insisting that 'What Aristotle actually says is "Therefore it is necessary for everything to be expressed in money, *tetimesthai*" ', 'Aristotle and Economic Analysis', 36, n. 35. Special magistrates regulated imports of grain, but there was no practice of authority setting prices, as Rackham and Burnet imply.

1133^{b}16: 'Money, then, acting as a measure, makes goods commensurate and equates them'; and a third time a few lines later: 'There must, then, be a unit . . . for it is this that makes all things commensurate, since all things are measured by money.'

This idea is inadequate and, though Aristotle appears to return to it once or twice in the ordering of the chapter as we have it, he finally drops it. It is inadequate because simply establishing a measure cannot itself create a commensurability between things that are in themselves incommensurable. Indeed, measure presupposes commensurability. The things must be commensurable in respect of some shared property in the first place, otherwise there would be nothing for the measure to measure. The possibility of a measure presupposes commensurability. The invention of money, by designating one commodity (say silver) as the money commodity, which will act as the equivalent of everything else, cannot create commensurability, because there is no logical difference between '5 beds = 1 house' and '5 beds = x amount of silver'. The second equation is just as problematical as the first, and in just the same way. Exchanging five beds for x amount of silver raises the same problem as exchanging five beds for one house.[17] Aristotle recognizes this: 'Let A be a house, B ten minae, C a bed. A is half of B, if the house is worth five minae or equal to them; the bed, C, is a tenth of B; it is plain, then, how many beds are equal to a house, viz. five. That exchange took place before there was money is plain; for it makes no difference whether it is five beds that exchange for a house, or the money value of five beds', 1133^{b}23–8. Furthermore, the possibility of a measure not only presupposes commensurability, but presupposes it in just the dimension where measurement is to be made. Aristotle says that 'the measure is always homogeneous with the thing measured; the measure of spatial magnitudes is

---

[17] Barker, one of the few writers to notice the problem of commensurability, confuses the matter by suggesting that money 'makes objects commensurable, and renders an equation possible', invoking a putative solution which Aristotle explicitly rejects at 1133^{b}27–8, *The Political Thought of Plato and Aristotle* (London, 1906), 379, n. 2. Barker's own analysis is discussed in Ch. 6.

a spatial magnitude, and in particular that of length is a length, that of breadth a breadth, that of articulate sound an articulate sound, that of weight a weight, that of units a unit', (*Met. I*, 1053ª24 ff.). A measure does not create the property in things which it measures. Measures of length do not create spatial extension.[18]

Aristotle's second idea runs alongside the first in the text of *Nicomachean Ethics* as we have it, but it is easily extracted, and it is clearly intended as an alternative solution. The idea is that the standard is in reality *chreia*, because this is what 'holds everything together'. But he observes that since *chreia* lacks a unit, it cannot serve as a measure, and for this reason Aristotle drops this second idea too. He passes immediately to the third idea.

Repeating the need for a common dimension and measure of things, he now separates the dimension (*chreia*) from the measure (money), and makes money a conventional representation of *chreia*.[19] We now appear to have not just a means of measurement (money), but a dimension of commensurability (need) for things to be measurable in; or to put it another way, we appear to have a commensurable dimension (need) which, though capable of variable magnitude, lacks a unit of measure until money provides one. 'This standard is in reality *chreia*, which is what holds everything together . . . but *chreia* has come to be conventionally represented as money' (1133ª 25–31).[20] He goes on a little later to argue for giving this role

---

[18] Mulgan fails to notice the problems Aristotle has with this first attempt at a solution, and identifies the attempt as the solution: 'In business relationships the process of equalizing [the relationship between the partners] is made easier by the use of units of money which allow the value of different goods to be compared numerically', *Aristotle's Political Theory* (Oxford, 1977), 14.

[19] Here, and in subsequent citations from Rackham and others, I have left the word *chreia* (need) in place of the translation 'demand', which, together with 'supply' (for which there is no real Greek equivalent), is now a theory-laden term carrying a weight of suggestion that cannot be attributed to a Greek author. The use of 'demand' might also suggest falsely that a modern subjective or utility theory of value might be attributable to Aristotle. Finley's criticism of the kind of anachronism exemplified in this use of 'demand' is cited below, in Ch. 2, and the nature of the anachronism is discussed in Ch. 8.

[20] Barker, again, is one of the few commentators to have noticed the connection that this discussion of *chreia* and money has to the problem of commensurability. But,

to *chreia:* 'That *chreia* holds everything together in a single unit is shown by the fact that when men do not need one another ... they do not exchange ... This equation must therefore be established' (1133ᵇ6–10). Something which 'holds things together' (*sunechei*), or which brings and holds the needy parties together in exchange, is not the same as a dimension in which the things exchanged are themselves commensurable (*summetra*), and Aristotle finally drops this second attempt at a solution for that reason. None the less, it is a stronger candidate than his first idea that the common measure of money creates commensurability out of thin air.

There are reasons for doubting, not only that *chreia* is the solution to Aristotle's problem, but also that Aristotle himself believed it to be the solution. First, Aristotle always frames his problem as having to do with the things exchanged (how can 1 house = 5 beds?), and *chreia*, though it may take those things as its objects, is a condition of the people exchanging them, not a property of the things. It is characteristic of the chapter as a whole, in its thought and in its textual detail, that it bears exclusively on products and not at all on persons except as makers of their different products. This will be argued in detail in Chapter 7, so it will only be mentioned here. There is nothing in the chapter to support the idea that Aristotle would be prepared to accept a solution based on *chreia*, and there is one passage, which we shall come to shortly, which decisively rules out any possibility of such a solution. Secondly, he never links

because he confuses Aristotle's *chreia* with the modern 'demand', he is led to confuse the commensurability of products with the 'holding together' (*sunechei*) of associations for exchange and of the association of the state (which Aristotle twice says is something that *chreia* or need does), and with the problem of a measure, which are quite separate problems, as I shall argue in Ch. 2. He writes: 'To Aristotle demand, or need χρεία ... Holding men together as a single principle ... is the one *common measure* by which the goods they exchange are valued. The nexus is also the standard. In a state of barter demand serves by itself as the measure of value, and makes couches commensurable with house, producing the equation 5 couches = 1 house. Except for demand, there is no commensurability and therefore no possibility of equation. But where men have passed from an economy in kind to a monetary economy, by agreeing upon a "currency", that currency may be said to form the concrete and objective form of the subjective standard formed by demand. It makes objects commensurable, and renders an equation possible—not in itself (for only demand can do that), but as the representative of demand', *Political Thought of Plato and Aristotle,* 379, n. 2.

chreia with commensurability (*summetria*). He has two other problems which he connects it with. He wants to know what is the 'one thing' by which all things are measured (δεῖ ἄρα ἑνί τινι πάντα μετρεῖσθαι, 1133ª25–6), and he suggests that this is in truth *chreia*. He also wants to know what it is that holds everything together (πάντα συνέχει; συνέχει ὥσπερ ἕν τι ὄν), by which he means what it is that brings and holds people together in associations for exchange, and he twice suggests that it is *chreia* that does this (1133ª27–8, 1133ᵇ6–7). But he never says of *chreia* (as he does of money) that it creates commensurability, and, since he frames the problem as having to do with the products rather than their owners, he would have been wrong if he had. These considerations do not decisively rule out *chreia* as Aristotle's solution to the problem, but they are strengthened in their tendency to do so by a third, which is decisive even on its own.

Aristotle does not produce a knock-down argument against a *chreia* solution, but he does produce a statement which unequivocally rules it out. At 1133ᵇ19–20 he says that 'really and in truth (τῇ μὲν οὖν ἀληθείᾳ) it is impossible for things so very different to become commensurate [*summetra*], but in respect of *chreia* they admit of being so sufficiently [*hikanôs*]'. Sufficiently for what? Rackham suggest that he means sufficiently 'for practical purposes', which seems reasonable since the implied contrast is with 'really and in truth'; or perhaps he means sufficiently for 'holding together' [*sunechei*] the association, which he twice says is something that *chreia* does (1133ª27–8, 1133ᵇ6–7). Either way, Aristotle's final thought is that for purposes of *epistêmê*, or scientific knowledge, houses, beds, shoes, and food, cannot really be commensurable at all. He had obviously been looking for an answer that would be satisfactory for *epistêmê*, and he is now admitting that he has not found one. *Chreia*, therefore, in Aristotle's view, provides no basis for an answer, any more than money did.

Aristotle is giving up as a bad job the attempt to explain commensurability, or, as it might be glossed today, to find a full metaphysical account of exchange value. His statement is tantamount to an admission that he does not know what is equalized in fair exchanges of food, shoes, and houses (though his theory of fair exchange still commits him to saying that something is), and that he does not know what exchange value is in his technical sense of 'what x is'. His admission of failure, and his reasons for making it, constitute a serious obstacle for those interpretations which have sought, on the basis of *chreia*, often mistranslated as 'demand', to read into Aristotle some version of modern subjective or utilitarian value-theory. Van Johnson, for instance, explicitly set out to overturn Marx's view that Aristotle formulates the problem of economic value but does not solve it. Van Johnson argues that Marx was wrong, because Aristotle held that ' "demand" ($\chi\rho\epsilon\acute{\iota}a$) . . . is at bottom the real unit of value', and that '$\chi\rho\epsilon\acute{\iota}a$ is as much a "concept of value" for Aristotle as labor is for Marx'.[21] But he fails to give any consideration to the passage in which Aristotle admits his inability to find any way in which products can be commensurable. Sir Ernest Barker, among many others, took a similar view: 'As Aristotle himself tells us, value depends on demand, on felt utility', and he too fails to consider Aristotle's explicit admission of failure.[22] (Aristotle's treatment of *chreia* will be dealt with separately in the next chapter.)

In the ordering of the chapter as we have it, Aristotle once again says of money that 'such a standard makes all things commensurable, since all things can be measured by money'. He follows this with the argument which really eliminates money as the solution: money does not create commensurability, because proportionate exchange existed before money did, and in any case the exchange value of a house is expressed *indifferently* by the five beds for which it exchanges, or by the money value (five minae) of five beds, and this is clearly in his mind in the passage at 1133ᵇ23–8 cited earlier: 'Let A, for instance, be a house, B ten minae, C a bed. A is half of B if a house is worth five minae or equal to them; and C, the bed, is a tenth of B. It is clear, then, how many beds are equal to one house—five. This is clearly how exchange was before there was

21 Van Johnson, 'Aristotle's Theory of Value', *American Journal of Philology*, 60 (1939), 450.

22 Barker, *Political Thought of Plato and Aristotle*, 384.

currency; for it does not matter whether a house is exchanged
for five beds or for the currency for which five beds are
exchanged'. The analysis ends at this point, and Aristotle
returns to the question of justice as a mean between too much
and too little, political justice, and so forth.

At the end of it all, he has succeeded in formulating a problem to which he can find no acceptable solution. We are still
in the dark about how to bring about fairness in an exchange,
because he has failed to explain either how exchangers are to
equalize proportions of their goods, or, since he cannot explain
the commensurability of products, how such equality is theo-
retically possible. None the less, the achievement of the chapter is formidable, since it formulates with unrivalled clarity the
problem which lies at the heart of the theory of value, and
hence at the heart of economic theory.

- Aristotle admitted he failed
@ defining exchange value
- He then relies on justice to
do the rationalizing of
exchange (fairness, but
he provides no
definition)

2

Chreia and Demand: *Nicomachean Ethics*, 5. 5

☞ 1 ☜

The most favoured of the economic interpretations of Aristotle portrays him as the father of subjective, utilitarian, or neo-classical value-theory.[1] The utilitarian interpretation itself will be dealt with in Chapter 6, but its main textual basis, the role of *chreia* in Aristotle's analysis, must be dealt with here because it depends on the interpretation of the text of *NE* 5. 5, which the previous chapter has been concerned with.

The founders of neo-classical theory—Jevons, Menger, and Walras—are often thought to have had only Gossen as their forebear. Both Kraus and Kauder, however, have suggested that the Austrians Menger and Böhm-Bawerk were both influenced by Aristotle.[2] Soudek offers the most detailed case for this sort of view, and he concludes that Aristotle 'anticipated by more than two thousand years Jevons' theory of exchange'.[3] This follows as a conclusion from Soudek's beliefs, first, that

---

[1] This view is heavily represented in Blaug's 1991 anthology, *Aristotle (384–322 BC)*, which collects fourteen articles on Aristotle's economic thought from the late nineteenth century to the present.

[2] E. Kauder, 'Genesis of the Marginal Utility Theory from Aristotle to the End of the Eighteenth Century', *Economic Journal*, 63 (1953), 638–50 (reprinted in Blaug (ed.), *Aristotle (384–322 BC)*, 42–54); O. Kraus, 'Die aristotelische Werttheorie in ihren Beziehungen zu den Lehren der modernen Psychologenschule', *Zeitschrift für die gesamte Staatswissenschaft*, 61 (1905), 573–92, and id., *Die Werttheorien* (Brünn, 1937) chs.3 and 40. A sceptical examination of the views of Kraus and Kauder is given by Spengler, 'Aristotle on Economic Imputation'. The influence of Aristotle on Menger is dealt with by Barry Smith, 'Aristotle, Menger, Mises: An Essay in the Metaphysics of Economics', *History of Political Economy*, suppl. to vol. 22 (1990), 263–88 (reprinted in B. Caldwell (ed.), *Carl Menger and his Legacy in Economics* (Durham, 1990), 263–88).

[3] Soudek, 'Aristotle's Theory of Exchange', 46.

Chreia *and* Demand: Nicomachean Ethics

Aristotle held *chreia* to be the commensurating element between commodities, and second, that Aristotle held also that what is equalized in exchange is 'want satisfaction'.[4] Van Johnson and Barker, among others, attribute the same sort of view to Aristotle.

The mistranslation of *chreia* as 'demand' helps this inter-pretation, and it has been very common since the last quarter of the nineteenth century. Grant, writing in 1874, and thinking Eudemus to be the author of Book 5 of the *Nicomachean Ethics*, thought that it showed 'indications that the Peripatetic School had been busy in working out the beginnings of political economy as made by Plato and Aristotle', and that ' "demand" (χρεία) . . . or in other words the higgling of the market . . . determines how many shoes are to be given for a house'.[5] Newman, in 1887, suggests that things exchanged 'even if in truth so diverse as to be incommensurable, must be commensurable in relation to demand'.[6] Barker, in 1907, suggests that 'To Aristotle demand, or need (χρεία), holds men together in an association for exchange.'[7]

Ross and Rackham both introduce 'demand' into their translations several times, including in a crucial context at 1133ª27, and the false suggestion has been readily followed by many commentators since. Hardie merely transmits Ross's mistaken speculation: 'Ross, in his note on 1133ª16 in the Oxford Translation, sees rightly, as had Ritchie, that the comparative values of producers *must* in Aristotle's view here mean the comparative values of their work done in the same time. He does not make *explicitly* the point that, since prices are fixed by the market, the value of the producer is only a disguised form of the demand for his product.'[8] Rackham goes to

---

[4] Ibid. and 60.   [5] Grant, *Ethics of Aristotle*, ii. 119 n.

[6] W. L. Newman, *The Politics of Aristotle* (4 vols.; Oxford, 1887–1902), i. 42.

[7] Barker, *Political Thought of Plato and Aristotle*, 379, n. 2.

[8] Hardie, *Aristotle's Ethical Theory*, 196, italics added. The 'value of producers', which Hardie mentions, is a reference to Aristotle's ratio of producers A : B, 'as builder to shoemaker', which is supposed to set the standard for the fair exchange of shoes and houses D : C, according to Aristotle's formula A : B :: D : C. This is discussed in Ch. 7 below. Even an author as careful as Langholm allows 'demand' as the translation of *chreia* to pass without comment; see his *Wealth and Money*, ch. 4. Irwin notes that Hardie (*Aristotle's Ethical Theory*, 198) 'moves from talk of needs to talk of

29

great lengths to inject the anachronism. He translates δεῖ ἄρα τοῦτο ἰσασθῆναι, ('this, then, must be equalised'—Irwin; 'this equation must therefore be established'—Ross) at 1133ᵇ10, as 'This inequality of demand has therefore to be equalised.' Aristotle has just been saying that the fact that exchange takes place depends on each producer needing the products of the other, so the context does not in the least suggest the reference of the demonstrative pronoun *touto* to be 'this inequality of demand', and at no point does Aristotle use such an expression for the pronoun to refer to in the first place. It is entirely a figment of Rackham's imagination. The reference is to equalizing the products δ and γ mentioned a few lines earlier at 1133ᵇ5.

There is greater sensitivity now than there used to be to the danger of anachronistically injecting the modern economic concept, partly due no doubt to Finley's warnings; he observes, for example, that 'the semantic cluster around *chreia* in Greek writers including Aristotle, includes "use", "advantage", "service", taking us even further from "demand" '.⁹ This traditional mistranslation, though it helps the utilitarian interpretation, is not essential to it. Soudek, himself a stout defender of that interpretation, notes with equanimity that 'The word ἡ χρεία has been persistently translated with "demand" '.¹⁰ Finley, even though he objects to the mistranslation of *chreia* as 'demand', nevertheless seems to endorse part of the utilitarian case in accepting that *chreia* has the central role of being that in virtue of which shoes and houses are commensurated and equalized: they must, he says, 'be "equalized somehow", by some common measure, and that is need

the " 'demand' which springs from those needs", without exploring the relation between demand and need', *Aristotle's First Principles* (Oxford, 1988), 626, n. 11.

⁹ Finley, 'Aristotle and Economic Analysis', 33, n. 22. See also Irwin's warning note on 1133ᵃ27 in his translation of the *Nicomachean Ethics*, 335. The mistranslation, and a utilitarian reading, is to be found also in Rowe, *Eudemian and Nicomachean Ethics*, 102. The utilitarian misreading of Aristotle has passed into other areas too; see e.g. Carver's view that Aristotle's equations of commodities 'are not equations in the strict mathematical sense, in his view, but useful expressions for a rough commensurability in terms of demand, a factor extrinsic to the thing itself', *Marx's Social Theory*, 88.

¹⁰ Soudek, 'Aristotle's Theory of Exchange', 60.

(*chreia*)', though the 'somehow' may well be intended to allow for Aristotle's final fall-back position of a non-epistemic commensurablity which is 'sufficient' for practical purposes.[11]

The case for the utilitarian interpretation rests entirely on the use Aristotle is alleged to make of the notion of *chreia* or need. It became clear in the previous chapter how little Aristotle is inclined to consider *chreia* as the property which makes houses, beds, shoes, and food commensurable. His search for an explanation of commensurability ended with the admission of frustration that 'really and in truth [τῇ μὲν οὖν ἀληθείᾳ] it is impossible for things that are so very different to become commensurate at all' (1133^{b}19–20). In an ideal world this would be enough to remove entirely the idea that Aristotle thought anything was the basis of commensurability, and *a fortiori* that he thought *chreia* was. But the little more that he has to say about *chreia* has been thought to provide enough to justify the claim that Aristotle was the father of the utility theory of value.

He does not identify *chreia* as the property which makes products commensurate 'really and in truth', but he does give it the role of making them commensurate 'sufficiently' (*hikanôs*, 1133^{b}20). It is not entirely clear what he means by this. Rackham, as we saw, suggests that he means sufficiently 'for practical purposes'.[12] This is reasonable because in the context 'sufficiently' is contrasted with 'really and in truth', so that Aristotle would be saying that for strict purposes of *epistêmê* or scientific knowledge, there is no commensurability, though for some other, non-epistemic purpose, perhaps a practical one, there is something like it. If that is what Aristotle is saying, then it is comparable with Adam Smith's handling of the incommensurablity of different sorts of labour. Smith did not establish a basis of commensuration for different labours,

---

[11] Finley, 'Aristotle and Economic Analysis', 33, with n. 22. Langholm gives *chreia* (*indigentia*) the role of that which is equalized: 'in the *Ethics* (as well as in the *Politics*, following Plato) he [Aristotle] makes it clear that it is the mutual needs of the exchangers which brings them together in the first place, and the arrangement of the text as we (and the scholastics) have it indicates that it is need (*indigentia*) which is the "equalizer" as well', *Wealth and Money*, 48.

[12] H. Rackham, *The Nicomachean Ethics* (London, 1926), 287.

Chreia ≠ commesurability
but it does make it
sufficient (practical)

but took what emerged from the higgling of the market as 'sufficient for carrying on the business of common life'.[13]

It is necessary to look carefully at the role Aristotle gives to *chreia* in *NE* 5. 5, and it will be useful to start by recapitulating the structure of his discussion. It involves four problems: equalizing, commensurability, measuring, and holding together. It is important to keep these apart until it is clear how Aristotle intends to connect them. The problems are: (1) explaining the equalizing, or making equal, of the proportions in which things are exchanged so that the condition of fairness is met, namely, equality of proportion (τὸ κατὰ τὴν ἀναλογίαν ἴσον, 1133ª10–11); (2) explaining the commensurability (*summetria*) which is logically presupposed by those equalities; (3) explaining the measure and the unit used in quantifying the commensurable dimension which is shared by products; (4) explaining the holding-together (*sunechei*) of divided labours within associations for exchange and within the association of the polis.

The first solution he suggests to the second of these problems, commensurability, is that money achieves it because it measures everything. Aristotle does not settle for this theory, and later in the chapter he rejects it with the observation that exchange took place before there was money, and that it makes no difference whether it is five beds that exchange for a house or the money equivalent of five beds (1133ᵇ26–8). So he thinks that products are commensurable independently of money. This accords with *Politics*, 1, where, as we shall see in Chapter 3, money itself is treated as a product of the development of exchange relations that are already established, and not as a condition of their coming into being, as the first theory would entail. He is right to reject the theory, because if a

---

[13] Smith writes that 'it is not easy to find an accurate measure either of hardship or ingenuity. In exchanging indeed the different productions of different sorts of labour some allowance is commonly made for both. It is adjusted, however, not by any accurate measure, but by the higgling and bargaining of the market, according to that sort of rough equality which, though not exact, is sufficient for carrying on the business of common life'. A. Smith, *The Wealth of Nations*, ed. Edwin Cannan (2 vols.; London, 1904), i. 33. Ricardo does the same in *The Principles of Political Economy and Taxation*, ed. P. Sraffa (Cambridge, 1986), 20; see Ch. 9 (1).

32

[margin annotations: "money ≠ make things equal"; "Exchange happened before $"]

range of things is effectively measured in some way, we may infer that they are commensurable, but they have to be commensurable first, otherwise measurement would not be possible. The measure cannot be what makes them commensurable.

Rackham interpolates the idea of a 'standard' indiscriminately into his translation of several of these passages in a way that invites confusion by obscuring the distinction between a measure and a commensurating property. He also suggests that this supposed standard is to be identified with *chreia* (which he translates as 'demand'), and this is misleading in giving a stronger theoretical role to *chreia* than is justified. For example, at 1133ᵇ6–10 Aristotle says ὅτι δ᾽ ἡ χρεία συνέχει ὥσπερ ἕν τι ὄν, δηλοῖ ὅτι ὅταν μὴ ἐν χρείᾳ ὦσιν ἀλλήλων, ἢ ἀμφότεροι ἢ ἅτερος, οὐκ ἀλλάττονται ... δεῖ ἄρα τοῦτο ἰσασθῆναι, which Rackham translates as 'That it is demand which, by serving as a single standard, holds such an association together, is shown by the fact that, when there is no demand for mutual service on the part of both or at least one of the parties, no exchange takes place between them ... This inequality of demand has therefore to be equalized'. Aristotle's ὥσπερ ἕν τι ὄν is not well translated as 'by serving as a single standard', and the expression 'as a single unit' given by Ross and Irwin is better. There is no reason to connect *on* with *chreia*, and if a connection had been intended, *on* would presumably have had the feminine form *ousa*. Aristotle never gives *chreia* the role of a standard, only the role of what 'holds things together' in the little *koinônia* of the exchange between A and B, and in the big *koinônia* of the polis.[14]

Aristotle starts his second attempt at a solution at 1133ᵃ25, saying that *chreia* is the one thing by which everything is

[14] Rackham falsely injects 'standard' again at 1133ᵃ25–6 in translating δεῖ ἄρα ἑνί τινι πάντα μετρεῖσθαι as 'it is therefore necessary that all commodities shall be measured by some one standard'. Ross's 'this equation must therefore be established' is a better translation of δεῖ ἄρα τοῦτο ἰσασθῆναι than Rackham's 'this inequality of demand has therefore to be equalized' (1133ᵇ10). Aristotle has not mentioned any inequality of *chreia* for the pronoun *touto* to refer to, and it refers rather to the equalization of shoes with food mentioned a few lines earlier at 1133ᵇ4–6. There is no indication in the text that Aristotle meant that *chreia* is what is equalized. Indeed he goes on to deny it.

measured (δεῖ ἄρα ἑνί τινι πάντα μετρεῖσθαι).[15] He says less about this theory than the first, and what he does say has to do with 'holding together' the associations in a single unit (ἡ χρεία, ἣ πάντα συνέχει, 1133ᵃ27; ἡ χρεία συνέχει ὥσπερ ἕν τι ὄν, 1133ᵇ6–7). At no point in the chapter does he connect *chreia* with *summetria*, or suggest that *chreia* is what makes products commensurable, except for the one passage in which he says that it makes them commensurable 'sufficiently' (*hikanôs*), and that idea immediately follows the admission that they are not 'really and in truth' commensurable at all (1133ᵇ19–20).

Chreia looks more promising as a suggestion about what might do the 'holding together', whether this is interpreted as meaning holding the two parties together in an exchange, or as holding together shoemaker, builder, farmer, and divided labour generally, in the polis, as might seem to be justified by 1133ᵇ6–7, 'now clearly need holds [an association] together as a single unit, since people with no need of each other, both of them or either one, do not exchange, as they exchange whenever another requires what one has oneself'. But it is less promising as a measure, which he suggests it to be at 1133ᵃ25 f, because, as he goes on to recognize, *chreia* lacks a unit.

Aristotle is in a difficulty. He has tried two solutions, neither of which works. The money solution is strong as a theory about the measure of values, but weak as a theory about commensurability. The *chreia* solution's strengths and weaknesses are the other way round. It is stronger-looking on commensurability but weak on the measure because *chreia* has no unit.

Aristotle tries to get out of his difficulty with a third idea, in which he tries to combine the strengths of the two failed attempts while avoiding their weaknesses. He proposes that money should be seen as the conventional representation of *chreia*, so that *chreia* is the basis of commensurability and money is the measure of it. He says that '*chreia* has come to be conventionally represented by money; this is why money is called *nomisma*, because it does not exist by nature but by custom (*nomos*)', 1133ᵃ28–31. This stroke seems to get round both

---

[15] The sections in which it is advanced are dislocated: 1133ᵃ26–33, 1133ᵇ6–8 and 18–20.

Chreia *and Demand:* Nicomachean Ethics

(1) the difficulty of having money as the basis of commensurability, and (2) the difficulty of having the unit-less *chreia* as the measure, by (3) combining the two theories deftly into a third with the strength of each and the weakness of neither. The idea would be this: *chreia,* not money as he suggested earlier, makes things commensurable, but it lacks a unit and so cannot be the measure. On the other hand, money cannot make things commensurable because things have to be commensurable before money can express their value, but it does have a unit and so can serve as the measure. If money and *chreia* are connected, one being said to be the conventional representation of the other, then the two together provide both commensurability and measure.[16] But Aristotle repudiates this solution too because 'in truth it is impossible for such different things to become commensurate' (*summetra*) epistemically and strictly speaking, 'but in respect of *chreia* they may admit of being so sufficiently' (1133ᵇ18–20).

This admission creates problems. First, why are products after all in truth incommensurable? The reason Aristotle gives is that they are too different. But that might not seem to be enough of a reason because he knew they were different from the beginning. Secondly, why can *chreia* only make them commensurable 'sufficiently', and sufficiently for what? Once these questions are asked, it may no longer seem certain or even clear which question *chreia* is meant to answer.

Aristotle's admission of failure at 1133ᵇ18–20 has to be taken at face value. It is unambiguous, it cannot be made to

---

[16] Moreau regards this as Aristotle's final position: 'Il est requis pour l'évaluation des objets échangés qu'ils soient tous commensurables; or, le principe de leur comparaison réciproque, c'est en réalité le besoin. C'est le besoin, ou son corrélatif l'utilité, qui est le dénominateur commun de tous les services', 'Aristote et la monnaie', *Revue des études grecques,* 82 (1969), 360. See also Éduard Will's view that 'Aristote est très précis: *ce n'est pas la monnaie en soi qui est la commune mesure, c'est le besoin;* la monnaie n'est qu'un étalon conventionnel destiné à exprimer en termes quantitatifs la valeur du besoin'. Will goes on to offer an interesting, but less than convincing, parallel between Aristotle and Marx: 'La pensée d'Aristote est ici curieusement parente de celle de Marx . . . Parenté plus dialectique que foncière, dira-t-on, car, si l'on substitue à la notion marxiste de *travail matérialisé* la notion aristotélicienne de *besoin matérialisé,* on enlève à la pensée de Marx son ferment révolutionnaire. Sans doute.' É. Will, 'De l'aspect éthique des origines grecques de la monnaie', *Revue historique,* 212 (1954), 219, original italics.

mean anything other than what it says, it cannot be wished away, and it is in a way just what we should have expected him to say. We might have expected him to think that products are incommensurable on general metaphysical grounds, at least if they are considered naturally, that is, in terms of the qualities that properly belong to them by nature. According to the theory of substance which is the anchor of his thought, each sort of thing has its own nature, form, *ergon, telos,* and definition, and these are specifically different from one kind of thing to another. The weight of his philosophy would be against a strong expectation of finding commensurability of the kind that would resolve the problem he sets himself in *NE* 5. 5, given the diversity of natures among products and activities, particularly if the commensurating property were thought to be one which products have by nature or *phusei.* (It is no doubt considerations of this kind that have led so many commentators to attribute a notion of 'labour' to Aristotle.[17])

What the metaphysics of substance and attribute leads us to expect is indeed the view of products that Aristotle takes in the *Politics,* as we shall see in Chapter 3. The point or *telos* of an artefact is to serve some purpose. Its nature as an entity lies in its natural properties, including those which make it useful, or in virtue of which it is a use value. Its nature does not include its exchange value, which is not in this sense a natural property. As use values, products differ in quality, but as exchange values they differ, not in quality, but only in quantity.

The problem is serious. Perhaps Aristotle was not after all asking the question (A), how different products can be strictly commensurable in the first place, or was not making it the primary objective of his inquiry. Perhaps he was asking another

---

[17] Ritchie, Ross, Hardie, Schumpeter, and Gordon do this; see Ch. 7 (2). Labour fits the bill well. Products are all artefacts and so products of labour, and this promises a commensurable property that the things themselves have by nature. However attractive the suggestion may be, it is no more than a conjecture, because there is not the slightest hint in the text that Aristotle intended it, in spite of the fact that the examples he considers are almost all artefacts. It is an unconvincing conjecture because the Greeks had nothing like a general notion of labour which is so commonly taken for granted today as a 'factor of production'. The impossibility of labour being given this commensurating function by Aristotle, for reasons to do with his theory of action, is discussed in Ch. 9 (1).

question altogether (B), how, or from what point of view, products can be treated as commensurable enough to allow exchange and the holding-together of the polis.

There is a case to be made for this view. 'Holding together' is, after all, a matter of serious concern to Aristotle. He knows that the division of labour and private exchange are fundamental conditions of polis life, where 'one man is a carpenter, another a farmer, another a shoemaker, and so on' (*Pol.* 3, 1280^{b}20 ff.). In Book 5 of the *Ethics* he is more concerned about fair exchange than about any other form of justice for that reason. He calls it 'the salvation of states' (1132^{b}33), and in later works he twice refers back to this judgement. He cites it more or less word for word in the *Politics* (1261^{a}30–1), with an explicit acknowledgement of its source in the *Ethics*, and a version of it appears in the *Magna Moralia*, 1194^{a}16 ff. If 'holding together' were really Aristotle's paramount concern, then strict epistemic commensurability would be secondary. And if that were so, then a property like *chreia*, which is no good for the strict commensurability of products because it inheres in the exchangers rather than the products, would do.

Other considerations too might seem to support such a view. (1) It is the second question, about holding together, rather than the first, about strict commensurability, which Aristotle's *chreia* finally answers. (2) He never explicitly says that *chreia* makes things commensurable, only that it holds together, and makes things commensurable sufficiently for that. (3) If he had been looking for an answer to the first question, that is, looking to find how things could be commensurable strictly or 'in truth', then he should be expected to search among the properties they have by nature. But this is not what he does. His first attempt is based on money, which, as he says twice, exists by convention not by nature, and his second is based on *chreia*, which is not a property of the products at all, but a state of those who buy and sell them. (4) It can be inferred that Aristotle distinguishes the two questions (A) and (B), and it would seem reasonable to suppose that he intends to address a problem he believes to be soluble, not one that he might be construed to believe to be insoluble. The view that products are incommensurable is one that we might in any case expect him to hold, and it seems unlikely that he realizes its application to his inquiry for the first time just at *NE* 5, 1133^{b}18–20. To suppose that he was asking the first question, it would seem, is to suppose that he was asking how incommensurable things can be commensurable. So he must really have been asking the second and soluble one, namely, how things can be sufficiently commensurable to make exchange and 'holding together' possible.

This reading could no doubt be made more plausible still, but there is no point trying, because it founders on the fact that Aristotle does ask the first question. He not only asks it, he organizes his entire inquiry around it. His conception of fairness in exchange requires it, since that conception entails equalizing the proportions of shoes and food to be exchanged. Everything in the chapter is based on the idea that exchange involves equations like '5 beds = 1 house = 5 minae', and he says that there would be no exchange without equality, and no equality without commensurability. If he were to follow singlemindedly what we might take to be the bent of his metaphysics in not asking the first question and denying commensurability, then he would have had to deny these equations, and there is no sign whatever that he wanted to do that. Quite the contrary: in holding that in exchange, products are related in equations as commensurable quantities, he had to accept that in exchange the beds do not differ in quality from the house. He had then to explain how that is possible; that is what the first question asks, and his whole inquiry is aimed at answering it. It is not possible to construe the logic of the chapter in any other way, and to construe it as having primarily to do with 'holding together' is not a serious possibility.

Such a reading would also entail a dramatic change of direction in Aristotle's thinking. The suggestion would be that he is shifting to something like a neo-classical notion of utility, which is concerned with the satisfaction a subject derives from possessing or consuming an object. But his entire analysis, in *Pol.* 1. 8–10 just as much as in *NE* 5. 5, is based on a contrast between exchange value and a classical notion of use value which is concerned with the object and not with the state of satisfaction of the consuming subject. No such change is flagged in the chapter, and his analysis, and indeed the bent of his philosophy, gives us no reason to expect one. This is too much to explain away, even if the text itself gave any direct support for the suggestion.

Aristotle is pressed from two sides: from the equalities ('5 beds = 1 house'), and from the doctrine of substance. He is attributing to products two natures which are incompatible: those products are on the one hand qualitatively different and incommensurable, and on the other hand they are qualitatively the same, commensurable, and differ only as quantities. The headway he makes in dealing with these relationships in the *Ethics* comes to a grinding halt with his conclusion at 1133^{b}18–20 that they cannot after all 'really and in truth' be commensurable at all. His claim that *chreia* makes things commensurable 'sufficiently' must be construed as an attempt to salvage what he can from the chapter.

Utilitarians, naturally, have interpreted Aristotle's *chreia* line as answering the first question, about strict commensurability. They have argued, or usually assumed, that Aristotle holds that *chreia* (construed as 'demand', 'utility', or 'want-satisfaction') makes products strictly or epistemically commensurable rather than just 'sufficiently', and in that way they have brought Aristotle broadly into line with the neo-classical theory of value.[18] This confusion has been made easier by the facts, first that in *NE* 5. 5 Aristotle has so many questions and so few answers, and secondly that he does not clearly or explicitly distinguish all the questions in his mind. The reader may easily persuade himself that an answer to one question is an answer to another. Aristotle wants to know (1) How do you get fairness and equality into exchange? (2) What is equalized in fair exchange? (3) What is commensurable between products? (4) How is the magnitude of the commensurating property measured? (5) What is the unit of measure? (6) What holds exchangers together? and (7) what holds the polis together?

[18] Von Leyden omits notice of the word 'sufficiently (*hikanôs*)' in his account of this passage, thus misrepresenting its meaning entirely, *Aristotle on Equality and Justice*, 15.

Chreia *and Demand:* Nicomachean Ethics

The utilitarian interpretation has not distinguished these questions carefully enough.

An apparent and tempting advantage of the *chreia* line is that it might give us a better idea idea of how to get fairness into exchange than the chapter otherwise provides. If it were *chreia* that is equalized between 5 beds and 1 house, then we would have some account of the equalization of proportions by which Aristotle specifies fairness. Even so, the account would be incomplete unless we also had a way of establishing that the *chreia* of one equals that of the other, and that would not be easy to find. We might imagine it to be brought about simply by the parties agreeing proportions for the transaction, but in that case, whatever they agree will be an equalization of *chreia* and so be fair. This is not very convincing. It would be strange if Aristotle were suggesting that whatever is agreed is fair. If that was what he had in mind, the chapter could have been a lot shorter, and it need have raised none of the questions that occupy him, particularly the question of how to make each exchange fair by making the things exchanged equal. We should need a lot of persuading that Aristotle thought, as modern writers of the epoch of market economy often have, that fair exchange and actual exchange necessarily coincide. Hobbes thought so, and he took a heavy swipe at the Aristotelians for being so obtuse as not to appreciate that nothing could be fairer than a contract.[19] Aristotle certainly held nothing of this kind, and it is difficult to imagine any Greek doing so. Aristotle's conception of the unjust man (*adikos*), who is 'grasping and unfair', is that he is 'unequal' (*anison*), and his act is unequal (*NE* 1129ᵃ32–3). He was well aware that

---

[19] 'Justice of Actions, is by Writers divided into *Commutative* and *Distributive*: and the former they say consisteth in proportion Arithmeticall; the latter in proportion Geometricall. Commutative therefore, they place in the equality of value of the things contracted for; And Distributive, in the distribution of equal benefit, to men of equall merit. As if it were Injustice to sell dearer than we buy; or to give more to a man than he merits. The value of all things contracted for, is measured by the Appetite of the Contractors: and therefore the just value, is that which they be contented to give . . . To speak properly, Commutative Justice, is the Justice of a Contractor; that is, a Performance of Covenant, in Buying, and Selling; Hiring, and Letting to Hire; Lending, and Borrowing; Exchanging, Bartering, and other acts of Contract.' *Leviathan*, ed. R. Tuck (Cambridge, 1991), 115.

although contracts are entered into voluntarily, they can nevertheless be unfair and unequal. This is partly what he has in mind in his account of Thales the Milesian, who, from his reading of the heavens, foresaw a bumper olive-harvest and surreptitiously rented the wine-presses ahead of time to give himself a temporary monopoly when the harvest came. He made a lot of money and confounded his taunters who had said his learning was obviously useless because he was poor. Aristotle also tells the story of the man of Sicily who made 11 talents by buying up all the iron from the mines so that when the merchants came he was the sole seller (*Pol.* 1, 1256ᵃ6–36).

The crucial question that a defender of the utilitarian interpretation has to answer is: how are we to understand Aristotle's statement that 'really and in truth it is impossible for things so very different to become commensurate, but in respect of *chreia* they admit of being so sufficiently' (*NE* 5, 1133ᵇ19–20)? Is it to be taken as (1) advancing a theory of value or commensurability based on need which is epistemically satisfactory in the strict sense, or as (2) an admission of frustration and failure in the attempt to find a theory of commensurability which is epistemically satisfactory in the strict sense? The first of these cannot be made to fit the chapter, and the cost of trying is to make nonsense of its logic and detail. *Chreia* does not have the position in Aristotle's argument which it would need to have if the utilitarian interpretation were to be made at all plausible. However roughly one is prepared to manipulate the text, and even on the most favourable assumptions, the *chreia* line still cannot be made to fit convincingly.

The utilitarian interpretation is not the only one which fails in this way. Any interpretation which seeks to find a theory of value in Aristotle must founder on the fact that he fails to find a solution to the problem of commensurability, and on his explicit admission of failure. If, as he says, things cannot really be commensurable at all because they are too different, then it follows that there is no commensurability, and in that case nothing can be the basis of it. *Chreia* is ruled out, but so too is labour, which several authors have tried to identify as

41

Aristotle's preferred basis of commensurability. In Chapter 6 we shall consider further the case against interpretations which try to attribute to Aristotle a utilitarian theory of value, and in Chapter 9 (1) I will argue against attributing a labour theory to him. There are only two possible bases on which to seek a solution to the problem of economic value, use and labour, since it is through the needs they satisfy and the efforts they embody that objects have human connections and become social objects. Since Aristotle rejects utility, and since he has no notion of labour, he cannot have a theory of economic value at all.

Aristotle cannot have a theory of economic value.

☞ 3 ☜
Exchange: *Politics*, 1

In *Politics* 1. 9 Aristotle looks at exchange in a different way. On the face of it he seems to be listing and distinguishing different forms of exchange: barter, or exchange without money; the use of money in exchange as a way of getting something that is needed; buying and selling to make money; and usury, or the lending of money at interest. This discussion of the types of exchange is usually treated as if it were a series of discrete discussions lacking proper theoretical cohesion. This is certainly wrong, because there is a strong theoretical unity in the chapter. Alternatively, if any kind of unity is perceived, it is thought to be a unity brought about solely by Aristotle's ethical concerns, and particularly by his concern with what is natural and unnatural. There is an important element of truth in this, but it cannot be clearly expressed, or the proper place of Aristotle's overriding ethical concerns rightly identified, unless the logic and structure of his analysis of exchange are correctly grasped in the first place.

Aristotle's discriminations between these different forms of exchange are not all of the same kind. They are not all discriminations between accidentally different ways of doing essentially the same thing, nor are they all discriminations between accidentally similar ways of doing things that are essentially different. He is discriminating in both ways at once. On the one hand he connects the different forms of exchange internally in a theoretical framework. The treatment consists partly in an analysis of the evolution of exchange relations over time through successive forms, which he sees as increasing in sophistication, and partly in an investigation of the nature of exchange value, which adds to that of *NE* 5. 5 by considering its effects on human thought and behaviour. On the other hand he subjects each form of exchange to an examination which is intended to reveal the end, aim, or *telos*, inherent in its form. In the course of this he finds that there is no single end which all forms of exchange serve alike. He finds that there are two distinct ends, and that some forms of exchange serve one and some the other. He evaluates the compatibility of each of these ends with the end of the *koinônia*, or community, of the polis, the good life for man. Aristotle's object is to show the nature of exchange value, the course of its development as it evolves through successive forms, the changing role of money in that evolution, and the effects these changes can have on *ethikê* and *politikê* in the polis, and on the ability of its citizens to see clearly what the proper end of polis life should be.

The general outline of Aristotle's discussion is familiar ground. The connecting theme is the process, which he sees as natural to man, in which people co-operate in the use of their common human capacities to make or grow things that will satisfy their needs. Today we would call this production. He calls it *oikonomikê*, or the art of household management. The word is a derivative of *oikos*, meaning a dwelling or household, and Aristotle means to suggest that *oikonomikê* is by nature the business of households, and households more or less like Greek ones. Greek writers tend not to distinguish between the family and the household as a productive unit. He holds that the family is a natural unit; that its parts include not only 'husband and wife, father and children', but master and slave as well; and that the polis 'is made up of households' (1253^{b}1 ff.). So where we might think of production in an abstract sense, free of any particular institutional implication, Aristotle thinks of it as connected with the *oikos* and the family.

The introductory discussion from *Pol.* 1, 1256^{a}1 to 1256^{b}26 is about the natural process of producing food and the other things required for life's needs so that there is 'enough'. The expression Aristotle uses at 1256^{b}4 is *to autarkês eînai*, and the usual translation of *autarkês* as 'self-sufficient' is not always appropriate. The main meaning Aristotle gives it is that of 'having enough', and its secondary meaning is that of being 'independent of others', though the priority in Greek is generally the other way round according to Liddell and Scott. Aristotle defines it as 'that which on its own makes life worthy of choice and lacking in nothing' (*NE* 1, 1097ᵇ14–15). When the term carries both meanings, it does not always carry them equally. The context should decide which meaning, if either, should be emphasized in translation, but in practice translators of the *Politics* often use 'self-sufficient' without regard to context. This causes Aristotle's thought to be rendered inaccurately in several places, and 1256ᵇ4 is one of them. The context of the discussion is deficiency, not dependency, and *autarkês* here primarily means having enough, and only secondarily, if at all, independence of others.[1] The difference can be important. To use as an example a set of connections that will be important later: Aristotle holds that a polis should be *autarkês*, that a polis needs wealth to be *autarkês*, that wealth is part of the good life, that wealth consists of tools or useful things, that these are limited in size and number by the ends they serve, with the consequence that the good life and its constitutive ends set the standard for deciding how much wealth is enough. This set of connections is not easily established if *autarkês* is translated as 'self-sufficient', with the suggestion that the independence of the polis is what is at issue.

Aristotle begins by considering the different kinds of food there are, and the different kinds of lives people lead

---

[1] Roll registers the point accurately in distinguishing Aristotle's two kinds of *chrêmatistikê*: 'Men may exchange without being engaged in the unnatural form of supply, the art of money-making. They would in that case exchange only until they had enough', *History of Economic Thought*, 35. Booth makes the point well, *Households*, 50–1. See also W. J. Ashley, 'Aristotle's Doctrine of Barter', *Quarterly Journal of Economics*, 9 (1895), 337: the natural sort of exchange ('ἡ μὲν τοιαύτη μεταβλητική,— he cannot help calling it μεταβλητική) "is not *against* nature (παρὰ φύσιν), and is not a variety of Crematistic (in the bad sense), since it is for the filling-up of that sufficiency which is according to nature" (εἰς ἀναπλήρωσιν γὰρ τῆς κατὰ φύσιν αὐταρκείας ἦν,—the making up of that full equipment of the household with the necessary implements of the art of οἰκονομική which he has just explained to be "*true* wealth"). Booth, who tends to emphasize independence ('autarky'), rather than 'having enough', in his account of *autarkês*, stresses none the less that 'the idea of the sufficiency of a certain level of wealth for autarky—for leisure and *ta kala* that fill it—and, correspondingly, of the idea of the uselessness within the household economy of surpluses beyond a certain threshold, is a note struck repeatedly in the *Politics* and the *Oeconomicus*', *Households*, 48.

according to which sort of food they get, and how. There is shepherding, which is the laziest life because shepherds 'get their food without trouble from tame animals'. There is hunting, which may be brigandage, or fishing—for those 'who live by lakes or marshes or rivers or a sea in which there are fish', or the pursuit of birds or wild beasts. And finally there is cultivating the soil, which is what most people do. These are 'the modes of subsistence of those whose industry springs up of itself, and whose food is not acquired by exchange [*allagê*] or trade [*kapêlikê*]' (1256ᵃ40 ff.). It is clear that Aristotle is talking about producing the means to living, and as long as we make the distinction, which he does not make, between the process of getting the means to living and the institution through which it happens to be done, according to him the *oikos*, there need be no confusion.[2]

Oikonomikê, he says, 'must either find ready to hand, or itself provide, such things necessary to life, and useful for the community of the family or state' (1256ᵇ27–30). Acquiring them is itself an art, the art of acquisition or *chrêmatistikê*, and 'it is easy to see that wealth-getting [*chrêmatistikê*] is not the same art as household management [*oikonomikê*], for the function of the former is to provide and that of the latter to use— for what will be the art that will use the contents of the house if not the art of household management?' (1256ᵃ10–13). The art of acquisition is part of the more general art of *oikonomikê*; it is subordinate to it as a part is to the whole, and it is natural: 'Of the art of acquisition then there is one kind which is by nature a part of the management of the household' because it provides the necessary means of *oikonomikê* (1256ᵇ27 f.).

But there is another kind of acquisition [*ktêtikê*] that is specially called wealth-getting [*chrêmatistikê*], and that is so called with justice; and to this kind it is due that there is thought to be no limit to riches and property. Owing to its affinity to the art of acquisition of which we spoke, it is supposed by many people to be one and the

---

[2] There is no reason to think, as it sometimes is thought, that the connection of *oikonomikê* with the *oikos* is an indication that Aristotle is espousing the values of the aristocratic *oikos* and therefore the political cause of the big landowners against that of the traders.

same as that; and as a matter of fact, while it is not the same as the acquisition spoken of, it is not far removed from it. One of them is natural, the other is not natural, but carried on rather by a certain acquired skill or art. (1256ᵇ40 ff.)

This kind is *chrêmatistikê* in the bad sense (1256ᵇ40–1257ᵃ5). It, too, is concerned with getting things, and because of that people confuse it with the first art. But it is really quite distinct from the natural *chrêmatistikê* that belongs to *oikonomikê*, because its end or *telos* is entirely different from the *telos* of *oikonomikê* which governs natural *chrêmatistikê*.

The source of the confusion is the near connection between the two kinds of wealth-getting; in either, the instrument is the same, although the use is different, and so they pass into one another; for each is a use of the same property, but with a difference: accumulation is the end in the one case, but there is a further end in the other. (1257ᵇ35 ff.)

According to Aristotle's theory of action, actions are defined by their aims or ends, and if two activities aim at different things they are different activities.

We have the beginnings of a distinction between two quite different patterns of acquisition and exchange. In these chapters of the *Politics* Aristotle deepens the distinction by uncovering its principle, and that principle governs the analysis of exchange that he goes on to give. He is beginning to apply in earnest the metaphysical gap he has opened up in the *Ethics* between use value and exchange value, and the division between these two species of exchange is its first major consequence. Natural *chrêmatistikê*, or natural exchange, aims at use value or getting useful things. Unnatural *chrêmatistikê*, which includes trade (*kapêlikê*), and a lot of other things too, as we shall see in Chapter 4 (1), aims at exchange value or getting money. In the *Ethics* Aristotle failed to discover the nature, or 'the what it is', of exchange value, but at least he established that it is a quantity, and that it is therefore in a different logical category from use value. His discussion in the *Politics* proceeds on that partial conclusion, largely unaffected by the failure of the metaphysical inquiry to explain fully the nature

47

of exchange value. The distinction of category is all that is needed to carry through the discussion of exchange, because it is all that is needed to ground the distinction between the two ends pursued in the different forms of exchange.

Aristotle next makes a distinction in the concept of wealth, and he draws it on just the same ground that he used to distinguish between the different kinds of exchange, good and bad *chrêmatistikê*. The two distinctions are connected. This is the second major consequence that follows from the metaphysical gap between use value and exchange value established in the *Ethics*. He distinguishes between, as we would put it today, wealth as available use-value, and wealth as available exchange-value (or money). 'True wealth' (*ho alêthinos ploutos*, 1256ᵇ30 f.) is 'the stock of things that are useful in the community [*koinônia*] of the household or the polis' (1256ᵇ30 f., and 36–7); that is, true wealth is defined as the available stock of useful things or use values. And it is this availability for use that is important, as distinct from the form of property through which the things become available for use. 'Wealth as a whole', he says in the *Rhetoric*, 'consists in using things rather than owning them; it is really the activity—that is, the use—of the property that constitutes wealth' (*Rhet.* 1361ᵃ23 f.). Unnatural *chrêmatistikê*, by its nature, does not belong to the art of acquiring true wealth, because its aim is wealth as a quantity of exchange value in the form of money, 'wealth of the spurious kind' (*Pol.* 1, 1257ᵇ29–30, Jowett).

Aristotle's division of the notion of wealth between the realms of use value and exchange value contrasts especially sharply with the definitions of wealth to be found in economic writing after, roughly, the middle of the nineteenth century. The classical political economists—Smith, Ricardo, and Marx—had each made the distinction in one way or another, if only by inference from the clear distinction drawn between use value and exchange value. But in the economics that followed classical political economy, it became usual in definitions of wealth to integrate, or conflate, use value and exchange value. Mill, for example, defines wealth as 'all useful or agreeable things, which possess exchangeable value'.[3] Marshall defines, not wealth, but 'a person's wealth'; and he defines it, not as Aristotle does in terms of use, but in terms of exchange or rights of transference: 'a person's wealth' consists in 'those material goods to which he has (by law or custom) private rights of property, and which are therefore transferable and exchangeable', and 'those immaterial goods which belong to him, are external to him, and serve directly as the means of enabling him to acquire material goods'.[4] Cairncross sees no substantial distinction, but only one of viewpoint, between wealth and capital; 'Social capital . . . includes not only trade capital, but also non-commercial assets that possess a money value . . . The distinction between social capital and wealth is one of standpoint. Capital is an agent in *production* . . . Wealth is a fund upon which we can draw in *consumption'*.[5] Samuelson gives no definition of wealth in the eighth edition of his textbook *Economics.* Aristotle distinguishes wealth from ownership and exchange, in contrast to Marshall and others who conflate them. In the passage from the *Rhetoric* cited above, Aristotle says that wealth 'consists in using things rather than owning them', and he adds that the 'definition of security is present possession in such a way that the owner has the use of the goods, and that of ownership is the right of alienation, whereby gift or sale is meant' (*Rhet.* 1361ª19 ff.).

Aristotle introduces the distinction between the two kinds of wealth at this early stage of the inquiry as the most forceful way of making his point about just how different the two forms of *chrêmatistikê* really are. The difference is not trivial, because it is one of ends; and the difference between the ends is not trivial either. The end is limited in the case of natural *chrêmatistikê*, and in the other case unlimited. The end sought by natural *chrêmatistikê*, true wealth, is limited because, being defined as the stock of things that are useful, a natural limit is reached when there are enough of them. 'Enough' meaning

---

[3] J. S. Mill, *Principles of Political Economy* (New York, 1969), 9. On Greek conceptions of wealth, see Booth, *Households*, 41–2, 48–51.

[4] A. Marshall, *Principles of Economics*[4] (London, 1898), 125.

[5] A. Cairncross, *Introduction to Economics*[3] (London, 1960), 67–8.

enough for the good life: 'They are the elements of true riches; for the amount of property which is needed for a good life is not unlimited' (*Pol.* 1, 1256ᵇ32). Aristotle considers what Solon says in one of his poems: 'No bound to riches has been fixed for man', and he comments that 'there is a boundary fixed, just as there is in the other arts; for the instruments of any art are never unlimited, either in number or size, and riches may be defined as the number of instruments to be used in a household or in a state' (1256ᵇ34 ff.).

The end sought by unnatural *chrêmatistikê*, however, is without a natural limit. Aristotle does not go deeper into the matter at this point, but he returns to it for a more detailed examination at 1257ᵇ17–1258ᵃ14. However, in the light both of what he says there and of his account of exchange value in the *Ethics*, the underlying thought at this point is that, since it is a quantity, exchange value (and its bodily form of money) has no inherent limit. This will be so, at least, where money is made the end, as it is in *chrêmatistikê* of the bad sort, for if it were used only as a means, there would be a limit, because 'of the means there is a limit, for the end is always the limit' (1257ᵇ28). The grounds on which he distinguishes the two aims of the two arts of *chrêmatistikê* become fully clear only later, in his analysis of the different forms of exchange that come into being as exchange relations between people develop. What he offers in that analysis amounts to an account of the coming-to-be of exchange value itself, and of its evolution through successive forms.

Aristotle's terminology is very loose, and perhaps because of this the translations do not always distinguish carefully or consistently between Aristotle's two sorts of wealth, or between the two distinct sorts of *chrêmatistikê* or wealth-getting which aim at them respectively. This is a common fault, which often obscures Aristotle's thought. Contrast Jowett with Ross and Rackham at 1256ᵇ41. Jowett, in his original edition of 1885, conveys the thought clearly: 'there is another variety of the art of acquisition which is commonly and rightly called the art of making money, and it has in fact suggested the notion that wealth and property have no limit'. Ross revised Jowett for the

1921 Oxford edition, and at this point, for reasons that are understandable in the context, he replaces Jowett's 'making money' as the translation of *chrêmatistikên* by 'wealth-getting', which, by being ambiguous between Aristotle's two senses of 'wealth', blunts the very point Aristotle is trying to make. Rackham does the same. When Aristotle criticizes 'getting wealth', he always means 'getting money' or spurious wealth, not getting use value or true wealth.

Rackham at times even translates *chrêmatistikê* as 'business', so that at 1257^b35, Aristotle's distinction between the two arts of wealth-getting becomes a quite opaque distinction between 'the two branches of the art of business', and Carnes Lord, in his translation *Aristotle: The Politics*, makes it even more misleadingly a distinction between two 'forms of expertise in business'. Both translations invite confusion of just those ends which Aristotle is at pains to distinguish systematically in the chapter. Finley writes that 'Polanyi . . . was right to insist that failure to distinguish between the two meanings of *chrêmatistikê* is fatal to an understanding of this section of the *Politics*'.[6] It is interesting that Aquinas was not tempted into any such confusion between the two arts of *chrêmatistikê* in his commentary on Book 1 of the *Politics* (Lectio 7, 111). Aquinas understands Aristotle to say that they are distinct arts: the first 'art of possessing . . . is the art of acquiring food and other things necessary for life'; the second is 'the art of money [*pecuniativa*], because it has to do with the acquisition of money'.

Exchange (*metablêtikê*) 'arises at first from what is natural, from the circumstance that some have too little, others too much' (1257^a15 ff.). Aristotle then introduces the first form of exchange (1257^a17–30), the form that is primitive both historically and logically, that is, barter, or the direct non-monetary exchange of one commodity against another, which will be

---

[6] Finley adds that 'Beginning with the Sophists, philosophers were faced with the problem of creating the vocabulary for systematic analysis out of everyday words. One increasingly common device was to employ the suffix *-ikos*. There are some seven hundred such words in Aristotle, many first employed by him'; see 'Aristotle and Economic Analysis', 41, n. 52, where Finley also refers to P. Chantraine, *La Formation des noms en grec ancien* (Paris, 1933), ch. 36.

represented as C–C′, to indicate the exchange of two commodities unmediated by money. (Exchange mediated by money will be represented as C–M–C′, in the case of selling in order to buy; and *kapêlikê*, buying in order to sell, will be represented as M–C–M′.)[7] He says that in the household, the first form of association where all things were held in common, there was no purpose for exchange to serve. That purpose arose with the increased scope of association of the village, whose members, he says, were more separated and had things to exchange; 'later, when the family divided into parts, the parts shared in many things, and different parts in different things, which they had to give in exchange for the things they wanted'. They did so in a direct way, as barbarian tribes still do, one useful thing for another (i.e. without money), 'giving and receiving wine, for example, in exchange for corn, and the like'. Such exchange 'is not part of the wealth-getting art [*chrêmatistikê* in the sense of getting money] and is not contrary to nature, but is needed for the satisfaction of men's natural wants [or having enough, *autarkeias*]' 1257ª30).

Aristotle explicitly introduces the second form of exchange,

[7] The notation using C and M to denote the circuits of commodities and money is due to Marx; see *Capital*, i, chs. 3 and 4, and his earlier *Contribution to a Critique of Political Economy*. Marx's analysis of these circuits follows Aristotle's closely. There are ample indications, especially in the *Contribution*, which was the forerunner of *Capital*, but also in *Capital* itself, that Marx derived the most basic elements of his own analysis from Aristotle (see ch. 1, n. 11), so it is not surprising that the notation should fit Aristotle's account so well. Where Marx differs most profoundly and originally from the entire tradition of economic thinking is in his view that use value and exchange value are quite different things, not roughly the same thing as they are considered to be in economic thought, and that the pursuit of one of them as an end of action leads to quite different results from the pursuit of the other, so that they must be regarded as alternative ends, rather than ends that can successfully be pursued together. This is precisely the upshot of Aristotle's analysis. The notation is to be found through all the volumes of *Capital* and *Theories of Surplus Value*, and the reason for this is that Marx's entire critique of political economy (the subtitle of *Capital* is *A Critique of Political Economy* or 'economics' as it would be called today), is based on a strict observance of the category distinction between use value and exchange value, as quality and quantity respectively. In Marx's view, capitalist enterprises, and a capitalist economy as a whole, are essentially organizations for the pursuit of M–C–M′, not C–M–C′. Keynes thought the same, unlike many economists; see Ch. 5 (5) below. A version of the notation was used by Defourney in 'Aristote: Théorie économique et politique sociale', *Annales de l'Institut supérieure de philosophie*, 3 (1914), 1–34.

C–M–C´, as a development out of the primitive one: 'the other or more complex form of exchange grew, as might have been inferred, out of the simpler' (1257ª30 f.). This form is the exchange of goods mediated by money. One commodity is exchanged for money, i.e. a sale (C–M), and money in turn for another commodity, i.e. a purchase (M–C´).

Aristotle explains the appearance of this form of exchange, and the appearance of money, in terms of a developing social reality which over time leads to the displacement of the less developed form of exchange-relations by the more developed (1257ª32–41). Such a form of explanation is entirely Aristotelian; it is an application of his metaphysics of substance, form, and change. In the *Ethics* he explains the advantage of the new form, and in doing so, as Roll notes, he gives the first clear statement of the function of money as a store of value:[8] 'money serves us as a guarantee of exchange in the future: supposing we need nothing at the moment, it ensures that exchange shall be possible when a need arises, for it meets the requirement of something we can produce in payment so as to obtain the thing we need' (*NE* 5, 1133ᵇ10–13). In C–C´ the acts of sale and purchase are fused into a single act. This can make it difficult to use what you have in order to get what you need. If you go to market with cabbages looking for corn and there is no corn, your cabbages might rot before you find any corn, and the exchange value of the cabbages perishes with them. But if you can realize the exchange value of your cabbages as a separate act from acquiring corn, then you can hold on to your exchange value safely until such time as you find corn. If one durable commodity, say silver, is accepted as the general equivalent of all the others, then this separation becomes possible. When cabbages and corn are bartered, the transaction compounds two acts into one: a sale of cabbages and a purchase of corn. Money separates the single act into two acts, C–M and M–C´, which is much more flexible because it allows the acts of sale (C–M) and purchase (M–C´) to be separated in time and place. It does this by making it possible for

---

[8] Roll, *History of Economic Thought*, 37.

the exchange value of the cabbages to be separated from the cabbages. Money gives exchange value an independent form of existence; it allows the exchange value of the cabbages to find an expression independently of the physical body of the cabbages themselves.

Aristotle takes as lenient a view of C–M–C′ as he does of C–C′. What is wrong with *chrêmatistikê* in the bad sense of *kapêlikê* is its end or aim: that the trader seeks wealth as exchange value or money, 'wealth of the spurious kind', rather than as useful things or 'true wealth', and the form of wealth he seeks has no limit, and his gain is another's loss. Barter is acceptable because of its end: meeting natural needs or having enough. Since the aim of the circuit C–M–C′ is the same as that of C–C′, Aristotle regards it as natural too. This seems to be confirmed when he recognizes the ethically acceptable use of money in C–M–C′ as a 'means of exchange', which he terms 'the necessary process of exchange', and describes as 'necessary and laudable' (*Pol.* 1, 1258ᵇ4).

But perhaps things are not quite so simple. There seem to be indications of a rather different attitude to C–M–C′ in Aristotle's mind. For example, he says that the use made of a shoe in selling it 'is not its proper and peculiar use', and the reason he gives is that 'the shoe has not been made for the purpose of being exchanged' (1257ᵃ6 ff.). In the *Eudemian Ethics* Aristotle distinguishes both the use of a thing for its natural purpose and its use for an unnatural one, and its *per se* use and its *per accidens* use. It is not immediately clear how he intends to connect these distinctions in general terms, but it is clear that he does not mean to suggest that all *per accidens* uses are necessarily for unnatural purposes. Using the eye for seeing well and using it badly in squinting are both uses of the eye as an eye, *per se* uses, 'but it was possible to use the eye in another way—*per accidens*, e.g. if one could sell or eat it' (*EE* 1246ᵃ26–31). There seems to be no clear or strong suggestion that these *per accidens* uses are necessarily wrong or unnatural.

He does not go so far as to say that the use of a thing in exchange is unnatural, but perhaps this only glosses over rather than removes a suggestion of incompatibility between the view that C–M–C′ is 'necessary and laudable', and the view that the use of an article in exchange is not the 'proper and peculiar use' conformable to the nature of the thing (*oikeia*). It is slightly surprising that he should allow this to pass without comment, because lack of conformity with a thing's nature is something he takes seriously. Although he does not use the term 'unnatural' (*para phusin*), the terms he does use (*kath' hauto, oikeia*) are enough to sustain at least the doubt.[9] Perhaps there is an ambivalence in Aristotle's mind towards exchange of the C–M–C′ form, so that he cannot make up his mind whether it is a good thing or a bad one. On the one hand he sees it as sharing the same natural end as C–C′. On the other hand he also sees it as leading naturally into M–C–M′ or *kapêlikê*, which he says arises out of it (*Pol.* 1, 1257ᵇ1–5). At any rate, having himself raised this hint of a problem, he carries on as if it were unimportant without saying why.

Perhaps we are meant to infer the reason, because it seems obvious. Just because a use of a thing is not its proper and peculiar use does not mean that this use is bad. The position Aristotle arrives at is that the use made of a thing in exchanging it is good or bad depending on the end served by the exchange. Exchanging a thing in the circuit C–M–C′ serves the end of bringing use values and needs together, and because the end is good the use is good too. But the use made of a thing in exchanging it in the M–C–M′ circuit is bad because the end is bad. Aristotle also thinks that the use made of money depends on ends in the same way. The end of C–M–C′ is good, and the use made of money in it is good too because of the end. The use made of money in M–C–M′ is bad because the end of M–C–M′ is bad.

The ethical vindication of the use made of a thing in exchange seems to be confirmed indirectly by his criticism of

---

[9] The impression that Aristotle has misgivings is stronger in Jowett's translation than in Rackham's. Jowett refers to the use of a shoe in exchange as 'improper', where Rackham says simply that it is not 'peculiar to' the shoe. The Greek is ἀμφότεραι δὲ καθ' αὐτὸ μὲν ἀλλ' οὐχ ὁμοίως καθ' αὐτό, ἀλλ' ἡ μὲν οἰκεία ἡ δ' οὐκ οἰκεία τοῦ πράγματος.

the niggardly 'smith who fashions the Delphian knife for many uses' when really 'every instrument is best made when intended for one and not for many uses' (1252^{b}1–5). The Delphian knife seems to have been a crude tool which could serve as a knife, a file, and a hammer, and its advantage was that it was cheap.[10] So what is wrong with the Delphian knife is not that it is used in exchange, but that it is made to be exchanged and is bad at its job for that reason. The construction of this 'tool' is therefore not part of the proper process of tool construction, where a thing is made to do a job. Hence it is not even really a tool, *a fortiori* not really a knife, and *a fortissimo* not a good knife. Its use value has been compromised and diminished by design out of considerations of exchange value. It has been deliberately constructed to perform more functions than it can perform well. Good tools are made to perform well and they are designed and made with that end only in view. This case confirms that the use made of a thing in exchange is not a target for Aristotle's censure. He distinguishes between using a thing in exchange and making it to be exchanged, and he criticizes the latter but not the former.

So perhaps Aristotle is not really ambivalent about C–M–C′ at all. The use made of a thing in exchanging it in this way may not be its proper use in the sense that the thing was not made to be exchanged. But it is a natural use, and 'he who gives a shoe in exchange for money or food to him who wants one, does indeed use the shoe as a shoe' (1257^{a}10 ff.). The distinction of ends he is relying on to distinguish C–M–C′ and M–C–M′ is an application of what is a quite general Aristotelian view. He distinguishes goods into the fine, the useful, and the pleasant (*NE* 2, 1104^{b}32); things we want for their own sake, things that we want for the sake of something else, and things we want because they are pleasant to us; their contraries being the shameful, the harmful, and the painful. Of things that are useful, their goodness *qua* useful depends on the end. So whether the use made of a shoe in exchange is good or not depends on the end; on the part the transaction plays in

---

[10] See F. Susemihl and D. R. Hicks, *The Politics of Aristotle* (New York, 1976), citing Aquinas and Oresme, 141–2.

human life. In C–M–C' the end is need or having enough, and that is part of the good life, so the use of the shoe here is good, 'necessary and laudable'. One sense of 'necessary' is 'anything without which it is not possible for good to exist or come to be, or for bad to be discarded or got rid of' (*Met. Δ*, 1015ᵃ 20 ff.); a thing is necessary if without it some good will not be brought about or some harm avoided. If, without exchange, someone will not have enough, but can have enough if he exchanges, then exchange is necessary. C–M–C' meets this test because its end is need, and it uses a shoe as a shoe. But using a shoe in M–C–M' is not using it as a shoe, and its end is not need but money. M–C–M' is not a means to the good life, so the use made of a shoe in *kapêlikê* is not good. Exchanging may be good and necessary, or not. It depends on the species of exchange and what its end is.

Things are more straightforward with *kapêlikê*, where people come to market, not to sell what they have grown or made in order to buy what they need to consume, but rather to buy in order to sell with a view to increasing their fund of exchange value, M–C–M'. Aristotle introduces this form too as a necessary development out of the preceding form C–M–C', and he understands it to have a development of its own.

When, in this way, a currency had once been instituted, there next arose, from the necessary process of exchange [i.e. exchange between commodities, with money merely serving as a measure], the other form of the art of acquisition, which consists in retail trade [conducted for profit]. At first, we may allow, it was perhaps practised in a simple way [that is to say, money was still regarded as a measure, and not treated as a source of profit]; but in the process of time, and as a result of experience, it was practised with a more studied technique, which sought to discover the sources from which, and the methods by which, the greatest profit could be made. (1257ᵇ1-5; the interpolations are Barker's[11])

The C–M–C' circuit begins and ends with use values. Its aim is to acquire something that is needed, and once it is acquired, that thing leaves the sphere of circulation altogether

---

[11] Barker, *The Politics of Aristotle* (Oxford, 1946).

57

and enters the sphere of consumption. Exchange here is an instrument falling within the first of Aristotle's two arts of acquisition, namely, that 'kind which is by nature part of the management of the household' (*Pol.* 1, 1256^b27, 1257^b20 f.). This is so because its aim is the acquisition of wealth as use-value not as exchange value; its object is wealth 'defined as a number of instruments to be used in a household or in a state' (1256^b37–8).

This form of exchange, however, makes possible another, *kapêlikê* (*chrêmatistikê* in the bad sense), which 'is concerned only with getting a fund of money, and that only by the method of conducting the exchange of commodities' (1257^b 21 f.). The owner comes to market, not with goods, but with money which he advances (rather than spends) against commodities, M–C, in order to resell them for a greater sum, C–M´. He does not stop there, however, because once he has finished one circuit, he still has as much reason for advancing the increased sum M´ as he had for advancing the original sum M in the first place, and it is just the same kind of reason.

This is the main contrast Aristotle draws between the circuits M–C–M´ and C–M–C´. He says that the aim or point of C–M–C´ lies in the fact that C and C´ are different use-values. The aim is to acquire the specific usefulness of C´ which is needed, and the sale of C is simply a means to that end. Once C´ is acquired in this way, exchange reaches a natural terminus, because the thing acquired now leaves the sphere of the circulation of exchange values, and enters the sphere of consumption, in which its use value is appropriated. But the M–C–M´ circuit has no natural terminus. It has no end outside of circulation. 'Money is the starting-point and the goal' of this form of activity, as Aristotle observes (1257^b22 f.), and since there is no difference of quality between one sum of money and another, the only possible difference being one of quantity, this quantitative growth of exchange value in the form of money is the only aim that M–C–M´ can have. But if M can be advanced to become M´, so can M´ be advanced to become M´´, and so on, without limit. Aristotle says of this kind of exchange that 'there is no limit to the end it seeks; and the end it seeks is wealth of the sort we have mentioned . . . the mere acquisition of currency' (1257^b28 f.); 'it is concerned only with getting a fund of money, and that only by the method of conducting the exchange of commodities' (1257^b 21 ff.); 'all who are engaged in acquisition increase their fund of money without any limit or pause' (1257^b33 f.). The two forms of exchange or acquisition, C–M–C′ and M–C–M′, 'overlap because they are both handling the same objects and acting in the same field of acquisition; but they move along different lines—the object of the one being simply accumulation, and that of the other something quite different' (1257^b34 f.). Aristotle makes no distinction between the petty trader or huckster and the grand trader. He is not concerned with scale but with the end of the activity. Roll comments that 'Aristotle's long discussion of the two arts of [*chrêmatistikê*] was not just an attempt to drive home an ethical distinction. It was also a true analysis of the two different forms in which money acts in the economic process: as a medium of exchange whose function is completed by the acquisition of the good required for the satisfaction of a want; and in the shape of money capital leading men to the desire for limitless accumulation.'[12]

This treatment connects with the conclusion, reached in the *Ethics*, that use value is essentially qualitative, heterogeneous, and unquantifiable, and exchange value is essentially quantitative and homogeneous, so that they are features of logically different kinds. In the *Politics* he is drawing some of the consequences of that conclusion. The logical difference of category carries forward into a difference of end. The actions to which people are led in pursuit of one are different from those to which they are led in pursuit of the other, and not the same as we might have expected had we held the common view that the two arts of aquisition are really one.

The relation, or lack of it, that Aristotle establishes between use value and exchange value, is fundamentally different from

---

[12] Roll, *History of Economic Thought*, 35.

the relation taken to hold between them in modern economics, where exchange value and use value are seen as necessarily connected. In economics, exchange value is treated either as a means to use value (the best or only means), or else as an end conjoint with use value, such that to pursue one is also to pursue the other. According to Aristotle, however, they are alternative ends, and in principle it is open to us to choose between them. In practice the choice is not always open, or at any rate it is not always an equal choice; he says that 'the life of money-making is one undertaken under compulsion' (*NE* 1, 1096ª5). But in principle, and sometimes in practice, there is a choice according to Aristotle. According to economics there is not. The effect of the economic view is that market economy as a whole is represented as the unavoidable, or the most efficient, means to the natural ends of living. On an Aristotelian view, this is an intellectual confusion with practical consequences because it involves a confusion of ends.

Aristotle still has to explain how C–M–C′ can be good, if it is a thing of such a kind that it leads naturally, as he thinks it does, into M–C–M′, which is bad. If the transition from one to the other were not to be thought of as a natural progression or development, there would be no problem. Aristotle often has half an eye on human wickedness, and if the explanation of this transition were to be that a good thing, C–M–C′, was perverted into an unnatural one because of human wickedness, then the transition would not be a natural one in the sense that is causing the problem. But this is not what Aristotle thinks. He does not say that human wickedness begets the idea that wealth is unlimited, and that people then abuse money by making it into a means of pursuing unlimited wealth. He says, on the contrary, that it is to unnatural *chrêmatistikê* that 'it is due that there is thought to be no limit to riches and property' (*Pol.* 1, 1256ᵇ40 ff.).

He seems to be saying that there is a natural line of development in exchange from one form to another. This is the point Ross seems to be missing in commenting on the transition from C–C′ to C–M–C′ that 'This notion of money as facilitating barter, instead of (practically) driving it out of the field, is a curious one.'[13] Susemihl and Hicks, by contrast, regard the transition as a 'natural development'.[14] Once C–C′ becomes a common form of activity, the obstacles it poses to successful exchange become common experiences, and the way to get round them is to make one commodity into a means of exchange, money. So money and C–M–C′ can be looked upon as an evolution within exchange, and this seems to be how Aristotle looks at it. It seems to be the way he looks at the transition from C–M–C′ to M–C–M′ too, and this is what generates the problem.

It is not surprising that Aristotle should take such a developmental view. He thinks that many important sorts of change are processes of change in an entity of some kind. Some events are accidental; for instance, those that arise from the interaction of two entities or systems. But others, such as growth, arise from the nature of an entity or substance, and in this case they are parts of a process, and they are not accidental. The polis itself is a natural growth (1252ª24), rather than an artificial body or association. He regards it as a *suntheton*, a compound whole formed by nature (1276ᵇ6 f.), and, like things that are full substances, it has a process of development, or coming-to-be, through which it reaches its mature form. He presents the development of exchange as part of the process of coming-to-be of the polis itself, as it emerges from the family and the village.

This Aristotelian view has not been prominent in the recent literature, perhaps because modern authors tend to prefer the Hobbesian and liberal view of society as an aggregate of individuals, rather than a view which attributes to society anything of the nature of a substance. Robinson insists, for instance, that 'As to his [Aristotle's] premiss that the city is a natural thing, the city looks much more like an artificial thing.' Robinson goes on to criticize Aristotle's 'armchair history' of the origin of the polis. This is presumably a reference to the

---

[13] W. D. Ross, *Aristotle*, rev. edn. (London, 1949), 213. Ross adds in mitigation that 'it must be remembered that in economics . . . Aristotle was almost the earliest worker'.

[14] Susemihl and Hicks, *Politics of Aristotle*, 29.

account of the social development from family, through village, to polis at 1252^{b}16–30. It is hard to imagine that the complaint could have been intended to cover Aristotle's closely associated account of the development of the forms of exchange and exchange value, which should certainly be considered part of his thought about the development of the polis.[15] It is still common to find commentators undermining or dismissing Aristotle's view that the polis is a natural growth by presenting it as a misplaced piece of biological thinking, or as involving an illicit 'biological analogy'. Mulgan suggests that Aristotle 'considers the polis as if it were a biological organism'. Day and Chambers suggest that the polis could be a natural growth only if it were a plant or an animal, and since it is neither, they conclude that 'Aristotle's language is metaphorical'.[16] There is no metaphor or analogy involved; Aristotle is doing no more than applying his substance–attribute metaphysics to the social realm. The polis has some of the important characteristics of a substance; it is a subject of predications, it has form and matter, it has a process of coming-to-be, and so forth. Aristotle considers the polis to be a *suntheton* or substance for that reason, and not because of an analogy with some other kind of substance.

There is nothing in the immediate context to indicate that Aristotle thought M–C–M′ should be banned, and given his

---

[15] R. Robinson, *Aristotle's Politics: Books III and IV* (Oxford, 1962), p. xxii. Robinson's introd. to this edn. of Books 3 and 4 of the *Politics* is marked by a strong political animus against Aristotle's view that the natural purpose of the polis, or the 'state', is to promote the flourishing of the citizens, which he dubs 'Aristotle's paternalism'. The liberal reading of Aristotle on the polis is quite recent. Earlier authors rightly tended to stress that for Aristotle the polis is a substance; see e.g. L. Robin, who gives a good sense of the structure of Aristotle's thought on the matter in his *Greek Thought* (London, 1928), 268 ff. A good outline account of Aristotle on individual and community is found in Irwin, *Aristotle's First Principles*, 352–4, 406–7. On the polis as a compound constituted by nature (*ta phusei sunestôta*), see Newman, *Politics of Aristotle*, i. 20, and 41 ff., who also has an excellent account of Aristotle's attitude to state and society, pp. 15–24. For a defence of the Aristotelian view of society as 'a natural growth' against the modern liberal view stemming from Hobbes and Locke, see my 'The Metaphysics of Substance in Marx', in T. Carver (ed.), *The Cambridge Companion to Marx* (Cambridge, 1991).

[16] Mulgan, *Aristotle's Political Theory*, 20; J. Day and M. Chambers, *Aristotle's History of Athenian Democracy* (Berkeley, 1962), 40–1.

view of the power that money has to influence the thought and
behaviour of people (discussed in Chapter 4 (1) and in Chapter
5), it hardly seems likely that he could have thought legislation
would have had a good chance of succeeding in its object, or
of avoiding making a bad situation worse. His attitude to
M–C–M′ may be more complicated than it appears at first
sight. Perhaps he thinks it is bad but inevitable. If so, its
inevitability would lie in the fact that once exchange value is
present in the form of C–M–C′, it is in its nature to develop
into the form of M–C–M′. If it has that capacity, as he seems
to think, it is no longer possible to say that there is nothing
more to be said about exchange value in C–M–C′ than that it
is natural because it is a means to true wealth. It is that, but it
is also M–C–M′ in embryo. It is no longer clear that Aristotle
should think any form of exchange value to be good without
qualification, though he may think that it is inevitable because
it springs from the growth of the family into the village, where
some have too much of x and too little of y and others have
too little of x and too much of y, which is what begets C–C′
and starts the whole development going.

The fourth form in the development of exchange value, and
the final one in Aristotle's account, is *obolostatikê*, 'the breeding of money from money' (1258ᵇ5), that is, usurer's interest
or M–M′. Trade, the process of getting wealth 'which consists
in exchange', is, he says, 'justly censured; for it is unnatural,
and a mode by which men gain from one another', but

the most hated sort [of bad *chrêmatistikê*, 1258ᵃ37], and with the
greatest reason, is usury, which makes a gain out of money itself, and
not from the natural object of it. For money was intended to be used
in exchange, but not to increase at interest. And this term interest
[*tokos*] which means the birth of money from money, is applied to
the breeding of money because the offspring resembles the parent.
Wherefore of all modes of getting wealth [*chrêmatistikê*] this is the
most unnatural. (1258ᵇ1–8)[17]

---

[17] The anti-usurious view that money is 'barren metal' has often been attributed to
Aristotle, but despite the conjecture, he does not use those words. None the less, they
have often been attributed to him. Shakespeare gives Antonio the lines: If thou wilt lend
this money, lend it not | As to thy friends: for when did friendship take | A breed of

In this brief treatment Aristotle confirms his decision to permit C–M–C'. He also recognizes a function for money that is natural because in C–M–C' it serves need, the end of *chrêmatistikê* in the good sense. The function of money specific to M–C–M' and M–M' stands condemned because of the end it serves.

The term 'usury' is often used these days to mean, not the taking of interest, which is what it always used to mean, but only the taking of excessive interest. Ross, perhaps with this in mind, implies that there is a distinction here which Aristotle has failed to make, and he complains that 'a justifiable moral prejudice against iniquitous usury blinds him to the economic services rendered by lenders of capital'.[18] It is true that Aristotle does not explicitly distinguish between usury and greater usury, though it is probably not a distinction he would object to. But a distinction between bad usury and even worse usury is not what Ross has in mind. He wants a distinction between bad usury and good usury. This is impossible on Aristotle's view, because his criticism of usury is a criticism of its end, and there is no difference of end between usury and iniquitous usury, only one of degree. This would be one of those actions, like adultery, which do not admit of a mean, and which 'are themselves bad, and not the excess or the deficiencies of them' (*NE* 2, 1107ª9–26).

Lending among Athenian citizens, as Paul Millett has

barren metal of his friend? (*Merchant of Venice*, I, iii). Bentham, in his *Defence of Usury*, claims that Aristotle ('that celebrated heathen'), 'notwithstanding the great number of pieces of money that had passed through his hands (more perhaps than ever passed through the hands of philosopher before or since), and notwithstanding the uncommon pains he had bestowed on the subject of generation, had never been able to discover, in any one piece of money, any organs for generating any other such piece. Emboldened by so strong a body of negative proof, he ventured to usher into the world the result of his observations, in the form of an universal proposition, *that all money is in its nature barren.*' Bentham's wit earns marks for effort but not for accuracy, because Aristotle does not say this. The question of who did first say it is the subject of a symposium by a constellation of scholars—E. Cannan, W. D. Ross, J. Bonar, and P. H. Wicksteed: 'Who said "Barren Metal"?', *Economica*, 5 (June 1922), 105–11. The mistaken attribution continues in spite of their efforts, and even Roll claims that Aristotle says that money 'is by nature barren metal', *History of Economic Thought*, 35.

[18] Ross, *Aristotle*, 243.

shown, was overwhelmingly *eranos* lending, and it was free of interest.[19] It was usually arranged between friends or acquaintances, and part of its effect was to help cement bonds of *philia* or friendship. The degree of altruism in this should not be exaggerated; a future return of some kind of help was expected, and naturally this expectation would not have been entirely absent from the lender's mind in making the loan in the first place.

Professional lending was not great either in extent or in the sums lent. Usurers (*obolostates, tokistai*) in Aristotle's world were confined to petty operators of a kind that we would call loan-sharks, who preyed mainly on stall-holders in the *agora* needing money to buy their wares for the day, and to a few metic 'bankers' (*trapezitai*) mostly in the Pireus and the *agora*, whose customers were also mostly metics or visiting traders with cash to be held safe. As metics, and often ex-slaves, they were marginal in a society based on citizenship. Citizens did not involve themselves in professional credit, and the clientele of 'bankers' were people to whom citizen-credit was not available, such as visiting traders, shipowners, and sightseers. The majority of deposits known from the surviving sources are deposits by traders. The Attic orators have only four cases of citizens making deposits, and two of them are untypical. 'Bankers' were lenders of last resort for citizens, and only a citizen known as a welsher would have to go to one, just because people did not trust him in normal reciprocity-lending.[20] Productive lending, or the advancing of capital at interest for productive enterprises (the 'economic services' Ross tries to defend), was practically non-existent.[21] Even on the most liberal definition of it, Millett is able to identify only eight cases

[19] For this and what follows, see Paul Millett's full study of the literary and epigraphic evidence, *Lending and Borrowing in Ancient Athens* (Cambridge, 1991).

[20] Millett notes (ibid. 35 and 188) that Athens preserved a high level of communal networks of credit relationships. He contrasts this with the heavy reliance on credit of modern urban populations living in labour markets. He cites studies which show that, in the last decade of the nineteenth century in the north of England, on average one working-class family in five was sued for debt in the county courts in the course of a year, and that in Britain as a whole before the First World War, on average every working-class family made at least one pledge per fortnight to pawnbrokers.

[21] Ibid., ch. 8.

in the literary and epigraphic evidence. So-called 'bankers' were scarcely worth the name, if by 'bank' we mean a financial institution whose assets are debts and whose liabilities are deposits, and whose lending of depositors' money at interest is mainly for productive investment.

Greek 'bankers' made their livings as money-changers and experts on coin, which were important functions, since each polis issued its own coinage. There is no clear evidence that they paid interest on deposits, and it may have been a breach of trust to lend it out for profit at all. The emphasis in the sources is on the inviolability of deposits. The evidence is consistent with the view that bankers' profits came from changing money, not from lending at interest. 'Bankers' often acted as brokers or agents, whereas modernists tend to assume that they did what modern bankers do with depositors' money. If interest was given on deposits, this was only by specific agreement. It is possible that 'bankers' lent only their own money, not that of depositors, which they may only have held in safe keeping, providing the well-to-do with an alternative to the common practice of hiding it or burying it in the ground.[22] Millett concludes that *trapezitai* were not primarily money-lenders. Their services were the safe-keeping of deposits, including valuables and documents, acting as witnesses and guarantors, changing money, and lending to metics, non-citizens, and the untrustworthy.

It is wholly misleading to write, as Barker does, of a process of 'economic development of Athens during the fourth century'. If Barker had been suggesting that the production of use values was developing, this would not have been seriously misleading, even if it were not true. But that is not what he is suggesting. He is suggesting that financial institutions were developing, and that money was extending a grip on social and productive activity: 'deposit banks, which made loans to merchants from their funds, were coming into existence; and the

---

[22] See Ste Croix's fundamental article, 'Greek and Roman Accounting', in A. C. Littleton and B. S. Yamey (eds.), *Studies in the History of Accounting* (London, 1956), 29; Millett, *Lending and Borrowing*, 163–70, 203–4, and 216. See Ch. 8 (4) below for a discussion of ancient hoarding.

Athenian banks were making Athens the principal money-market of Greece'.[23] The suggestion is not that productive activity was increasing, but that it was changing its form by becoming 'economic activity' as that is understood today, namely, productive and distributive activity systematically regulated by money. The evidence uniformly contradicts this Whig wishful thinking.

[23] Barker, *Politics of Aristotle,* 29, n. 2.

The Integrity of the Analysis

⫷ 1 ⫸

Nicomachean Ethics, 5. 5 and *Politics*, 1 are usually held to be hodgepodges of insights and prejudices, some showing economic precocity, others economic backwardness, social hauteur, and political reaction. Taken together, they are generally thought to lack any serious overall intellectual cohesion. This view is shared by schools of thought which agree on very little else. It is held by those, like Finley, who think Aristotle did no economic thinking at all, and by Barker and his many followers, who think Aristotle did primitive neo-classical economics. The incoherence attributed to Aristotle is entirely a product of misconstruction and oversight. There is a tight organization across both of Aristotle's discussions which brings them into a theoretical unity whose fundamental principle is the analysis of use value and exchange value, and the metaphysical gulf he opens up between them. The positions he adopts on wealth, exchange, and interest, are arrived at by consistently applying that principle, and the same is true, though in a more devious way, of his accounts of money and trade. The object of evaluation should be this theoretical structure, not the rag-bag so often attributed to him.

The treatment of trade in the *Politics* is often regarded as especially fatuous. It is not usually recognized as having any connection with his analysis of exchange value in the *Ethics*, and it is commonly regarded as merely expressing attitudes of snobbery and political prejudice against trade and money-makers. The Greeks often regarded trade as a degrading thing for a free man to engage in, and Sparta, admittedly an odd place, banned citizens from it altogether, as Plato does from his ideal polis. It would be surprising if Aristotle's view of trade and money-makers were entirely unconnected with this Greek sensibility, but there should be something more than a loose general affinity if a charge of prejudice is to be taken seriously. A balance of hostile judgements over argued cases to back them up would be some sort of evidence for prejudice, and prima-facie evidence against would be anything like a theory from which the hostile judgements followed as conclusions. Theories can be concocted to give the required conclusions, of course, and then we have to try to decide how serious the theory is. It comes to this: is there so little in the reasons Aristotle gives for his condemnation of trade that they may be convincingly explained away and belittled as no more than expressions of attitudes?

Ross thought so, and he concluded that Aristotle's 'view is too much a reflexion of the ordinary Greek prejudice against trade as an illiberal occupation'.[1] Mulgan finds Aristotle's view to be 'of interest as an expression of the aristocratic attitude towards wealth, with its preference for landed property and its prejudice against trade and commerce'.[2] Judgements of this kind suggest more modern disputes, into which Aristotle is being dragged.

Plato's criticisms are aimed at the moral qualities of the traders themselves, at the destructive effects their activities have on relationships in the community, and on the behaviour and attitudes of the citizens. Trade 'fills the land with wholesaling and retailing, breeds shifty and deceitful habits in a man's soul and makes the citizens distrustful and hostile' (*Laws*, 705a). But Aristotle's account, as we saw in Chapter 3, is not of this kind. The criticism he offers of trade (*kapêlikê*) goes well beyond anything that can be attributed to taste, tradition, and prejudice. It has roots deep in his metaphysics, ethics, and theory of action, and the fact that this has gone so largely unnoticed is a lacuna. Certainly, he does not refrain from observing that *kapêlikê* 'is justly discredited (for it is not in accordance with nature, but involves men's taking things from one another)', *Pol.* 1, 1258^{b}1–2, and one can argue about whether the trader (*kapêlos*) just grubs for money or performs

---

[1] Ross, *Aristotle*, 243.   [2] Mulgan, *Aristotle's Political Theory*, 49.

a service, as commentators repeatedly have in defence of commerce. But such criticisms are strikingly absent from the four chapters that make up Aristotle's economic thought. His criticism is aimed not at *kapêlikê*, but at its end, the getting of wealth as exchange value or money. This is an end shared by many pursuits besides trade, and Aristotle seems to think that trade is not even the most ignoble way of pursuing it.

Kapêlikê is certainly one way of pursuing that end, but there are lots of others. Almost all the activities that make up ethical and political life can be made into means for pursuing it. Philosophy itself can be used in this way, and Aristotle says that this is just what the Sophists do, for the Sophist 'is one who makes money from an apparent but unreal wisdom' (*S. El.* 165ᵃ23). The quality of the wisdom may be a separate criticism, or it may be connected with the fact that the Sophist designs his 'product' for sale, like the maker of the Delphian knife, with the result that he produces 'philosophy' which stands to the real article as the Delphian pseudo-knife stands to a real knife that can do what it is meant to do properly. Aristotle gives no explicit indication which form of the criticism he has in mind, though he probably means the latter, because he says that sophistry itself 'is, as we said, a kind of money-making' (171ᵇ28), rather than a kind of philosophy. (He also thinks that Sophists are well advised to take cash in advance 'because no one would give money for the things they know', *NE* 9, 1164ᵃ27 ff.).

Activities that look alike may be different, and if they have different ends they are different. What he says of *chrêmatistikê* in the *Politics*, he says of sophistry in the *Metaphysics*. Just as good and bad *chrêmatistikê* look alike because 'in either, the instrument is the same', when really they are quite different because 'the use is different' and is aimed at a different end (*heteron telos*, 1257ᵇ34 ff.), so sophistry looks like philosophy because it 'turns on the same class of things as philosophy', but differs from it 'in respect of the purpose of the philosophic life' (*Met. Γ*, 1004ᵇ17 ff.). The same sort of thing can be said of any profession or activity which is capable of being used for the pursuit of money, or 'making a living'.

The Integrity of the Analysis

The point that needs to be emphasized is that Aristotle sees the pursuit of exchange value or money as a distinct activity with a distinct end all of its own. It is distinct from trade or any other particular way of pursuing it. When it becomes connected with the conduct of another art A, as it always does, it is not merely an accidental accompaniment of A which is neutral or indifferent to the nature of the art, or to its point or aim, or to what that aim would dictate to be the proper conduct of the art. If it were neutral in that way it would conjoin with art A, but leave the conduct of that art unaffected. In Aristotle's view, it is itself a distinct art, and because of that it introduces another end, an end quite distinct from the end of the art A and different from it. The difference is such that a conflict of ends arises, as a result of which something must happen to the end of art A; it can be compromised, or subordinated, or, in the worst case, entirely replaced by the end of getting money.

Complaints about money-making are familiar in ancient literature. Xenophon's Socrates speaks contemptuously of 'the traffickers in the market-place who think of nothing but buying cheap and selling dear', and Plato's Socrates charmingly complains of the 'little bald-headed tinker who has made money'. Plato criticizes the confusion of aims that money introduces into the practice of the arts (*Republic*, 342), though not as lucidly as Aristotle does here, and he bans citizens from taking part in money-making or trade (*Laws*, 846d–847b, 915d–920d). Aristotle may well have shared similar sentiments, but he does not air them much, and his more penetrating criticism goes beyond Plato's sentiments of disgust.

People may pursue the aim of expanding exchange value, or 'enjoyable excess', by means of *kapêlikê*, and then they are not living well for the familiar Aristotelian reasons. But if they cannot pursue it by that means, 'they try to do so by some other means, employing each of the faculties in an unnatural way [and] make all these faculties means for the business of providing wealth [*chrêmatistikas*, that is, in the context, money-getting], in the belief that wealth is the end and that everything must be directed to the end' (*Pol.* 1, 1258ᵃ8–14). Aristotle instances the military and medical arts, but the list

71

can be extended a long way, as he clearly intended it should be. 'For it is not the function of courage to produce wealth, but to inspire daring; nor is it the function of the military art nor of the medical art, but it belongs to the former to bring victory and to the latter to cause health. Yet these people make all these faculties means for the business of providing wealth' (1258^{a}11 ff.). Each of these activities has an end or point for the sake of which it is pursued, and by which it is defined; causing people to be healthy, for instance, or causing them to be educated. But they can all be pursued for the sake of exchange value as well as for the sake of their own intrinsic end, or sometimes instead of it. When that happens, their own real point or end can become no more than a means to the end of exchange value, namely, its quantitative expansion. Since this single end is something quite different from their specific and intrinsic ends, these activities can be transformed, and their real points can be compromised or even destroyed.

The object of the medical art is health. But if the medical profession pursues it for the sake of exchange value, then health is no longer its only aim. The practitioners will now be pursuing two ends at the same time. Those ends can be combined in different proportions by individual practitioners. In the best case the practitioner will give the greatest priority to health and the least to money. Even in this case the aim is still not simply health, but a minimum compromise between health and the other end. In the worst case the practitioner gives the greatest priority to exchange value and the least to health. In this case he cannot disregard health altogether, because the pursuit of exchange value here is parasitic on the pursuit of health, and there is a threshold in the pursuit of health below which he cannot go and still effectively use the art for the pursuit of exchange value. He is using the medical art as a means to another end altogether. In both the best and the worst cases, and at every point on the spectrum between them, the practitioners are no longer pursuing health alone, and they will not do the same things they would have done if they had been.

In practice, the two ends will not be clearly distinguished, and the practice of the art of medicine will not aim in any simple way at either one end or the other. Rather, the two activities will 'pass into one another', as Aristotle says the two distinct arts of *chrêmatistikê* do. What he says of *chrêmatistikê* applies equally to medicine, and to any other art practised in this ambiguous way. The ambiguity and confusion arise from the differences between the two distinct kinds of wealth that are being pursued at the same time. Both are called 'wealth', and they are not clearly distinguished, but rather merged: 'The source of the confusion is the near connection between the two kinds of wealth-getting; in either, the instrument is the same, although the use is different, and so they pass into one another; for each is a use of the same property, but with a difference: accumulation is the end in the one case, but there is a further end in the other' (1257b34 ff.).

There is little to suggest that Aristotle regards this sort of misuse of an art primarily as a personal failing on the part of the individual practitioner. In *De Sophisticis Elenchis* he is hard on the Sophists for their misuse of philosophy, but he had his own reasons for doing that, and they may well be a special case. In the *Politics* he does not subject doctors, soldiers, or any other professionals to harsh words for misusing their professions. And contrary to what commentators have often suggested, he even spares the traders the sort of treatment he gives the Sophists. Plato is much rougher with traders, castigating their miserable qualities of soul, and the damage their activities do to life and relationships in the city. Aristotle is not being unduly delicate in witholding criticism of this sort. He does not indulge in it because it would be irrelevant to the nature of the problem as he understands it. It is not in any immediate way a problem of individual conscience, to be dealt with by individual practitioners resolving to avoid shameful behaviour in future. He regards these misuses as aspects of a more general kind of problem, and it is characteristic that he should do this. He believed that people generally act above all according to their interests, or, as we might put it today, according to their 'economic position'.[3] People have to live,

---

[3] See Ste Croix, *The Class Struggle in the Ancient Greek World* (London, 1981), 71, 73, 78, 79. Ste Croix argues that Aristotle 'takes it for granted that men will act,

and if in order to live they must get money, as they must in an exchange-based society, and get it through the practice of the art they have been trained in, then that is what they will have to do; 'the life of money-making is one undertaken under compulsion' (*NE* 1, 1096ᵃ5). These social arrangements are not of their making, and as individuals they have no choice but to accommodate to them. Aristotle is concerned with the nature of those social arrangements and the consequences of their operation before he is concerned with personal behaviour.

He is concerned with personal behaviour too, of course, but in this context he is concerned with it inasmuch as it is affected by those arrangements of money. He says of the boaster that 'he who claims more than he has with no ulterior object is a contemptible sort of fellow (otherwise he would not have delighted in falsehood), but seems futile rather than bad'. Boasting with an object in mind is worse, but it makes a difference what the object is: 'he who does it for the sake of reputation or honour is (for a boaster) not very much to be blamed'. On the other hand, 'he who does it for money, or the things that lead to money, is an uglier character' (*NE* 4, 1127ᵇ9–13). Money, as the universal equivalent, acts as a universal ulterior object that can enter into the doing of almost anything, and into almost any sort of relationship, so that personal behaviour can be systematically affected by its presence.

What goes for the medical art goes for all the other arts and faculties that can be used in the same ambiguous way. Aristotle is concerned not only about exchange value compromising the single activity of *chrêmatistikê*, but about its invasion of the whole of ethical and political life. The activity of pursuing money has a capacity to attach itself to other activities, to infiltrate its aim into theirs, and to subordinate their ends to its own. This makes it a danger to Aristotle's conception of the sort of life fitting for creatures having the capacities humans have, and living a polis life. Aristotle does not make

politically or otherwise, above all according to their economic position', ibid. 79. See also the discussion of Sainte Croix in Irwin, 'Moral Science and Political Theory in Aristotle', in P. A. Cartledge and F. D. Harvey (eds.), *Crux: Essays Presented to G. E. M. de Ste. Croix on his 75th Birthday, History of Political Thought*, 7/1–2 (1985).

the point himself, but it is obvious that this is something that could undermine the rational ordering of ends set out in the first pages of the *Nicomachean Ethics* (1, 1094ª1–1094ᵇ11). Aristotle holds that the arts and their ends can and should be arranged in a hierarchy, some more serious than others. Those that are less serious are pursued, not for their own sakes, but for the sake of others that are more serious; 'as bridle-making and the other arts concerned with the equipment of horses fall under the art of riding, and this and every military action under strategy, in the same way other arts fall under yet others—in all of these the ends of the master arts are to be preferred to all the subordinate ends; for it is for the sake of the former that the latter are pursued' (*NE* 1, 1094ª10–15). The master art is *politikê* or politics, because its end is the good for man, and so its end includes all the other arts and their ends, and while they are pursued for its sake, it is not pursued for the sake of anything else. If these arts are infiltrated by the pursuit of exchange value, and their ends compromised, confused, or subverted, in the ways considered above in relation to medicine, there can be little hope of their being rationally ordered. The polis itself, Aristotle says, comes into existence for the sake of life, but it exists for the sake of the good life (*Pol.* 1, 1252ᵇ30–1; *Pol.* 3, 1280ª31–2); it is not merely for defence and exchanging goods, it is a partnership in living well (*Pol.* 3, 1280ᵇ29–35). 'Even if people living near each other had laws to prevent them wronging each other in the exchange of products—for instance, if one man were a carpenter, another a farmer, another a shoemaker, and others producers of other goods—and the whole population numbered ten thousand, still, if they associated in nothing more than military alliance and the exchange of goods, this would not be a polis' (*Pol.* 3, 1280ᵇ17–23). The pursuit of wealth as exchange value is not good enough for Aristotle, but worse than that, it undermines his understanding of the fitting use of human capacities, the good for man, and the point of the polis and of political life.

Aristotle is more inclined than modern writers to rely on psychological and moral factors to explain social and political change. He criticizes those who see private property as the cause of social evils, and suggests that the cause really lies in human wickedness (*Pol.* 2, 1263^{b}15–27). But in his account of the development of exchange value, he handles the interaction of personal motivation and social forms and institutions more subtly. He argues that there is an end built into the circuits of exchange value, partly present perhaps in C–M–C' and fully fledged in M–C–M', to which people adapt themselves and their behaviour. He does not think money and monetary exchange are neutral devices which human wickedness abuses by putting them to vicious ends. He thinks the vicious end is inherent in the institution itself. He holds that wealth ('true wealth') is in its nature limited (*Pol.* 1, 1256^{b}27 ff.), but he observes that there exists an erroneous idea that wealth is unlimited. He does not, however, find the origin of this idea in vicious human propensities, as we might have expected, perhaps, but in the existence of the form of exchange value. He defines the good kind of *chrêmatistikê* by its end, to provide a stock of useful things, and he contrasts it with the bad kind: 'there is another variety of the art of acquisition which is commonly and rightly called the art of making money [*chrêmatistikên*]'. The end of bad *chrêmatistikê* is getting money, and it is this that 'has in fact suggested the notion that wealth and property have no limit' (*Pol.* 1, 1256^{b}40 ff.).

'Limit' (*peras*) is an important Aristotelian idea, and it is a serious matter for Aristotle that in the pursuit of wealth as exchange value 'there is no limit to the end it seeks; and the end it seeks is wealth of the sort we have mentioned . . . the mere acquisition of money' (*Pol.* 1, 1257^{b}33 ff.).[4] In the context of 'virtue as a kind of mean' he says that 'evil belongs to the class of the unlimited [*apeiron*], as the Pythagoreans conjectured, and good to that of the limited' (*NE* 2, 1106^{b}29 ff.). This does not apply to ends that are constitutive of the good life, because 'there is no limit to the pursuit of health, and as in the other arts there is no limit to the pursuit of their several ends, for they aim at accomplishing their ends to the uttermost (but of the means there is a limit, for the end is always the

---

[4] Plato's main objection to trade was that it made it possible for the pursuit of gain to be unlimited, see *Laws*, 736e, 741e, 847d, and 918d.

limit)' (*Pol.* 1, 1257^{b}25 ff.). But, as he says, it always applies to means. Aristotle holds as a general principle that an end imposes a limit on means. Every art has an end, and the means to that end are not unlimited, but limited to those means that are needed to attain it. True wealth is not an end but a set of means for attaining ends: 'For the amount of such property sufficient in itself for a good life is not unlimited, as Solon says that it is in the verse "But of riches no bound has been fixed or revealed to men"; for a limit has been fixed, as with the other arts, since no tool belonging to any art is without a limit whether in number or in size, and riches are a collection of tools for the householder or the statesman' (*Pol.* 1, 1256^{b}31–8); 'external goods have a limit, as has any instrument (and everything useful is useful for something)' (*Pol.* 7, 1323^{b}7–8).[5] Wealth in the order of nature (*ho ploutos ho kata phusin*, that is, use value, 'true wealth', *ho alêthinos ploutos*) consists in 'those goods capable of accumulation which are necessary for life and useful for the community of the city or household', and are therefore not unlimited in number and size, but limited to those needed to attain the ends of those communities.

We get the idea that wealth is unlimited, Aristotle says, from the fact that wealth has come to take the form of exchange value or money (*Pol.* 1, 1256^{b}40 f.). The limits set to wealth as use value are imposed by the particular arts and their ends, to which wealth in this sense is the means. But wealth as exchange value is not a means, either to the arts and their immediate ends, or to the end that the arts themselves serve or constitute, the good life. That is enough to condemn it in Aristotle's view. But the position is even worse than this. When exchange value is well developed in society, it itself becomes the end, and the arts and their ends become means to it, instead of means to the good life. He says that 'all these faculties become means for the business of providing wealth [sc. as money], in the belief that wealth is the end and that everything must be directed to the end' (1258^{a}8–14). Wealth of this

---

[5] See the discussion of 'external goods' (*ta ektos agatha*) by J. M. Cooper, 'Aristotle on the Goods of Fortune', *Philosophical Review*, 94/2 (1985), 173–96, which does not, however, discuss their being limited.

kind has no limit imposed from without because it is not a means subordinate to an end; and since it is itself a purely quantitative feature, it has no limit of its own; so it has no limit at all.

Ross objects that Aristotle overlooks the fact that people were able to seek unlimited wealth before money came into existence. Aristotle 'does not notice that the pursuit of wealth for its own sake may arise even at his earliest stage, where goods are accumulated and exchange has not begun, and that in barter no less than in the exchange of goods for money profiteering is possible'.[6] The implication is that money can hardly be blamed for the idea of unlimited wealth, and that Aristotle should have blamed human greed for it instead. But the thought that people could have wanted too much before money was invented, is, it has to be said, such an obvious one that it is hard to imagine that Aristotle did not think of it; particularly since *pleonexia*, or the desire for too much, is such a familiar Aristotelian theme. In any case, *pleonexia* is not the same thing as a devised general form of wealth which is in its nature without a limit. The desire for too much is always there to cause bad behaviour, and Aristotle is not one to forget it. But that is not what he has in mind. His point is that C–M–C′, as an institution or form of behaviour, has a limit built into in its form. It is difficult to suppose that he imagines this fact is a guarantee against greed, and that when exchange was confined to the C–M–C′ form people behaved only in ungrasping ways. His point is about the nature of the activity and the end it embodies. It is in the nature of M–C–M′ that it has no limit built into its form. For that reason, those who pursue it are engaged in a form of activity whose end is of such a kind that it has no limit. Whatever the degree of their personal propensity to greed may be, the nature of the end of the activity they are engaged in will usually ensure that their behaviour is greedy.

It is no defence against Aristotle's criticism of money-making to object, as Barker and Ross do, that the trader performs

---

[6] Ross, *Aristotle*, 243.

a service. According to Ross, Aristotle 'does not see that the commercial class, which he condemns, renders a useful public service and makes its profits only because it does so', and according to Barker, Aristotle, like the Physiocrats, 'forgot . . . that production is a process which does not stop till the article reaches the consumer; and they failed to realise that every stage of this process is equally valuable, and equally "productive".'[7] This is no defence, because Aristotle's criticism is aimed not at the trader, but at money and the effect it has on the arts when they are pursued for the sake of it. Those arts include most things that could be described as 'rendering a useful public service'. Making money is a distinct end and art, but it is not a distinct activity.

There is no activity of 'making money' which can be conducted on its own, independently of the conduct of another art or useful activity, except in the literal sense of coining or printing legal tender. Making money is an end which can be pursued only by its being latched onto the conduct of some other art. This applies even to trade. Trade, in so far as it is a useful service, is the art of getting useful things to where they are needed. That art is transformed into 'trade' in the more familiar sense by its being used as a way of making money. Ross's argument seems convincing only if the two arts and ends are conflated, and on Aristotle's view they have to be distinguished, as the two arts of good and bad *chrêmatistikê* have to be distinguished. The term 'trade' now has such strong commercial connotations that it can be difficult to detach them, but the distinction between the two sorts or arts of 'trade', the movement of use values and the movement of exchange values, can be important. Failure to observe it can lead to confusion in assessing ancient evidence, and Garnsey and Saller have occasion to note that 'Polanyi, and more recently, Finley, have reminded us that not all commodity movement in antiquity is properly described as trade in the sense of market exchange. In particular, the transport of goods under the order of or under the control of the state, "redistribution", or "administered

---

[7] Ibid.; Barker, *Political Thought of Plato and Aristotle*, 390, n. 1.

trade", was of singular importance under the Roman empire. Insofar as rich investors were caught up in the transport to the city of Rome or the Roman armies of massive quantities of goods, especially tax grain, this would tell us little about the importance of trade in the Roman world.'[8]

Aristotle may blame money rather than human frailty for the evils of exchange value, but human frailty has a share in the blame. The forms of exchange value, which are socially devised, exacerbate what are already human propensities for seeking pleasure and acting on shallow ideas of human well-being, and those natural propensities in turn reinforce the social forms: 'The many, the most vulgar, would seem to conceive the good and happiness as pleasure, and hence they also like the life of gratification. Here they appear completely slavish, since the life they decide on is a life for grazing animals' (*NE* 1, 1095^{b}16 ff.). We can get some sort of proportion into judging the qualities of this treatment by comparing it with Adam Smith's in *The Wealth of Nations*. Smith, despite having all the benefits of hindsight, takes exchange value largely for granted, offers little or no analysis of it, and for explanation postulates a natural and universal human 'propensity to truck, barter and exchange'.[9]

Aristotle does not project into the future to estimate the character and scale of the danger posed to the polis by exchange value. He was not a Whig in history, and he did not have the modern idea of progress any more than any other

---

[8] P. Garnsey and R. Saller, *The Roman Empire* (London, 1990), 48. The word 'commodity' has strong connotations of exchange value, and by using it unguardedly the authors do not add to the clarity of the point they are making. It is characteristic of much economic vocabulary to be ambiguous in this way between a use-value and an exchange-value meaning; the ambiguity is touched on in Ch. 8.

[9] A. Smith, *Wealth of Nations*, i. 15. This propensity to exchange is, according to Smith, a natural propensity 'in human nature', and it is what marks us off from non-human animals, 'which seem to know neither this nor any other species of contracts'; 'Two greyhounds, in running down the same hare, have sometimes the appearance of acting in some sort of concert. Each turns her towards his companion, or endeavours to intercept her when his companion turns her towards himself. This, however, is not the effect of any contract, but of the accidental concurrence of their passions in the same object at that particular time. Nobody ever saw a dog make a fair and deliberate exchange of one bone for another with another dog.'

The Integrity of the Analysis

Greek.[10] Naturally he did not conceive of capitalist market economy, nor of its fundamental condition: that human capacities in general might themselves come to be supplied in the form of an exchange value to be bought and sold. He believed that all possible political institutions had already been discovered, and that the polis was the highest of them. He also believed that all the arts had been discovered and forgotten many times in the course of history (*Met. A*, 1074^{b}10 ff.). He seems to see exchange value as an obstacle to polis dwellers in moving from mere life to the good life.

☞ 2 ☜

There are contrasts to be drawn between the discussion in the *Ethics* and that in the *Politics*, and Finley draws some of them in the course of his endeavours to expose the anachronism of the many attempts that have made to give a neo-classical reading of Aristotle. Those efforts have indeed been unconvincing, and they will be looked at in Chapter 6, but in order to show their weaknesses it is not necessary to go to the length of claiming, as Finley does, that Aristotle's chapters contain only ethics, to the exclusion of anything that could be regarded as reflection on what today would usually be called 'economic' matters. There would have been no need for this exaggerated thesis if Finley had distinguished between economic inquiries, that is, inquiries that are in their nature economic, and inquiries which, though not in their nature economic, concern matters which today we would call 'economic'. Finley is led to exploit in exaggerated ways the contrasts he rightly draws between the two discussions, because of the exaggerated thesis he is trying to make them support.

---

[10] In *The Idea of Progress*, Bury wrote that 'the Greeks, who were so fertile in their speculations on human life, did not hit upon an idea which seems so simple and obvious to us as the idea of Progress'. This view has been challenged by Edelstein, *The Idea of Progress in Classical Antiquity* (Baltimore, 1967). Finley repudiates Edelstein's attribution of an idea of progress to the Greeks on the ground that Edelstein's work is vitiated by 'neglect of the fundamental distinction between material and cultural progress', 'Aristotle and Economic Analysis', 47, n. 76.

The Integrity of the Analysis

The salient difference between the passages from the *Ethics* and the *Politics* is that the *Ethics* contains no discussion of *kapêlikê* or trade. Finley regards this as a critical difference. The *Politics* goes through four forms, C–C′, C–M–C′, M–C–M′ and M–M′, but the *Ethics* is confined to C–M–C′, that is, exchange between two producers without the intervention of a middleman. Furthermore, Aristotle never uses any of the usual Greek terms for 'trade' and 'trader' (*kapêlikê, kapêlos*), as he often does in the *Politics*, but sticks to the neutral word *metadosis*.

These features would certainly appear to be odd if the discussion really had been intended as economic analysis. Trade, both *kapêlikê* and *emporikê* or mercantile trade, were commonplace in Aristotle's world, and he knew perfectly well that a large volume of goods circulated in the M–C–M′ manner and not in the C–M–C′ manner, and their absence from the discussion in the *Ethics* needs some sort of explanation. It might appear to be a deliberate lack of realism on Aristotle's part, and if that is what it is, then it would be difficult to explain on the supposition that he had been trying to do economic analysis, and easier to explain on the supposition that he had been doing ethics, at least as that term is usually understood today. This is the gist of Finley's case.[11]

The first of these suggestions is that if Aristotle had been attempting economic analysis in the *Ethics*, then he would have discussed such a familiar thing as trade. The tacit premiss here is that economic analysis deals only with familiar things like trade. This is, indeed, a view commonly taken of their subject by economists. Schumpeter, for instance, whom Finley explicitly follows in this, defines economic analysis as 'intellectual efforts made to *understand* economic phenomena', and he identifies that with 'analysing actual market mechanisms'.[12] Aristotle is plainly not doing that kind of thing in *NE* 5. 5, so it follows, given a definition of this kind, that his attempted analysis of the commensurability of products as exchange val-

---

[11] He makes it in 'Aristotle and Economic Analysis', 9, n. 26, and 13–15.

[12] Schumpeter, *History of Economic Analysis*, 1 and 60; cited by Finley, 'Aristotle and Economic Analysis', 26 and 44.

ues is not economic analysis. Part of the problem is that it is difficult to see what other name to give it. If one is determined to hold that Aristotle did no economics, as Finley was, it would be tempting to overlook Aristotle's attempted analysis altogether, as Finley does. On the other hand, it is equally difficult to see how the problem of commensurability might be solved by attending to 'actual market mechanisms'; and if Aristotle's problem falls outside the domain which an authority like Schumpeter regards as 'economics', one might conclude that the problem is not an economic one, and that an attempt at solving it is not 'economic analysis'. Aristotle's text leads the commentator into the notoriously disputed and tangled question of how 'economics' is to be defined, and it is easy to see the attractions of a simple insistence that Aristotle's chapter is ethical and nothing more.

The second suggestion is that Aristotle deliberately excluded trade because, the subject of the chapter being, according to Finley's view, the justice of each having 'their own' in the community (*koinônia*), Aristotle cannot introduce the *kapêlos* or trader, since justice in exchange is achieved when 'each have their own', when, in other words, there is no gain from anyone else's loss.[13] Aristotle's insistence on the unnaturalness of commercial gain, Finley suggests, rules out the possibility of a discussion of profit-making exchange M–C–M′ in the *Ethics*.

The *Ethics* chapter, however, is not simply about the justice of each having 'their own'. It is mostly about how goods can possibly be commensurable, or how it can be possible that a proportion of one good might be equal to some proportion of any other you care to choose, however different: 5 beds = 1 house = so much money (1133^b27–28). Naturally, since Aristotle was aware of the successive forms of exchange relations, he studied his problem against the setting of the form of exchange in which that relation of equality is expressed, C–M–C′, and not a form in which an inequality is expressed, M–C–M′. That is why Aristotle is talking exclusively of an exchange between two producers without the intervention of a

[13] The Greek expression *ta hautôn ekhein* (having your own) is often used by Aristotle, and it means roughly what is yours, or what you have, or ought to have.

middleman. Consideration of M–C–M′ would have done nothing to advance the solution of this problem. The objective nature of the circuit M–C–M′, which becomes the subjective aim of the *kapêlos* engaging in it, lies, as Aristotle himself explains, in the fact that unequals are exchanged; the sum advanced is exceeded by the sum extracted. This is a subordinate species of exchange. Aristotle is aware of the fact, and he makes the point explicitly in the *Politics* that this is a derivative form of exchange (1257^b1–5). In the *Ethics* he has uncovered a more general problem to do with the possibility of exchange of any kind. That being so, he has no need to discuss subordinate species, so he does not discuss them. To put the point another way, it is impossible to come to understand the later and derivative form of the exchange of unequals until one has understood what equality in exchange means; and it is impossible to come to understand that until one has solved the underlying problem of commensurability, which is the presupposition of systematic exchange-relations existing at all. Aristotle is not concerned with the forms through which they pass in the development of exchange value. That matter is gone into in the *Politics*. That is why trade (M–C–M′) is discussed there and not in the *Ethics*. Indeed, this very disposition of material between the two works reveals his awareness of the different levels of generality.

It is true, as Finley says, that in the *Ethics* unlike the *Politics* Aristotle tends to prefer the neutral word for exchange (*metadosis*), and to avoid the terms usually associated with trade (*kapêlikê*). It is hardly convincing to suggest that the reason for this is that Aristotle cannot introduce *kapêlikê* because justice in exchange is achieved when 'each have their own' and there is no gain from anyone else's loss. Even if the fairness of each having 'their own' really had been the main subject of the chapter, as Finley insists it is, this need not be thought to have given Aristotle reason to avoid the use of *kapêlos* and *kapêlikê*. It might be thought to have given him better reason for using them ruthlessly, since the *kapêlos* is a prime example of unfairness, and Aristotle is unsparing about unfairness. Whatever one's preferred intuition in the matter, Aristotle's silence about trade in the *Ethics* cannot be explained by supposing his concern to have been ethical, in the straightforward way Finley supposes, because that supposition, even if it were correct, would explain the presence as well as the absence of a discussion of trade. If the *Ethics* had contained such a discussion, the explanation would explain this too.

☞ 3 ☜

The analyses Aristotle offers in *NE* 5. 5 and *Pol.* 1. 8–10 form an integral whole, and one with obvious metaphysical depth and conceptual penetration. Aristotle's ideas about exchange, wealth, money, and interest cohere as a theoretical whole because they all derive systematically from the categorical distinction he establishes between use value and exchange value which he makes the foundation of his thought about matters which we would call 'economic'.

That metaphysical difference, established in the *Ethics*, carries though into the difference of end, established in the *Politics*, between the pursuit of use value and the pursuit of exchange value. It provides the explanation of the divergent courses of action taken by the doctor who pursues health and by the doctor who pursues money—and so on for all the other arts and faculties that are used in this ambiguous way. It provides the basis of the distinction he draws between the different aims of the evolving forms of exchange: the circuits C–C' and C–M–C' have use value as their aim, and M–C–M' and M–M' aim at exchange value. It also leads him to offer two definitions—a use-value definition and an exchange-value one—of each of the economic notions of wealth, exchange, and, in a way, of money too, as we shall see in Chapter 5.

Aristotle's metaphysics reinforces the treatment in another way also. In his account, use value and exchange value fall on different sides of the Greek distinction between nature and convention, *phusis* and *nomos*. Use value is natural and belongs to *phusis*, because the usefulness of a product is explained by the natural properties in virtue of which it serves the purpose for which it was made. Exchange value is conventional, and belongs to *nomos*, because it arises in the course of people developing their ways of handling or exchanging products. The two values are logically distinct and cannot be internally connected; at most they can exist side by side, and that only so long as the conventions that give existence to exchange value continue to hold. These conventions need not hold, and they do not hold in the 'Arcadian kind of life', for example (1261ª29 ff.), or, as Aristotle knew and Herodotus makes clear, in the Persian empire.[14] It is not clear that, on the neoclassical account, it is possible for exchange value to be treated ultimately as conventional rather than natural, because according to that account the two are not categorically distinguished but fused together.

There is demonstrably a formidable theoretical cohesion uniting *NE* 5. 5 and *Pol.* 1. 8–10, and the account as a whole is supported in depth by Aristotle's system of metaphysics. It is remarkable that his chapters should have been so undervalued in modern times, and so frequently dismissed as desultory, superficial, primitive, ideological, or pompous common-sense platitudes.

In utilitarian or neo-classical economics, use value and exchange value are conceptually connected in the notion of utility. In Aristotle's analysis, however, exchange value cannot be an aspect of use value, or be conceptually connected with it, in the way that it is understood to be in neo-classical economics, and for quite general logical and metaphysical reasons. It is not obvious that the metaphysical support for the neoclassical view is equally solid.

---

[14] Herodotus tells the story of the Spartan herald who warns Cyrus the Great against causing harm to Greek cities in Asia Minor. Cyrus replies that he has never yet been frightened by men who, in the middle of their cities, set up places where they gather to cheat each other with oaths. Hdt., 1. 152–3.

☞ 5 ☜
Money: *Politics,* 1. 8–10

Joseph Schumpeter considered Aristotle's treatment of money in *Politics,* 1. 8–10 to be 'the basis of the bulk of all analytical work in the field of money'.[1] Schumpeter was among Aristotle's shrewdest economic commentators and in some ways the most critically hostile, yet he regarded the analysis as penetrating and precocious. But it is perhaps more penetrating than he thought and more deeply and interestingly flawed. The analysis is ethical as well as economic, and these two aspects are in a tension which leads Aristotle to attribute two natures to money, that of a means and that of an end. His official position is that it has only one of these natures, that of a means of exchange, and he ignores the other without giving a reason. Modern condescension should not be precipitate, however, because the tension is not one that can easily be avoided from what might be thought the high vantage-point of modern economic thinking about money, which is just as deeply divided and in just the same way.

Tensions were beginning to show in Aristotle's treatment of exchange and money in *Pol.* 1. 8–10, which was looked at in Chapter 3. The ethical and the economic aspects of the analysis had seemed to fit together neatly in the earlier parts of his account. But as the thought developed, they seemed to be meshing less and less perfectly, though the nature of the tension and its underlying source were not immediately apparent. The early hint of a possible reservation on Aristotle's part

[1] Schumpeter adds that 'it prevailed substantially until the end of the nineteenth century and even beyond', and that three of the four functions of money traditionally listed in nineteenth-century textbooks of economics can be traced back to Aristotle, namely, money as medium of exchange, as measure of value, and as store of value. The absence of the fourth, money as a standard of deferred payments, can hardly be held against Aristotle, since there were no deferred payments in the ancient world, though Schumpeter does not offer this excuse; *History of Economic Analysis,* 62–3.

about the use made of a thing in exchange is a symptom of what becomes a deep ambivalence running through the entire analysis. It erupts in three connected problems which pull the basis of his ethical verdicts on the different sorts of exchange away from his analysis of their evolution. These problems centre on the nature of money.

In his account of the evolution of exchange, Aristotle distinguishes four forms: C–C´, C–M–C´, M–C–M´, and M–M´. But interwoven with this is an analysis, which today might be called 'ethical' rather than 'economic', in which he examines the end of each form. He finds that there are two ends, not one, and he concludes that though they appear to be different ways of doing the same thing, they are really similar ways of doing different things.

The key to the ethical side of his treatment is the distinction he draws between those two ends. C–C´ is acceptable because its end is consumption, the bringing together of needs with the use values that will satisfy them, and he judges this to be natural and necessary by the usual criterion of having 'enough' (*autarkês*). C–M–C´ is acceptable too, because it shares the same end. But the end shared by M–C–M´ and M–M´ is the accumulation of money, and the aim here is not that of having enough. Using money in this way is not to use it as a means subordinate to a natural end, but to make money itself the end, and to make natural ends a means of making money. As an end, it is without a limit and so it is irrational.

If this distinction of ends should fail, Aristotle would face a very unpalatable choice between holding that all the forms of exchange are equally acceptable, including the 'hated' usury or M–M´, and holding that they are all equally unacceptable, including the 'necessary and laudable' C–M–C´. And if the distinction should fail for reasons arising from his analysis of exchange and money, then he would face the choice of holding on to his analysis and facing up to the unpalatable ethical choice that would follow from it, or ditching the entire analysis of the three chapters, which would leave him with nothing at all.

☞ 1 ☜

Aristotle's complaint about the Delphian knife was, as we saw, that it is not good enough to do its job properly, and that it has this deficiency because it has been deliberately constructed to perform more functions than it can perform well (it is a knife, a file, and a hammer) in order to sell cheaply.[2] It has been made to be exchanged rather than to do a job. The one who makes it shows a 'niggardly' spirit (*penikhrôs*). But it is difficult to be sure just how this is to be understood. It might amount to no more than a complaint about one particular kind of product and those who make it, and, if that is all it is, we should not read too much into it. But it might be a particular illustration of an implied general criticism of the deleterious effects that exchange can have on the quality of the things produced, when they are made in order to be exchanged for money. If that is Aristotle's point, then the implications are more serious. This would be a criticism of the effects of money on production.[3]

The danger of anachronism is obvious. We are excessively familiar today with the commercially inspired adulteration of use values: foods lacking in nutrition or actually being poisonous, consumer durables with obsolescence and decay built into their design specification, unnecessary surgical operations done because they pay, education being made into training, and so forth. Care must be taken not to project this sort of thing back without evidence. But things of a similar nature were not altogether unknown in the ancient world. Lots of shoddy things were produced, coin debased, and products adulterated. The Delphian knife finds a parallel in the product of 'the coppersmith who for cheapness makes a spit and a

---

[2] Aristotle is not proposing that all tools be made only to the highest imaginable standards of perfection; e.g. that all tools be made only of the best materials, regardless of how scarce they may be. He is simply suggesting that you do the best with what you've got. He thinks that even with what you've got, anyone can do better than the miserable Delphian knife.

[3] See Moreau, 'Aristote et la monnaie', 358.

lampholder in one' (*De Part. An.* 4, 683ª22 ff.).[4] Aristotle himself is concerned about the effects of exchange value or money relations on the practice of the professional arts, as we saw in Chapter 4 (1). People not themselves engaged in trade (*kapêlikê*) but who wish to pursue money 'do so by some other means, employing each of the faculties in an unnatural way [and] make all these faculties means for the business of providing wealth [*chrêmatistikê*, that is, in the context, money-getting], in the belief that wealth [sc. 'of the spurious kind'] is the end and that everything must be directed to the end' (*Pol.* 1, 1258ª8–14). Aristotle cites the military and medical arts, and even philosophy, as examples of this, and he takes a dim view of it.

It is true that ancient society was not a market economy, and that fact must always be held firmly in mind in considering matters of this kind. The product of labour did not universally take the form of a commodity or exchange value, since a sizeable proportion of production was undertaken for direct consumption rather than for sale. The common culture was quite inhospitable to the values of commerce, and they were not admired or publicly applauded, nor was public policy constructed with them at its heart. But even making due allowance for these great differences, and for avoiding modernist exaggerations and false assimilations of ancient practices to modern ones, there was still quite enough of that kind of behaviour to make it a perfectly realistic possibility that Aristotle might have intended the example of the Delphian knife to illustrate an implied general criticism.

The conditions prevailing in fourth-century Athens do not make such a criticism impossible or even unlikely, but even so it is still possible that Aristotle did not intend it. He does not explicitly draw the implication himself, and the best we can do is to decide how likely or unlikely it is that he had it in mind. There are two questions to be asked. Is there better reason to think that Aristotle intended it than there is to think that he

---

[4] See Newman's long note, *Politics of Aristotle*, ii. 109–10. See also Ross's note on the implement made by the coppersmith, in the Oxford trans. of *De Part. An.* 683ª22, n. 1.

didn't? And, whether he intended it or not, was it a thought he could easily have had, and should have had if he didn't?

As to the first question, there is little explicit indication that he wants to extend the criticism of the smith to the makers of things generally. He is not short of opportunities, and the single criticism of the coppersmith in *De Partibus Animalium* is not enough to suggest that he was particularly anxious to pursue them. Against this it can be said that, given all that he has to say about the drawbacks and dangers of money-seeking behaviour, which after all is his theme in *Pol* 1. 8–10, it is not very likely that he simply meant to criticize the makers of one or two particular items rather than a tendency they illustrate.

As to the second question, if Aristotle did not think of the idea, we are entitled to ask why. It would have been an obvious and natural application of his view of true and false wealth, of his idea of wealth as use which he develops in the *Rhetoric*, of his criticisms of the end aimed at in M–C–M′ behaviour, and of the abuse of the arts for making money. Given all that, it would be astonishing if the idea had never so much as crossed his mind. It is an obvious generalization of criticisms he already advances, and, given the character of the rest of his theory, it is certainly one that he should have added. It is easier to believe that he suppressed it for some reason than that it never ocurred to him.

The defects of the Delphian knife are not due to personal shortcomings of the individual smith, his skills, 'niggardliness', or honesty. Nor are they due to deficiencies in his materials. They are due to a social cause that operates systematically where there is money, namely, that goods tend to be produced in order to be exchanged against money. Aristotle's reason for saying that the use made of a shoe in exchange is not its 'proper or peculiar use' was that 'the shoe has not been made for the purpose of being exchanged' (*Pol.* 1, 1257ᵃ6 ff.). But where there is money, this is all too likely to be the purpose for which a thing has been made. The Delphian knife illustrates the kind of failure this typically leads to, and it is difficult to see that Aristotle could be making any other point. His allusion to the 'niggardliness' of the smith (*penikhrôs*, or the 'spirit of stint', as Newman puts it) should not draw attention away from the systematic nature of the failure. The smith's spirit of stint is not to be compared with the personal failing of the boaster who boasts with no ulterior purpose and is futile rather than bad. Nor is it like the act of the man who boasts with the purpose of getting honour and reputation, who is not to be blamed much. Those are human failings. It is to be compared with the calculating man who boasts with the purpose of 'getting money or the things that lead to money', who 'is an uglier character' (*NE* 4, 1127^{b}9–13), and with the Sophist who sells 'philosophy' for money, or the doctor who sells 'medical services'.

So it seems that C–M–C′ is not as innocent as Aristotle says. Its end is not to be so simply characterized as 'providing use value' or 'meeting need'. The fuller story will have to incorporate the possibility of the use value of products being systematically compromised by the fact that those products are also made to be exchange values. That possibility is systematically present where products are circulating against money. But telling this fuller story would undercut the ground on which Aristotle passes C–M–C′ as 'necessary and laudable', and the function of money that goes with it as ethically acceptable.

The ground was the distinction of ends he drew between C–M–C′ and M–C–M′, and the example of the Delphian knife shows that this cannot be drawn in the simple way he draws it, as one between use value and exchange value. The end of M–C–M′ remains the accumulation of wealth as money, but it is no longer so easy to exclude that from the definition of the end of C–M–C′. If the shorthand expression C–M–C′ is written in full, and its acts of sale and purchase are represented separately, as C–M/M–C′, then in the sale C–M, we see the smith aiming to maximize M by exchanging a 'knife' which he designed and made with that aim in mind. The Delphian knife has the defects Aristotle complains of just because M is its maker's aim. If M is at least partly the smith's aim, not simply C as Aristotle suggests, then the order of the smith's acts of sale and purchase may reasonably be reversed to give M–C/C–M′. The activity he is pursuing is at least partly M–C–M′ and not simply C–M–C′. Over time his activity has the form C–M–C–M–C–M–C–M–C . . ., and it can no longer be neatly divided up to make a sequence of repetitions of C–M–C′ thus: C–M–C/C–M–C/C–M–C . . . There is just as much reason now to divide it up as C–M/M–C–M/ M–C–M/M–C–M/M–C . . . Unless we are to say that he only makes money not knives, as the Sophist makes money not philosophy, it no longer seems clear how we are to distinguish making money and making knives.

Aristotle's decision to allow C–M–C′ and disallow M–C–M′ now looks shaky because the distinction of ends has become blurred. If Aristotle should not want to accept behaviour of this kind, in which the two ends merge or 'pass into one another', as he puts it, it would be open to him simply to insist on applying the distinction: the smith is able to do M–C–M′ and make bad 'knives', but he shouldn't. If he wants to act well he should stick to C–M–C′ and make proper knives. But if getting 'enough' means, in the circumstances, getting enough money to buy things, as it does in a money economy, it might well be the case that in acting on Aristotle's advice the smith cannot get 'enough', or 'make a living'. This is not something Aristotle could, or would want to, deny him the ability to do. In that case Aristotle would be in a difficulty which he could get out of only by dropping the advice to avoid M–C–M′.

Money-getting is a distinct art because it has a distinct end, and Aristotle says himself that when a professional art like medicine is pursued for the sake of money, the ends of the two arts of medicine and money-getting 'pass into one another; for each is a use of the same thing', and this compromises the pursuit of health (1257ᵇ34 ff.). But he never explicitly admits that the same applies to the artisan arts too. His ethical verdicts seem more reasonable if it is supposed, as it usually is, that the activity of the trader (*kapêlos*) is the only case of M–C–M′ behaviour that Aristotle sets out to criticize, and that the presence of money leaves the ends of all other activities unaffected. But this supposition is clearly wrong, as we saw in

Chapter 4 (1). So it must be asked how far along the line of activities he thinks the presence of money exerts its influence in making the end of the activity at best ambiguous between the pursuit of C and the pursuit of M. There is no reason to think the maker of knives is any different in this respect from the maker of anything else, or that artisans are any better than professionals like the doctor and the philosopher, so there is no reason to think that any sort of activity should remain immune if it involves money. His criticism of the smith is a criticism of just the same kind, and it seems strange that he neither develops it explicitly, nor shows any inclination to extend it to the makers of other things.

It is difficult to imagine that in this one field of the artisan arts, Aristotle simply forgot about the confusion of ends which occurs when an art is pursued for the sake of wealth as money. He shows the smith misusing knife-making in just the way that the Sophist misuses philosophy and the doctor misuses medicine. It is puzzling that Aristotle does not connect the smith into this line of criticism. The Delphian knife is such an obvious example of the same kind of shortcoming that his failure to relate it explicitly to his criticism of the effects of money as the spurious form of wealth seems to need some more convincing explanation than that he simply went to sleep at that point. It is tempting to suppose that he had a reason for deliberately excluding such considerations in this case.

If he had been determined to approve the function of money in C–M–C´, but to disbar its use in M–C–M´, it would have been necessary to keep a clear line of demarcation between them. He had strong reasons for wanting to allow C–M–C´, and the function of money as a means of exchange. Without them, money would have no legitimate function at all, and only barter, C–C´, would be legitimate. In holding this he would have become more unrealistic and a more extreme Laconizer than even Plato, who never went so far (*Laws*, 742a–c) in spite of the fact that money was prohibited in Sparta. This would have been an uncomfortable position for Aristotle to have to occupy. His inclination was to accommodate to deeply entrenched practices which there was little chance of changing, even if this entailed some cost to more basic positions he held. His strange defence of slavery, so at odds with his view that the best *politeia* is one where 'anyone at all [*hostisoun*] might do best and lead a flourishing life' (*Pol.* 7, 1324ª23–5), shows that he was capable of bending over backwards to do this, and Athens was hardly the place in which to expect unrealistic proposals about the use of money to be best received. To have pressed further than he did with the implications of the Delphian knife case would have forced him to choose between, on the one hand, dropping his objections to M–C–M′ and M–M′, together with the entire analysis of use value, exchange value, wealth, and exchange from which those objections follow, and on the other hand denying the legitimacy of money in any of its functions. The course he chooses manages to accommodate two common and entrenched sentiments: the usefulness of money for getting things, and the dislike of traders and money-lenders.

☞ 2 ☜

Aristotle is inconsistent in his treatment of money. His clearest explicit statement is that 'money was invented to be used in exchange' (*Pol.* 1, 1258ᵇ4–5), and mainly on the strength of this he has usually been understood to hold that money is in its nature an instrument or means for the circulation of use values, whose usefulness lies in helping to get use values to where they are needed. But his theory equally supports attributing to money the entirely different nature of an end, and obvious as this is, he ignores it and gives no reason for choosing the first view.

Roll rightly observes that according to Aristotle's own account of the development of exchange 'The natural purpose of exchange, the more abundant satisfaction of wants, is lost sight of; the accumulation of money becomes an end in itself.'[5] According to Aristotle, money becomes the universal form of wealth, because 'everything can be expressed [*tetimesthai*] in

---

[5] Roll, *History of Economic Thought*, 35.

money' (*NE* 5, 1133^{b}14–15), and many activities, perhaps most, come to be done for the sake of it as well as for the sake of their own intrinsic ends, or instead of them. What was introduced to be a means to human ends becomes an end itself, and the human ends it was meant to serve become means to it. We might have expected Aristotle to conclude that what money finally becomes is its *telos* or nature. In that case he would have had to conclude that when people introduced money believing it to be a means, they did not fully understand what they were doing. But he does not take this course. He insists that the true nature of money is to be what it was originally intended to be, a means, and that its development into an end is a perversion.

Aristotle often gives origins this kind of importance. He holds that they are a good guide in identifying the natures of things: 'he who considers things in their first growth and origin, whether a state or anything else, will obtain the clearest view of them' (*Pol.* 1, 1252^{a}24). So it is in character for Aristotle to identify the nature of money by means of its origin. But looking at origins is not the only way we have of identifying the natures of things, and it is just as typically Aristotelian to find out what something really is by looking for its mature form. What a thing develops into (its *telos* and its final cause) is the nature, for 'what each thing is when fully developed we call its nature, whether we are speaking of a man, a horse or a family' (*Pol.* 1, 1252^{b}32 f.). What a thing of a kind does when it is mature is the *ergon* of that kind of thing, as sight is the *ergon* of the eye (*EE* 1219^{a}16). It is also its *telos* (*De Gen. An.* 778^{a}33 f.), for 'each thing's *ergon* is its *telos*' (*EE* 1219^{a}8), and 'the *ergon* is the end, and the activity the *ergon*' (*Met.* Θ, 1050^{a}22). If Aristotle had chosen to determine the nature of money by this method, he should have arrived at the conclusion that it is in the nature of money to become an end, as he recognizes it does in M–C–M′ and M–M′. His own theory, then, contains what is needed to deduce, by familiar Aristotelian devices in each case, two quite different accounts of the nature of money. But a thing cannot ultimately be both a means and an end.

He might have drawn the conclusion that money has two natures, one as a means and the other as an end. In some ways this would not have been a surprising conclusion. He gives two definitions for each of the other major economic concepts, wealth and exchange (*chrêmatistikê*), a use-value definition and an exchange-value definition. This doubling-up of definitions is fundamental to his theory, because it is required by his metaphysical analysis, which established a difference of category between use value as qualitative, and exchange value as quantitative. So it would not have been surprising if he had concluded that money has two natures, or that there are two sorts of money, and given two definitions of this too. A distinction between use-value money and exchange-value money might also seem to fit, because the end of the good use of money in C–M–C′ is use value, and the end of its bad use in M–C–M′ is exchange value.

But this would have been nonsense, because money is exchange value. Its job is to express the exchange value of each commodity independently of that commodity's own physical body. The use value of a thing is undetachable from its physical body, but its exchange value can be represented in the physical body of the money commodity, and Aristotle knew this.[6] If gold is the money commodity then it has two use values: firstly as the substance of wedding rings, and secondly as the substance that is useful as a means of exchange and store of value. Aristotle knew this too.[7] Money is exchange value from the start, and it has this character in C–M–C′ just as

[6] The exchange value of the cabbages disappears with the decay of the cabbages and of their use value, but if they are sold, their exchange value lives on in the sum of money they realize. Aristotle says that the usefulness of money lies in the fact that it, unlike the perishable cabbages, 'serves as a guarantee of exchange for the future: supposing we need nothing at the moment, it ensures that exchange shall be possible when a need arises, for it meets the requirement of something we can produce in payment so as to obtain the thing we need' (*NE* 5, 1133^{b}10 ff.).

[7] Aristotle says that 'men agreed to employ in their dealings with each other something intrinsically useful and easily applicable to the purposes of life, for example, iron, silver and the like' (*Pol.* 1, 1257^{a}35 ff.); 'In the satisfaction of wants money became the medium of exchange by agreement. And for that reason it bears the name *nomisma*, because it owes its existence, not to nature, but to law [*nomô*], and it is in our power to change it and make it void' (*NE* 5, 1133^{a}28–31). See the discussion by Moreau, 'Aristote et la monnaie', 362.

much as in M–C–M′ and M–M′. Each of these forms of exchange depends on the exchange value of C being represented independently of the physical body of C. But if money has only the nature of exchange value, then it cannot have the use-value nature he wants for C–M–C′.

⌐ 3 ⌐

Each form of exchange realizes a potential in the nature of money, or rather, in the nature of exchange value, whose independent representative money is. In seeing those forms, from C–C′, through C–M–C′ and M–C–M′ to M–M′, as related in a process of development, as he does in *Politics*, 1, Aristotle is committed to holding something like this. According to his own account, once C–C′ became possible with the advent of the village, it came into being because it helped people to get 'enough'. Money arose next, because it made such exchange easier, and so C–M–C′ came into being. Once that in turn had developed, and its operation had become sufficiently understood, it gave rise to M–C–M′ and M–M′. Each transition from one form to the next is a part of the evolution of exchange, and each results from people pursuing the possibilities in the relations and institutions they have created.

Aristotle tends to think of change as a process of generation and maturation in some kind of entity, so it is natural that he should present the development of exchange in the way he does. But it is strange that in the course of such a process the entity should change its nature and become something else altogether, and this seems to be what is supposed to happen between C–M–C′ and M–C–M′, when money ceases to be a means and becomes an end. The idea is incoherent, because a process of development is necessarily undergone by some kind of unitary nature, and in the absence of such a unity there cannot be such a process. The identification of a unity is usually a matter of identifying an end or *telos*.[8] But in his account of

---

[8] See the discussion of wholes and ends in S. R. L. Clark, *Aristotle's Man: Speculations upon Aristotelian Anthropology* (Oxford, 1975), ch. II. 3.

the development of exchange, he explicitly identifies not one end but two, so it is hard to see what the requisite unity can consist in, and without that there cannot really be a single process of development at all. Aristotle subsequently implies that this is a single process only from C–C′ to C–M–C′, and a perversion thereafter, but this is another way of putting what has so far seemed unconvincing in his account.

Aristotle's ambiguity about the nature of money and its end is registered by Ross in his contribution to a little-known symposium with three economists, Cannan, Bonar, and Wicksteed, on the question of who should be given the credit for being the first to say that money is 'barren metal', and whether in particular the credit should go to Aristotle. On the one hand, Ross says of Aristotle's view of interest and M–M′ that 'I don't think he means that it is by an unnatural convention that money breeds money. He appears to regard it as the normal course of things that it should.' This is surely right if we have in mind Aristotle's account of the development of exchange and money. What happens in 'the normal course of things' is the result of the operations of some nature, and the appearance of interest in the course of that development is as much a part of the process as any other. It might even be said that M–M′, or interest, realizes a potential in the nature of money.

On the other hand, Ross also observes, 'money produces interest, but that this is not what it was invented to do—it was invented to be used in exchange. The yielding of interest is an unintended by-product. And since Aristotle identifies the nature of a thing with the end it is intended to fulfil, it is a legitimate gloss to say that interest-bearing is according to Aristotle no part of the nature of money.'[9] This is surely right too, if we have in mind Aristotle's ethical verdicts and their basis in the distinction of ends. The conclusion is, though Ross did not draw it, that the bearing of interest is part of the nature of money and that it is not.

---

[9] Ross's contribution to Cannan's symposium 'Barren Metal', 107.

~ 4 ~

Aristotle takes sides in the current debate about whether it is a good or a bad thing for a city to be located by the sea, and in opposition to Plato he decides that on the balance of advantage it is a good thing. But he is careful to make a distinction. It is a good thing for a city to engage in *emporikê* or sea-borne trade, because 'it is necessary that they should import from abroad what is not to be found in their own country, and that they should export what they have in excess'. But it is not good to engage in entrepôt trade. 'Those who make themselves a market for the world only do so for the sake of revenue, and if a state ought not to desire profit of this kind it ought not to have such an emporium' (*Pol.* 7, 1327ª25–31). He recognizes a danger that unless commercial activity is restrained, a port may develop willy-nilly into an entrepôt, and he is prepared to envisage legislation to regulate the behaviour of merchants in the port: 'any disadvantage which may threaten can easily be met by laws defining the persons who may, or may not, have dealings with one another'.

Since he is willing to envisage legislation to control dealings in the port in Book 7 of the *Politics*, it seems odd that in Book 1 he never so much as raises the question of legislation to regulate M–C–M′ behaviour in the city itself. This may be simply a matter of proportion. Such behaviour in the city was largely confined to a retail trade that was very restricted in scale and effect compared with what we know today, and the commercial values it represented did not penetrate deeply into the social relationships of the polis, in spite of Plato's bitter complaints in the *Laws*. But the big extension of commerce that would have followed permitting entrepôt trade would have been a more serious affair. Perhaps Aristotle was going for a compromise. It seems fairly consistent with what he says and does not say that he should be prepared to put up with a certain amount of behaviour of this kind by individuals, while being against any big extension of it.

It would be easier to believe in this compromise if Aristotle had believed that M–C–M′ behaviour arose from individual shortcomings rather from the systemic effects of money, but he did not, as we saw in Chapters 3 and 4 (1). He regards such behaviour as systemic because he believes it arises from the development of money, and what is primarily wrong with it lies in the unlimited nature of the end of M–C–M′, 'wealth of the spurious kind', rather than in the *pleonexia* of individuals. The common and damaging idea that wealth is unlimited does not arise from human wickedness, but from the existence of M–C–M′, which is 'commonly and rightly called the art of making money, and has in fact suggested the notion that wealth and property have no limit' (1256^{b}40 ff.). The perversion of the arts is not primarily the result of individual failings but of the need for money (1258^{a}8–14); 'the life of money-making is one undertaken under compulsion' (*NE* 1, 1096^{a}5). Aristotle does not regard money as a technical device, something morally neutral, which we pervert by turning it to wicked ends; he argues that money and C–M–C′ beget M–C–M′, and that there is an end built into M–C–M′ to which people have to adapt themselves and their behaviour. The problem is whether Aristotle's belief in the systemic character of the threat posed to the community by money is consistent with the view, implicit in the putative compromise, that money-seeking behaviour in the city can be contained without laws.

The moral ethos of Greek life was unfavourable to the values of commerce. Nearly all lending was *eranos* lending, and Aristotle himself tells us that a temple of the Graces was put up in a prominent place in the city to remind citizens that grace required that 'we should serve in return one who has shown grace to us, and should another time take the initiative in showing it' (*NE* 5, 1133^{a}3 ff.). *Chrêmatistikê* existed, so it was a known danger, and in spite of its systemic origin, Aristotle would perhaps have been justified in thinking that it could be contained by ethical precept, or by public intervention, as in the case of entrepôt trade. He did not have a crystal ball in which to foresee the full-blooded assertion of the capacity of money to erode *koinônia* and the values in *ethikê* and *politikê* which he knew and expounded, and no serious hint of its potency showed at any time in antiquity.

⪦ 5 ⪧

Aristotle is in two minds about money. His official view of its nature is that it is a means, but this is a stipulation rather than a conclusion, because he does not argue for it. The view that money is an end is just as integral to his analysis, and his attempt to exclude it as a perversion is inconsistent with his account of the development of exchange, where both views of money are integrated. It is not his analysis of exchange which pushes him towards the stipulation; the impetus from there would be towards the view that it is in the nature of money to become an end. The impetus comes from elsewhere. His decision to identify its nature by its origins rather than by its *telos* is crucial in securing the stipulation, and since he does not argue for that either, the decision looks arbitrary until it is noticed how well its consequence suits the ethical and political requirements of his wider position: money cannot be abolished, so there had better be an acceptable use of it; but it causes harm, and those who live by pursuing it are unpopular, so there had better be an unacceptable use of it.

Aristotle's analysis throws up a host of considerations with bearings on two still-contentious and unresolved questions: the nature of money and the relation between ethics and economics. His difficulty about the nature of money is not an elementary one which can be resolved easily with the resources of modern economic thought, because the same duality is present there too. It is the chief bone of contention between the friends and foes of market economy.

Adam Smith holds, as Aristotle finally decides to do, that use value or 'consumption is the sole end and purpose of all production'.[10] Smith recognizes that money becomes the end for those engaged in business, that their operations are of the

---

[10] A. Smith, *Wealth of Nations*, i. 159.

M–C–M′ character, and he thinks that they need to be publicly regulated for that reason (unlike some of his twentieth-century *soi-disant* disciples). But he thinks that the totality of those operations, though they have that character individually, result in an outcome for the society that is C–M–C′ in character, and he resolves the tension between money as a means and as an end in that way. So the pursuit of exchange value, in spite of appearances, really serves the end of use value.

In Marx's view, market economy is a lawlike system of exchange value and it can be interfered with to make it serve human ends better only to a limited degree. Use value is not the end but a means, and money or exchange value is not a means but the end. The system inhibits wealth and potential wealth being put to human ends because its end is something quite different, the quantitative expansion of exchange value, M–C–M′. Wealth cannot be both use value at the service of the natural ends of human living, and at the same time take the form of exchange value and serve the end of expanding exchange-value. These are alternatives between which we must choose. They may be made to intersect to a limited extent, but they cannot be made to intersect enough for human flourishing.

Keynes's project was to increase the extent of that intersection. He also takes the view that money becomes an end, though he regards this as due mainly to ethical perversion in the use people make of money, rather than, as Marx thought, to something in the nature of money which produces ethical perversion in the behaviour of people. The money motive, Keynes says, is a 'disgusting morbidity, one of those semi-criminal, semi-pathological propensities which one hands over with a shudder to the specialists in mental disease'. But it is a perversion we shall be able to overcome once we have enough, or in economic parlance, when there has been sufficient accumulation, and he thinks that time will come in the lifetimes of the grandchildren of his own generation.[11] He writes:

---

[11] J. M. Keynes, *Essays in Persuasion* (London, 1931), 369.

Money: Politics

The distinction between a cooperative economy and an entrepreneur economy bears some relation to a pregnant observation made by Karl Marx,—though the subsequent use to which he put this observation was highly illogical. He pointed out that the nature of production in the actual world is not, as economists seem to suppose, a case of C–M–C´, i.e. of exchanging commodity (or effort) for money in order to obtain another commodity (or effort). That may be the standpoint of the private consumer. But it is not the attitude of business, which is a case of M–C–M´, i.e. of parting with money for commodity (or effort) in order to obtain more money.[12]

In Keynes's view it is possible both to continue with money and M–C–M´, and to bring the money motive under moral control, thus transforming money from an end into a means.

❀ 6 ❀

The tension between ethics and economics, visible in a way in Aristotle's account, is also reproduced in modern economic thinking.

The pseudo-Aristotelian *Oeconomica*, as Finley has argued, deals simply with the production of use values.[13] It strikes a modern reader as quite un-'economic', because it lacks any discussion of investment, labour costs, profit maximization, turnover, etc.; it lacks even the notions of these things. The Greeks and Romans had no system of double-entry bookkeeping; the evidence, legal, literary, and documentary, for Greek and Roman accounting, shows that they lacked even the ideas of debit and credit. What we might mistake for accounts are no more than inventories of use values and checks on embezzlement. [14] Serious concern with exchange value and awareness of its categories are almost entirely absent. There is little or nothing in Greek literature that we should want to call 'economic' writing. All the extracts in Laistner's collection,

---

[12] Id., *The Collected Works of John Maynard Keynes*, xxix (London, 1971), 81.

[13] See Finley's review of Aristotle, *Économique*, ed. B. A. van Groningen and A. Wartelle (1968), *Classical Review*, 20 (1970), 315–19. Finley attacks what he rightly sees as wholly false injections of 'economic overtones' into the work.

[14] See Ste Croix, 'Greek and Roman Accounting'.

misleadingly entitled '*Greek Economics*', have the same character as the *Oeconomica*. This is not surprising, since the ancient world was not based on market economy. It was, as Finley has argued, a world primarily of use value in which markets played only a peripheral role, and if economics is the science of exchange value, it is not surprising that the Greeks did not invent it.[15]

Since Aristotle's time, or rather in the last few hundred years, exchange value has grown from being an end which individuals may pursue into an end which whole societies are organized to pursue. It has become the regulator of those societies through the system of markets, and, in the form of 'the economy', it has become the pre-eminent source of reasons for decision-making in the public realm. These changes had profound effects on ethics, on the very conception of what ethics is, of its place in human affairs, and on conceptions of human good and even of human identity—effects which are to be found in the works traditionally anthologized under the title of the 'British Moralists'.[16] Their accompaniment was the rise of economics to the position of an independent science.

If economics is to be seen as the science of exchange value, its magnitudes and movements, its interaction with use value, and of the requirements of its pursuit as the primary end, then the place of use value in it is that of a means rather than an

---

[15] Lowry has given the best and most detailed case for the view that the Greeks did invent economics in *The Archaeology of Economic Ideas* (Durham, 1987). Some of the problems in arguing a case of this kind are discussed in Ch. 8 below.

[16] Selby-Bigge's *British Moralists* was published by the Clarendon Press in 1897, and it became well known to students of moral philosophy. Selby-Bigge confined himself mainly to authors of the eighteenth century, with the exception of Cudworth and a few extracts from Hobbes and Locke 'for convenience of reference'. This rather arbitrary constraint made it difficult to convey the coherence of the development of the moral, social, and political thought of the era of market economy, and David Raphael, though he would probably not have wanted to describe his purpose in just those terms, thought the constraint unreasonable. Raphael extended both the period and the range of authors, adding Cumberland, Hume, Hartley, and Reid, but omitting John Clarke, John Brown, and Lord Kames, whom Selby-Bigge had included. Raphael's anthology appeared in two volumes entitled *British Moralists: 1650–1800* (Oxford, 1969). Raphael's authors are Hobbes, Cumberland, Cudworth, Locke, Lord Shaftesbury, Samuel Clarke, Mandeville, Wollaston, Hutcheson, Bishop Butler, Balguy, Gay, Hume, Hartley, Price, Adam Smith, Paley, Reid, and Bentham.

end. The growth of economic thinking and of the values implicit in it, to be found in authors like Petty, were fiercely resisted and parodied by moralists like Swift, and what emerged was a discrete science which contested much of the ground previously occupied by *ethikê* and *politikê* in public decision-making.

The tricky relationship between ethics and the new science was dealt with in a number of different ways. Keynes had an ethical theory which stood outside of economics.[17] In one of his essays, Keynes addresses the questions 'What can we reasonably expect the level of our economic life to be a hundred years hence? What are the economic possibilities for our grandchildren?' He foresees, among other things, a working day of three hours:

There are changes in other spheres too which we must expect to come. When the accumulation of wealth is no longer of high social importance, there will be great changes in the code of morals. We shall be able to rid ourselves of many of the pseudo-moral principles which have hag-ridden us for two hundred years, by which we have exalted some of the most distasteful of human qualities into the position of the highest virtues. We shall be able to afford to dare to assess the money-motive at its true value. The love of money as a possession—as distinguished from the love of money as a means to the enjoyments and realities of life—will be recognised for what it is, a somewhat disgusting morbidity, one of those semi-criminal, semi-pathological propensities which one hands over with a shudder to the specialists in mental disease. All kinds of social customs and economic practices, affecting the distribution of wealth and of economic rewards and penalties, which we now maintain at all costs, however distasteful and unjust they may be in themselves, because they are tremendously useful in promoting the accumulation of capital, we shall then be free, at last, to discard.[18]

Keynes was set aside from the mainstream of economic writing by virtue of having an ethical theory which was independent of economics. Most economic writing has had a particular ethical theory integrated into it: utilitarianism. This theory fit-

---

[17] See Fitzgibbons, *Keynes's Vision*, esp. ch. 3.
[18] Keynes, *Essays in Persuasion*, 360 and 369.

ted neatly because it had been designed for this supporting and subordinate role in the first place. The origin of utilitarianism in Bentham was associated with the ambition of providing political economy with a system of ethics, or something that looked like ethics, which could be fully integrated into political economy. This was desirable because actual morality stood outside of economics, and was constantly making difficulties for it, and setting down conditions which economics might have difficulty meeting, or not be able to meet at all. Testimony to this origin is seen in the fact, argued by Bernard Williams, that although utilitarianism serves the purposes of economics well, it can do really quite little of what a real morality is supposed to do. [19]

Utilitarianism, unsurprisingly, fits the requirements of economics well. There is only one end, pleasure or utility, and all actions are means to it. They are therefore to be judged only on their efficacy in promoting that end, so that only the consequences of actions are significant, not the actions themselves. Utilitarianism provides economics with a simulacrum of ethics in which it is not difficult to arrange a close association between utility maximization and the maximization of exchange value. Utilitarians might deny that they are committed to the view that the common currency of happiness is money. But, as Bernard Williams observes, 'they are committed to something which in practice has those implications: that there are no ultimately incommensurable values'. Williams adds that it is not an accidental feature of the utilitarian outlook that the presumption is in favour of the monetarily quantifiable, and that other values are forced into an apologetic dilemma: 'It is not an accident, because (for one thing) utilitarianism is the value system for a society in which economic values are supreme; and also, at the theoretical level, because

---

[19] See Macpherson, essays 9 and 10 in his *Democratic Theory: Essays in Retrieval* (Oxford, 1973), and esp. 'The Economic Penetration of Political Theory', in *The Rise and Fall of Economic Justice* (Oxford, 1985). On how little utilitarianism does of what an ethics is supposed to do, see Bernard Williams, *Morality* (Cambridge, 1972), 96–112. See also MacIntyre's remarks about emotivism, in *After Virtue* (London, 1981), chs. 2 and 3, esp. p. 33, and McMylor's discussion in *Alasdair MacIntyre: A Critic of Modernity* (London, 1994), ch. 3.

quantification in money is the only obvious form of what utilitarianism insists upon, the commensurability of value.'[20]

A second reaction to these changes has been the view that economics and ethics have little or nothing to do with one another, which Lionel Robbins championed in his famous study *The Nature and Significance of Economic Science*: 'Between the generalisations of positive and normative studies', he wrote, 'there is a logical gulf fixed which no ingenuity can disguise and no juxtaposition in space or time bridge over.' He concluded that regarding economics and ethics 'it does not seem logically possible to associate the two studies in any form but mere juxtaposition . . . the two fields of enquiry are not on the same plane of discourse'.[21] Few economists accepted his conclusions when they were published in 1932, but today most do.

Some economists are concerned that economics should have developed in the way that it has, proceeding on unrealistic assumptions about human nature and motivation, and apparently incomprehending of the intrinsic points of non-economic activities and the values they embody. Amartya Sen finds 'something quite extraordinary in the fact that economics has in fact evolved in this way'—a way which he describes as 'the self-consciously "non-ethical" character of modern economics'.[22] Adam Smith was after all, he points out, a Professor of Moral Philosophy, and economics was for a long time seen as something like a branch of ethics.

Looked at from an Aristotelian perspective, however, the divorce between ethics and economics seems inevitable rather than extraordinary. The activities they study aim at different ends, use value and exchange value, whose compatibility is

---

[20] B. Williams, *Morality*, 103.

[21] L. Robbins, *The Nature and Significance of Economic Science* (London, 1932), 132. Robbins derived this conclusion, not because he held economics to be the science of the pursuit of exchange value as an end, rather than of use value and human good as an end, but because he held it to be 'neutral as between ends' (ibid. 131), and he held this because he virtually identified economics as the science of means–end rationality in general. In one of the most quoted phrases in recent economic literature, Robbins wrote that 'Economics is the science which studies human behaviour as a relationship between ends and scarce means which have alternative uses', ibid. 15.

[22] A. Sen, *On Ethics and Economics* (Oxford, 1987), 1–2.

limited. Neo-classical economics draws a conceptual connection between use value and exchange value through the notion of utility, so that the two appear inseparable and the question of whether money is a means or an end cannot be clearly formulated. For this reason neo-classical economists would deny that economics is the science of exchange value only or primarily. On Aristotelian metaphysics, however, no such conceptual connection is possible, because use value and exchange value fall into the different categories of quality and quantity, and pursuing them as ends requires different courses of action in each case. So the Aristotelian view must be that economics is the science of exchange value only or primarily, not of both equally. Ethics and economics are competitors over the same ground, and one can prosper only at the expense of the other. From an Aristotelian point of view it can hardly seem surprising that ethics and economics should have come apart, or that once they had, they should have proved so hard to reconcile. What should seem surprising is that they should ever have been thought to be connected.

6

Neo-Classical Interpretation

Adam Smith makes three references to Aristotle in *The Wealth of Nations*, none of which concerns the economic writings, *Nicomachean Ethics*, 5. 5 and *Politics*, 1. 8–10. The references deal with political or historical points, and they seem to have been drawn from Smith's reading of Pufendorf and Montesquieu rather than from a study of Aristotle himself. Ricardo, in the *Principles*, makes no reference to Aristotle at all. The first examination of Aristotle's inquiries subsequent to the rise of economics was Marx's, offered originally in the *Contribution* and then eight years later in *Capital* itself.[1] Marx did not claim that Aristotle was an economist, or that he was the father of any school of economics, even Marx's own, but understandably his endorsement of most of Aristotle's conclusions was construed as a claim of Aristotelian paternity on behalf of his own theory.[2] Marx had inaugurated a contest, and in time subsequent orthodoxies in economics sought to establish Aristotelian paternity too.

The arrival of neo-classical theory gave rise to many such suits, the best-argued of which were those of Barker, Van Johnson, Soudek, and Schumpeter. These authors were keenly aware that Aristotle had incautiously laid himself open to—doubtless unintended—socialist interpretation, and Van Johnson explicitly set out to overturn Marx's conclusion that Aristotle

---

[1] The observation is made by Gianfranco Lotito, 'Aristotele su moneta scambio bisogni (Eth. Nic. v 5)', *Materiali e discussioni per l'analisi dei testi classici*, 4–6 (Pisa, 1978), 125.

[2] It is arguable that Marx was not an economist at all. His work is a critique of economics as a whole, not of any particular school of economics. If he set out to pursue an aim of that kind, as he did, then it would be curious if he were to have done economics himself. I have argued elsewhere that *Capital* is not a work of economics, but a work of metaphysics and ethics, see 'Was Marx an Economist?', in P. Dunleavy and J. Stanyer (eds.), *Contemporary Political Studies 1994* (Proceedings of the Political Studies Annual Conference; Belfast, 1994), 923–33.

had failed to arrive at a theory of economic value. On the contrary, Van Johnson argued, Aristotle had arrived at a neo-classical one. Soudek concluded that Aristotle 'anticipated by more than two thousand years Jevons' theory of exchange', and Gordon praised Kauder for having proved Aristotle's anticipation of 'the Austrian value theorists of the nineteenth century'.[3] Schumpeter argued a different neo-classical case: Marx had been right about Aristotle, but that just shows how little Aristotle has to offer for economics: no more than 'decorous, pedestrian, slightly mediocre, and more than slightly pompous common-sense'.[4] This case, though subtler, has found little favour, perhaps because it unattractively concedes the paternity suit.

☞ 1 ☜

The object of neo-classical theory, Schumpeter wrote, was to show 'what A. Smith, Ricardo, and Marx had believed to be impossible, namely, that exchange value can be explained in terms of use value. Jevons, Menger, and Walras would all of them have approved of this statement.'[5] Schumpeter knew perfectly well that no such view could be attributed to Aristotle, any more than to Smith, Ricardo, and Marx, though at best he grasped only intuitively that in Aristotle's case the most basic reason for this was the irreducible category-distinction Aristotle draws between use value and exchange value.

Schumpeter recognizes that Aristotle held exchange value and use value to depend on intrinsic properties possessed by products, rather than on extrinsic ones, or on relations. Since he does not share that view himself, he rejects Aristotle's theory and others like it. His reasons for rejecting Aristotle's view may be good or bad, and that will be considered later, but at

---

[3] Soudek, 'Aristotle's Theory of Exchange', 46. B. J. Gordon, 'Aristotle and the Development of Value Theory', *Quarterly Journal of Economics*, 78 (1964) (reprinted in Blaug (ed.), *Aristotle (384–322 BC)*, 113–26), 115. Kauder, 'Genesis of the Marginal Utility Theory', 638.

[4] Schumpeter, *History of Economic Analysis*, 57.   [5] Ibid. 911–12.

least the view he attributes to Aristotle is the view that Aristotle held. The same cannot be said of Barker's interpretation.

Schumpeter regards Aristotle's view as perverse and ungrounded. He has little grasp of Aristotle's substance–attribute metaphysics, or of his theory of categories, and for that reason he is unable to appreciate the logic of Aristotle's argument, which consists in applying that metaphysics to the analysis of use value, and to the relation of exchange values '5 beds = 1 house'. He probably would not have been very impressed if he had known more about it because, although he is fairly unimpressed by philosophy generally, he is particularly unimpressed by Aristotelian philosophy. In spite of his philosophical disclaimers, it is obvious from his work that he shared sufficiently the Humean and anti-Aristotelian beliefs and prejudices of the positivist movement of the first half of the twentieth century. Schumpeter writes as if it were a sufficient rebuttal of Aristotle's view that value is intrinsic, simply to counterpose to it the current orthodoxy that value is extrinsic, relational, and accidental. He uses the neo-classical view as if it were a yardstick against which Aristotle's view may be judged to be a failure. But it is unconvincing, and ought to be unconvincing even to adherents of neo-classical theory, to represent the neo-classical theory of value as itself beyond any need of metaphysical clarification and justification. Some of Aristotle's beliefs have been superseded by more accurate observation or better theory. Observation has led us to ignore his belief that the bison defends itself from hunters by discharging its burning excrement over a distance of eight yards and scorching the hairs off the hounds (*HA* 630^{b}8–11). Better observation and theoretical advances in mechanics have caused Aristotle's beliefs about the trajectory of missiles to be superseded by the theory of parabolic motion. But the neo-classical theory of value is not the sort of thing that could be vindicated by observation, and it cannot be claimed on its behalf that it has the standing of an established scientific theory which can fairly be regarded as putting other theories out of contention, as mechanics or the theory of evolution have.

Schumpeter's case rests on an insensitivity in metaphysics. Aristotle derives his theory of value from his metaphysics, and refuting it would require identifying some flaw in the metaphysics, or else some flaw in the reasoning by which it is derived from that metaphysics.[6] Schumpeter, not appreciating this, is unable to produce a serious attempt at argument because he fails to see the need for one. Metaphysical insensitivity has had an important role in the discussion of Aristotle's attempt to analyse economic value, as it has in the discussion of value generally, and a lot of it has centred on the notion of a capacity.

Aristotle's inquiry into exchange value is aimed at explaining a capacity: the capacity products come to have for exchanging in proportions as quantities. According to his theory of capacities, a capacity has to be distinguished from the exercise of that capacity. This accords with our ordinary way of talking about capacities or powers; someone who can speak French is normally said to have that capacity even when he or she is asleep, speaking English, or just keeping quiet. Having the capacity is one thing, but using it in actually speaking French is another. 'Value', as the term is used in economics, is the name of whatever it is by virtue of which products can behave in exchange in the way that they do, that is, exchange in proportions as quantities. (This holds independently of theories about what the substance of value consists in. It holds for the utility theory of value just as it does for the labour theory of value.) What a thing can do, it has a capacity to do, so the exchangeability of products is a capacity, and it has to be explained as a capacity is explained. It is in order to explain

[6] Schumpeter is uneasy about his handling of intrinsic value in Aristotle and in Marx, and he repeatedly worries away at it in his various works in ways that do not convince the reader—or, apparently, himself. Schumpeter is not well placed to carry the matter through. He is strongly inclined, as many other economists of the time were, to dismiss the idea of intrinsic value out of hand as 'metaphysical', in the special sense of the term that was favoured by the Logical Positivists, that is, as something that ought to be eliminated. He also has a sceptical attitude to philosophy generally which would not incline him to take seriously the kind of metaphysical inquiry required to settle the issue of whether value involved an intrinsic or extrinsic property.

this that Aristotle is looking for an explanation of the commensurability of products. The view that value is intrinsic is unavoidable on Aristotelian metaphysics. If a thing has a capacity, its possessing that capacity implies actual properties in the thing. In Aristotle, and in the Aristotelian tradition, things are identified as things of a kind, and that identification can involve capacities as well as qualities. What a thing is can be partly a matter of what it can do. The litmus test for acids, for example, decides whether something is an acid by determining whether or not it has the capacity to turn red litmus-paper blue.[7] Since attributing value to products is attributing a capacity to them, value must be intrinsic to them. (The same conclusion follows from Aristotle's analysis of the commensurability which is implied by the fact that a relation of equality is involved in exchange.)

The Humean position is different at every point, and the fact is significant because the metaphysical sensibilities of modern economics are overwhelmingly Humean. According to Humean metaphysics, there is no distinction to be drawn between a capacity and its exercise. Hume's position in the *Treatise* is that 'The distinction, which we often make betwixt *power* and the *exercise* of it, is . . . without foundation.'[8] To say that something can do something—that is, that it has a capacity to do it—is just to say that it does do it. If there is held to be no distinction between a capacity and its exercise, then the fact that products do exchange in non-arbitrary proportions is all there is to saying that they can. From this it has been inferred that it is not necessary or even possible to seek an explanation of the capacity, of how things that are exchanged are capable of being equated in proportions, that is, of how they can be commensurable.

This is broadly the position drawn upon by Bailey who,

---

[7] For an explanation of this view see Geach's article 'Aquinas', in G. E. M. Anscombe and P. T. Geach, *Three Philosophers* (Oxford, 1963), 101–4. For a development of the view in relation to the identity of natural kinds, see David Wiggins, *Sameness and Substance* (Oxford, 1980), esp. 77–86.

[8] Hume, *Treatise of Human Nature*, 171. For a critical discussion of the Humean view of capacities, see R. Harré and E. H. Madden, *Causal Powers* (Oxford, 1975), 1–25, 82–100, 101–16.

writing in 1825, just as economics is beginning to replace classical political economy, insists that 'value is the exchange relation of commodities and consequently is not anything different from this relation ... Value denotes nothing positive and intrinsic, but merely the relation in which two objects stand to each other as exchangeable commodities.'[9] This view has passed into the neo-classical canon.

Bailey seems to be saying that exchange value cannot be a property because it is a relation, namely, the relation of exchange. Such a position could not be Aristotle's, because on his metaphysics things that are in a relation cannot also be the relation they are in. Thus, exchange values, being the things related in the exchange relation 'x of A = y of B', cannot be the relation relating them, that is, the relation of equality. The suggestion is incomprehensible.

Bailey might also have it somewhere in mind to argue, not that exchange value is not a property at all, but that it is a property which cannot exist outside the exchange relation. This is an intelligible suggestion, unlike the first, and it has been echoed by later writers. Schumpeter, for instance, writes that Marx 'was under the same delusion as Aristotle, viz., that value [is] ... something that is different from, and exists independently of, relative prices or exchange relations.'[10] The argument would be that exchange value is a property like that of 'being married', which property depends on the relation 'being married to . . .' in the sense that one cannot have the property unless one has the relation to someone. The case would be that unless some product or good stands in the exchange relation to some other, then it can't be an exchange value; just as a person cannot be married unless he or she stands in the relation of being married to someone. This is a better argument, but the problem now is to see how it might be an objection to the view it is intended to damage. The analogy with a property like

[9] S. Bailey, *A Critical Dissertation on the Nature, Measures, and Causes of Value* (London, 1825), 4–5. The view is often regarded as a post-Marxian insight and therefore as something Marx could not have considered. In fact he considers it in *Theories of Surplus Value*, ii (Moscow, 1968), 140–7.
[10] J. Schumpeter, *Capitalism, Socialism and Democracy*[4] (London, 1952), 23, n. 2.

'being married', even if correct, is clearly not the whole story, because 'being married' is not a quantity and does not enter into relations of equality. Schumpeter and others, in any case, want to combine the objection with the view that the basis of exchange value is utility, which itself is not a property that exists only in the exchange relation. Aristotle explains in the *Categories* that 'All relatives, then, are spoken of in relation to correlatives that reciprocate, *provided* they are properly given . . . For example, if a slave is given as of—not a master, but—a man or a biped or anything else like that, then there is not reciprocation; for it has not been given properly' (7ª22–30). If goods are to be related by equality, as they are in '5 beds = 1 house', they must be given as quantities; not quantities of goods, e.g. 5 beds, but quantities of whatever it is that 5 beds has in equal amount with 1 house, that is, exchange value.

Schumpeter says of Marx, in the passage just cited:

> He was under the same delusion as Aristotle, viz., that value, though a factor in the determination of relative prices, is yet something that is different from, and exists independently of, relative prices or exchange relations. The proposition that the value of a commodity is the amount of labour embodied in it can hardly mean anything else. If so, then there is a difference between Ricardo and Marx, since Ricardo's values are simply exchange values or relative prices. It is worth while to mention this because, if we could accept this view of value [sc. as a common property intrinsic to commodities], much of his theory that seems to us untenable or even meaningless would cease to be so. Of course we cannot.

The mention of labour is immaterial to the argument, which is about whether or not value is intrinsic. If Schumpeter is to be taken at his word, then it would seem that all that prevented him from agreeing in essentials with Aristotle and Marx was his adoption of the Humean rather than the Aristotelian analysis of capacities.[11]

The same metaphysical predilections seem to underlie Joan Robinson's view that 'one of the great metaphysical ideas in

---

[11] The Humean view has not fared well in recent philosophical work on capacities; see, e.g. M. Ayers, *The Refutation of Determinism* (London, 1968), 55–75 and 80–95, and A. J. P. Kenny, *Will, Freedom and Power* (Oxford, 1975), 122–44.

economics is expressed by the word "value" . . . like all meta-physical ideas, when you try to pin it down, it turns out to be just a word'.[12] She is using the term 'metaphysics' here in the special opprobrious sense which was part of the fashion of the time for the Humean metaphysics of Logical Positivism, and not in its usual philosophical sense. Pareto is less restrained in his Humean sarcasm:

In a recently published book, it is said that 'price is the concrete manifestation of value'. We have had incarnation of Buddha, here we have incarnation of *value*. What indeed can this mysterious entity be? It is, it appears, 'the capacity which a good has to be exchanged with other goods.' This is to define one unknown thing by another still less known; for what indeed can this 'capacity' be? And, what is still more important, how is it measured? Of this 'capacity' or its homonym 'value' we know only the 'concrete manifestation' which is the price; truly then it is useless to entangle ourselves with these metaphysical entities, and we can stick to the prices.[13]

⮠ 2 ⮐

Where the first line of utilitarian interpretation recognizes that Aristotle held value to be intrinsic, the second line attributes to him the neo-classical view that value is extrinsic, and that exchange value can be explained in terms of use value. This line has been much commoner, and few commentators, not even Finley, have managed to stay clear of it altogether. Joseph put it succinctly: 'Aristotle, *Nicomachean Ethics*, V. v. ii, 1133ᵃ25–31, finds in demand or need the real source of exchange value.'[14]

Barker sees that Aristotle's definition of wealth involves the antithesis of nature and convention. He also observes how different Aristotle is, in defining wealth as use value to the

[12] J. Robinson, *Economic Philosophy* (London, 1964), 29.

[13] V. Pareto, *Manual of Political Economy*, trans. A. Schwier, ed. A. Schwier and A. Page (London, 1971), 177.

[14] H. W. B. Joseph, *The Labour Theory of Value in Karl Marx* (Oxford, 1923), 9, n. 1.

exclusion of exchange value, from moderns like Mill who define it in ways that involve exchange value.[15] Mill's *Principles of Political Economy* was the standard university textbook until it was replaced by Marshall's *Principles of Economics*, and Mill is the authority Barker cites. Mill defines wealth as 'all useful or agreeable things, which possess exchangeable value'.[16] But Barker misunderstands and rejects Aristotle's view of wealth, and thinks it is justified simply to insist that Aristotle should have collapsed the *nomos–phusis* distinction here, and should have held instead that 'Nature and art are really one'. Aristotle has metaphysical reasons for not doing this, but Barker overlooks them; he shows insensitivity to the metaphysics of Aristotle's discussion, here and elsewhere, as many anglophone Aristotelian scholars were apt to do at that time.[17] Finding no better basis for it, Barker attributes Aristotle's view to the fact that he 'deprecated exchange' because of his 'reactionary archaism' and his snobbish prejudice against money-makers. The elements of Barker's position need to be separated.

Barker does not overlook, as Schumpeter did, the arguments about value in which Aristotle establishes the philosophical basis of his economic thought, he misunderstands them, and the mistranslation of *chreia* as 'demand' is at the centre of the misunderstanding. He says, directly contrary to what Aristotle says at *NE* 5, 1133^{b}18–20, that 'To Aristotle "demand", or need ($\chi\rho\epsilon i a$) . . . makes couches commensurable with houses, producing the equation 5 couches = 1 house. Except for demand, there is no commensurability and therefore no possibility of equation.'[18] He goes on to connect demand with money: money forms 'the concrete and objective form of the subjective standard formed by demand. It makes objects commensurable.' The notion of demand is logically connected with the notion of exchange value, and Barker is justified in connecting them as he does. But by substituting 'demand' for 'need' (*chreia*) in the first place, Barker is moving very far from

[15] Barker, *Political Thought of Plato and Aristotle*, 374.
[16] Mill, *Principles of Political Economy*, 9.
[17] Barker, *Political Thought of Plato and Aristotle*, 376.   [18] Ibid. 379, n. 2.

Aristotle's own position in two ways. First, since 'demand' is an aggregation of wants or revealed preferences, he is implying an identity between needs and wants which is conceptually mistaken and contrary to Aristotle. Secondly, insinuating 'demand' introduces a bridging device between use value and exchange value. These points will be taken in turn.

The notion of need is not usually liked by economists, particularly those of liberal temper. The mention of it is, Wiggins observes, apt to produce a standardized professional response: 'What do you mean by a need? Is a need just something you want, but aren't prepared to pay for?'[19] Needs, however, are logically distinguishable from wants. 'Need' is not an intentional verb but 'want' is. What I need does not depend on what I believe, as what I want does.[20] Need is, in a specifiable sense, an objective state, not a subjective one, and in some of its uses 'need' denotes an absolute or categorical state, not an instrumental one conditional upon entertaining some particular purpose.[21]

Aristotle does not confuse needs with wants by thinking of them as rationalized strong desires. His view of them is made

---

[19] For this and what follows, see Wiggins's article 'Claims of Need', in his *Needs, Values, Truth* (Oxford, 1987), esp. 5–9, 25–6. Economists' dislike of needs is often the result of associating the idea with 'totalitarianism', or more precisely with Stalinist 'communism', and with the 'paternalism' of social-democratic governments. Wants, and aggregates of them (i.e. 'demand'), are supposed to be democratic things, because everyone is supposed to be an authority on what he or she wants. But it is possible to be mistaken about what one needs in a way that is not possible about what one wants, so that doing social philosophy and social policy in terms of needs is thought to lend itself to the authoritarianism of intellectuals who hold theories about what humans 'really' need, even though they may not know it, and even if it goes against what they want. See Wiggins's further discussion of Pareto, ibid. 319–28.

[20] Wiggins writes, ibid. 6: 'If I want to have x and $x = y$, then I do not necessarily want to have y. If I want to eat that oyster, and that oyster is the oyster that will consign me to oblivion, it doesn't follow that I want to eat the oyster that will consign me to oblivion. But with needs it is different. I can only need to have x if anything identical with x is something that I need. Unlike "desire" or "want" then, "need" is not evidently an intentional verb. What I need depends not on thought or the workings of my mind (or not only on these) but on the way the world is. Again, if one wants something because it is F, one believes or suspects that it is F. But if one needs something because it is F, it must really be F, whether or not one believes that it is.'

[21] Ibid. 6–11.

clearer by what he says in *Met. Δ* about the Greek word for 'necessary' (*anagkaion*).

We call necessary (*a*) that without which, as a joint cause, it is not possible to live, as for instance breathing and nourishing are necessary for an animal, because it is incapable of existing without them: and (*b*) anything without which it is not possible for good to exist or come to be, or for bad to be discarded or got rid of, as for instance drinking medicine is necessary so as not to be ill, and sailing to Aegina so as to get money. (1015ª20 ff., trans. Kirwan)[22]

The word has never been translated here as 'needed', as Wiggins remarks, and for good reason, because the chapter is seen as Aristotle's only entry for several senses of the word for 'necessary'. But it could have been translated in that way, and it would have been beneficial in one way if it had been: 'In the presence of an Aristotelian elucidation', Wiggins suggests, 'the reductive, rationalised strong desires conception of need might not have passed so long without serious challenge.'

What is necessary or needed is thus connected with Aristotle's idea of flourishing as a thing of a kind. Anscombe brings out the connection: 'To say that an organism needs that environment is not to say, e.g. that you want it to have that environment, but that it won't flourish unless it has it. Certainly, it all depends whether you *want* it to flourish! as Hume would say. But what "all depends" on whether you want it to flourish is whether the fact that it needs that environment, or won't flourish without it, has the slightest influence on your actions.'[23] 'Demand' does not have this connection with flourishing, and it cannot be used to represent the Aristotelian idea of need without destroying a tissue of connections that are vital to Aristotle's philosophy.

The modern economic notion of 'demand for *x*' ranges indiscriminately over things that are wanted and things that are needed. But not all needs for *x*, or even all wants for *x*, constitute parts of the demand for *x*. 'Demand' means 'effective demand', that is, demand which registers in the market

---

[22] C. Kirwan, *Metaphysics: Books Γ, Δ, and E* (Oxford, 1993).
[23] G. E. M. Anscombe, 'Modern Moral Philosophy', *Philosophy*, 33 (1958), 7.

because it is backed by money. Needs and wants come apart from demand because needs and wants that are not backed by money do not count as demand. When Aristotle speaks of *chreia* he means needs not wants, though a case could be made that he means needs and some wants, but it is certain that he does not mean that subset of needs and wants that are satisfiable because their possessors have money.[24] Even if Aristotle had had the notion of demand, which he did not, he could not have given it the place in his theory that he gives to *chreia*. *Chreia* exists by nature (*phusis*), but 'demand' exists by convention (*nomos*) because it presupposes those very conventions of exchange value which need not exist, and which, in the case of M–C–M´, he is explicitly opposed to. By introducing demand, Barker bridges the *nomos–phusis* gap which Aristotle establishes between use value and exchange value, contrary to the letter and spirit of his economic theory (if it can be called 'economic'), and of his metaphysics.

Barker is attributing a neo-classical view of value to Aristotle in which use value and exchange value are inherently linked, and for that reason Aristotle's views of wealth, exchange, and so forth, since they are based on use value to the exclusion of exchange value, appear to be inconsistent with it. They also appear to be without any intellectual foundation, since the foundation Aristotle gave them has been removed by misinterpretation, and so Barker finds another foundation for them in moral and political prejudice. Aristotle's views of wealth, his use of the nature–convention distinction, his analysis of exchange and trade, and his views on the proper use of the arts and faculties, then come to appear not only as inconsistencies on Aristotle's part, but as poorly motivated as well.

Barker censures Aristotle for being 'as reactionary in economics as was Plato', whose views he characterizes by the motto 'Back to the simple and primitive', and for believing in an ideal economic society which comes 'perilously near the

---

[24] For a discussion of the place of need and flourishing in Aristotle's conception of the end of the polis, see Martha Nussbaum, 'Nature, Function, and Capability: Aristotle on Political Distribution', *Oxford Studies in Ancient Philosophy*, suppl. vol. (1988), 145–84.

"golden" age—"When wild in woods the noble savage ran" '.[25] The constructions Barker puts on Aristotle here are likely to appear exaggerated to readers today. Their desperate quality connects with a striking feature of Barker's discussion in his chapter IX, entitled 'Aristotle's Principles of Economics'. The greater part of that chapter is a barely disguised effort to justify modern, or bourgeois, conceptions of wealth, value, exchange, money, and profit, in the face of Aristotle's theory, which Barker seems to fear might be thought to imply criticism of them.[26] He shows the same sensitivity in drawing likenesses between Aristotle and the Physiocrats, who held that exchange is not 'productive': 'It may be remarked that the Physiocrats, with these views, were not socialists; nor need we therefore make Aristotle, with the same views, into a socialist.' Such sensitivity is common, particularly in the anglophone literature. Ross, for instance, defends what he calls 'the commercial class' on the ground, which is beside the point of Aristotle's principal criticism, that it 'renders a useful public service and makes its profits only because it does so'. It was not generally appreciated at the time Ross was writing either that there was no 'productive lending' in the ancient world (that is, there was no credit for establishing productive enterprises as opposed to lending for consumption), or that money in general did not function as capital.[27] So Ross saw no obstacle to extending the defence of the commercial interest to encompass also the protection of commercial banking from Aristotle's criticism of usury.[28]

[25] Barker, *Political Thought of Plato and Aristotle*, 374–7.

[26] He may have got that idea from von Pöhlmann, whom he cites on p. 385, n. 2, though without giving a title for Pöhlmann's work. It may have been *Geschichte des antiken Sozialismus und Kommunismus*, a work of the Marxist tradition which appeared in two volumes in 1893 and 1901, went to a second edition in 1912, and a third in 1925 under the title *Geschichte der Sozialen Frage und des Sozialismus in der antiken Welt*.

[27] On 'productive lending' in the ancient world, see Millett, *Lending and Borrowing*, 73–4, 96, 195. On the use of money in ship's bottomry, see Ste Croix, 'Ancient Greek and Roman Maritime Loans', in H. Edey and B. S. Yamey (eds.), *Debits, Credits, Finance and Profits* (London, 1974).

[28] Ross, *Aristotle*, 243. For Ross's discussion of usury, see the end of Ch. 3.

☞ 3 ☜

Rejections of Aristotle's views on grounds of this kind have become the rule rather than the exception. Mulgan too conceives Aristotle primarily as an enemy of improvement and technology, in something like the spirit of a nineteenth-century English poetaster contrasting a greenery-yallery pastoral idyll with the devilry of the iron masters. He thinks that Aristotle's distinction between natural and unnatural wealth is to be interpreted as meaning that natural wealth (*ho alêthinos ploutos*) 'is confined to the products of land or sea, such as farm animals and their by-products, crops, fruit and fish', and unnatural wealth is whatever (in Aristotle's phrase at *Pol.* 1, 1257ª3–5, taken quite against the context to be a reference to technology) 'is gained by experience and skill'.[29] So he thinks that Aristotle is making a case for the 'claim that agriculture is closer than commerce to nature', and he concedes that in a sense this is so, 'if we mean that it is concerned more directly with products and processes of natural growth which do not depend on technology'. But of course agriculture too involves technology, and Mulgan suggests that Aristotle overlooks this in supposedly arguing that 'what is natural in the sense of primitive and unaffected by human technology is therefore best for man'. It is difficult to recognize Aristotle in any of this. Not surprisingly, Mulgan comes to the conclusion that the arguments making up Aristotle's case about true and unnatural wealth are not worth much and hardly do more than express attitudes.[30]

[29] Barker makes the comparable but slightly different point that Aristotle has a Physiocratic view of 'productive labour'. He suggests that, like Aristotle, the Physiocrats 'too "confined the epithet 'productive' to *agricultural* labour, and denied it to every other class of labour". They too felt that it is agriculture, and similar extractive occupations, "that furnish the materials for all wealth; and that all other labour is merely engaged in the working of these materials" (Gide, *Political Economy*, E. T., p. 113)', Barker, *Political Thought of Plato and Aristotle*, 390, n. 1. The likeness is unconvincing since, as is argued later, Aristotle did not have a notion of labour, and he did not have the notion of productivity either, any more than any other Greek writer.

[30] Mulgan, *Aristotle's Political Theory*, 48–50. Lewis also argues that Aristotle holds that the 'direct working of the land is the most natural [form of production and acquisition], followed by extractive production such as mining'; 'Acquisition and Anxiety:

Schumpeter is an exception, because he is inclined to look harder for serious analytical content in Aristotle. He does not like the analysis he finds there, but he does not rely heavily for his criticism on attributing ideological class-attitudes to Aristotle. He reproduces the common opinion that Aristotle has 'the ideological preconceptions to be expected of a man who lived in, and wrote for, a cultivated leisure class, which held work and business pursuits in contempt and, of course, loved the farmer who fed it and hated the money lender who exploited it', but this is an aside and not the main thrust of his evaluation of Aristotle's argument.[31]

Ross, as we saw earlier, simply finds that Aristotle's 'view is too much a reflexion of the ordinary Greek prejudice against trade as an illiberal occupation.'[32] Mulgan, again without noticing the philosophical basis of Aristotle's views, finds them 'of interest as an expression of the aristocratic attitude towards wealth, with its preference for landed property and its prejudice against trade and commerce.'[33] Judgements of this kind obviously do no justice at all to the philosophical depth of Aristotle's position. But they are unbalanced in other ways too, because such attitudes as Aristotle evinces are not particularly Greek, aristocratic, or necessarily prejudiced.

Contempt for commercial values is hardly a cultural quirk peculiar to the ancient Greek aristocracy. Historically it has been a common enough sentiment wherever there has been significant money-economy. The antipathy of ancient authors is exceeded by that of medieval ones, whose views are well summarized by Tawney.[34] The Catholic Church continued to denounce them unequivocally up until the encyclical *Vix Pervenit* of 1745, and it still keeps them at arm's length.[35] Such

---

Aristotle's Case against the Market', *Canadian Journal of Economics*, 11 (1978) (reprinted in Blaug (ed.), *Aristotle (384–322 BC)*, 173–94), 76.

[31] Schumpeter, *History of Economic Analysis*, 60.   [32] Ross, *Aristotle*, 243.

[33] Mulgan, *Aristotle's Political Theory*, 49.

[34] R. H. Tawney, *Religion and the Rise of Capitalism* (London, 1926), ch. 1.

[35] According to *Vix Pervenit*, in the return of a loan of money, it is always wrong to demand any extra sum of money, however small, over and above the principal. It is allowed that it can be right, in some circumstances, to demand a consideration, but those circumstances do not include the mere making of the loan in itself. The

antipathy is common enough today, and not only among socialists.

The evidence usually adduced for the view that Aristotle espoused a cause of opposition against traders comes from *Politics*, 1. 8–10 (looked at earlier, in Chapters 3 and 4 (1)). It is true that Aristotle has little good to say about traders in the *Politics*, but he has little bad to say about them either. He is critical of the activity of trade, but unlike Plato he has nothing to say about the moral qualities of those who engage in it. Traders are not really the target of his criticism. His target is exchange value in general, and the effects it has on *ethikê* and *politikê* in the polis. His criticism of this is too general, and its social application is too wide, for it to be at all plausible to suggest that the purpose of the discussion in the *Politics* is to mount a political attack on the trader in particular. Aristotle's criticism is directed at wealth-getting in the sense of money-making, and he is explicit that the trader is not the only one who does this, because doctors, philosophers, soldiers, and other professionals do it too. All the arts and faculties can be put to this unnatural end. It is not even particularly clear that he thinks the trader is worse than the others, because even if the trader practises an ignoble art, so do they, and at least he is not perverting a noble one in the process. Aristotle does not explicitly make this point, but it is an obvious implication, and it is clearly in his mind when he condemns the Sophists for abusing philosophy by turning it into money-making.

It cannot even be said that he picks on traders as offenders more often than he picks on others, or that he subjects them to any special opprobrium. The target of his criticism is *chrê-matistikê* in the bad sense of money-making, and this is the

encyclical concludes that 'It must be carefully noted that anyone who says that there are always such grounds attached to a loan would be rashly persuading himself of a falsehood.' (Denzinger's *Enchiridion Symbolorum*, 2546–50, pp. 506–8). See the encyclicals *Rerum Novarum* (1891) and *Quadragesimo Anno* (1931), and the accounts given of them in J.-Y. Calvez and J. Perrin, *The Church and Social Justice* (London, 1961). The encyclical of 1993, *Veritatis Splendor*, reiterating the Second Vatican Council, condemns as 'intrinsically evil' and 'a disgrace', economic evils including bad housing and 'degrading conditions of work which treat labourers as mere instruments of profit' (p. 123), though these have usually received less attention than other things more offensive to liberal sentiment, as indeed they do in the encyclical itself.

term he uses, not only for trade, but also for what the Sophists do and what is done by those who misuse the medical and military arts. *Kapêlikê* or trade is only one of a number of examples of *chrêmatistikê* which Aristotle singles out for mention. It is true that *kapêlikê* has a special place in his analysis of exchange in *Politics*, 1, but this is only because he thought it had a special place in the genesis of bad *chrêmatistikê* as a general phenomenon which includes *kapêlikê* but is not exhausted by it. The context of that discussion is an examination of wealth, and when Aristotle distinguishes 'true wealth' from 'wealth of the spurious kind' or money, the trader is not especially prominent as an example of the pursuer of spurious wealth; the professions are at least as prominent if not more so, and the artisan is implicated too by inference from the case of the 'niggardly' smith who makes the Delphian knife. This hardly amounts to evidence that the chapters constitute a political attack on traders. The discussion of fairness in exchange in the *Ethics* furnishes Aristotle with a golden opportunity to heap obloquy on the trader's head, since he thinks that *kapêlikê* involves people 'taking things from one another'; but he does not avail himself of it. The usual terms for trade and trader, *kapêlikê* and *kapêlos*, do not occur at all in *NE* 5. 5. There may be more than one reason for this (see Chapter 4 (2)), but even so it hardly suggests that a cause of political opposition to the class of traders was close to Aristotle's heart, even if there were reason to think that he entertained one. The only reason given for thinking that he did is this supposed evidence from *Politics*, 1.

It is not very convincing to accuse Aristotle of sharing the mindless prejudices of the Greek landowning class. His criticisms apply not only to the trader, the presumed object of Greek aristocratic contempt, but to professionals generally, the very class Aristotle was brought up in. His own father was a doctor, and he himself, although he had privileges at Athens, remained a metic or resident alien, a class which was almost entirely engaged in trade and manufacture. The charge of prejudice is particularly unfair, because the criticisms Aristotle actually makes, as opposed to the ones Mulgan puts into his

nce, if any were needed, of his detachment
ess rather than of prejudice.

ıy of knowing for certain whether the views
money-wealth and money-makers were peculiarly aristocratic ones. These views may have been much
commoner than that. It would not be very surprising if the
peasants of the *chôra* and the non-aristocratic city-dwellers
held such views, because some of them would have had as
much reason as anyone to resent the living made by traders
and usurers. But practically nothing is known of what they
thought about anything, so describing Aristotle's views as
specifically 'aristocratic' can be little more than conjecture.
Even if it were fair to describe the view he held of money-
wealth as an 'aristocratic' one, it would certainly fit no kind of
pattern in his opinions and principles. The thrust of so many
of Aristotle's political convictions, in constitutional matters
and in others, favours the middle kind of people. Just to take
a few random examples: the best *politeia* is not governed exclusively either by the rich or by the poor (*Pol.* 4, 1294^{b}37 f.);
those in between the rich and poor 'are most ready to follow
rational principle' (*Pol.* 4, 1295^{b}5 f.), and where they exist in
numbers, there is more likely to be a better *politeia* (*Pol.* 4,
1296^{a}23) and one which confines the strife between rich and
poor within limits (*Pol.* 4, 1294^{a}35 f.; 1297^{a}38 f.). Aristotle's
account of the best *politeia* hardly embodies an aristocratic
principle. On the contrary, he says that 'it is evident that the
best *politeia* is that arrangement according to which anyone
whatsoever [*hostisoun*] might do best and live a flourishing life'
(*Pol.* 8, 1324^{a}23–5).[36] Certainly slaves and foreigners were
excluded from this, but even making full allowance for the
exclusions, Aristotle's vision of a polis which promotes the
human flourishing of all its members is not an aristocratic one.
He reports with typical detachment the contending opinions
about what 'desert' should mean in the principle, 'agreed by
all', that honours and other things belonging to the community should be distributed according to desert, hinting at the

[36] See Nussbaum's discussion of this in 'Nature, Function and Capability'.

self-interestedness of the definitions: 'democrats make the cr̲ terion free birth; those of oligarchic sympathies, wealth', and aristocrats are not spared the irony, for 'upholders of aristocracy make it virtue' (*NE* 5, 1131ᵃ24 ff.).

In any case, there is no reason to believe that there was any serious antagonism between the commercial class and the landed aristocracy, though that claim has often been made, and even more often hinted at and implied. Schumpeter suggests that in Plato and Aristotle, the 'examination of the various economic functions reflects the attitudes of an aristocracy which is confronted by a rising merchant class'.[37] Soudek's suggestion that 'the author of the *Laws* . . . had made his peace with money-making and plutocracy, while Aristotle never gave up his opposition to this class', misunderstands both Plato and Aristotle; but it strikes another false note too, and Finley comments that beneath the misunderstandings there 'lies an equally fantastic picture of a sharp class struggle in Greece between wealthy landowners and merchants'.[38]

On the whole there is little to be got out of attempting to evaluate the first book of the *Politics* in terms of Aristotle's real or imagined class-loyalties, and the attempts that have been made at it have seldom been entirely free of the taint of ideology themselves. Aristotle's criticism of exchange value and its associated behaviour is at a conceptual level to which responses of this order cannot penetrate. His attack may seem more pertinent to the market economies of today, now that *ethikê* and *politikê* have been so thoroughly penetrated by exchange value, and the confusion of ends has reached so deeply into everything. In recent times, however, his criticism has been taken more trivially rather than more seriously.

---

[37] J. Schumpeter, *Economic Doctrine and Method*, trans. R. Aris (London, 1954), 11.
[38] Soudek, 'Aristotle's Theory of Exchange', 71–2; Finley, 'Aristotle and Economic Analysis', 43, n. 60.

7

Justice in Exchange:
'As Builder to Shoemaker'

The interpretation of *Nicomachean Ethics*, 5. 5 has been bedev-
illed by unsuccessful attempts to get a theory of fair exchange
out of it, by finding some meaning for the formula Aristotle
gives for fair exchange: 'as builder to shoemaker, so many
shoes to a house' (1133ª23–5). There is nothing wrong with
looking for a theory of fair exchange in the chapter. That, after
all, is ostensibly what the chapter is about, and that is why it
is included in the *Ethics* at all, rather than in the *Politics*. But
these attempts have focused attention obsessively on the formula, to the exclusion of the inquiry into economic value,
which is what is actually in the chapter. The fact that the formula has been the subject of such a large number of unsatisfactory interpretations, which few but their authors have ever
found convincing, has not done much to encourage the idea
that the chapter is particularly worthy of attention.

☞ 1 ☜

The subject of *Ethics* Book 5 is justice (*dikaiosunê*). Aristotle
first distinguishes universal justice from particular justice, and
he then goes on to examine particular justice in detail. He
divides it into two kinds. The first is distributive justice (*to
dianemêtikon dikaion*), which is to be used in the distribution
of honours and other public goods among those 'with a share
in the constitution'. He says it causes quarrels if equal persons
are given unequal shares of these things, or unequal persons
equal shares, and so the point of distributive justice is to match
the share with the worth of the person. The second kind is

corrective justice (*to diorthôtikon dikaion*), and this concerns private relations and goods rather than public ones. Its point is to rectify (the literal meaning of *diorthôtikos* is 'straightening out') an unfair imbalance of good or advantage that has arisen in private affairs, by removing the unfair gain and restoring the unfair loss. The worth of persons does not count here, and Aristotle says that the parties are treated as equals.

When he finishes with the analysis of distributive and corrective justice, Aristotle launches into the discussion of fairness in exchange. In the nineteenth century, commentators generally treated fair exchange as merely a third subdivision of particular justice alongside the other two, distributive and corrective justice. Ritchie argued convincingly in an article of 1894, that to treat it in that way is to give it less importance than Aristotle intended it to have.[1] Justice between exchangers, or 'catallactic justice' as Ritchie called it, lay at the foundation of the polis in a way that the particular justices did not, important though they were. Commercial buying and selling had, indeed, replaced archaic mutual gift-giving long before Aristotle's time. The division of labour was sufficiently advanced and important in the polis for Plato to be able to represent it as a not-very-original opinion that the polis came into existence in the first place because of the greater abundance of material goods that the social division of labour makes possible (*Rep.* 2, 369e–371b). Private exchange is the inseparable correlate of the private division of labour, and Aristotle, as Ritchie observes, gives fair exchange primacy over the other forms of justice in Book 5 of the *Ethics* just because it provided a form of *philia* for an activity which he knew to be more basic than any other in the life of the polis. He calls it 'the salvation of states' (*NE* 5, 1132^{b}33). The judgement is referred back to, and repeated more or less word for word in the *Politics*: 'Wherefore the principle of reciprocity [*to ison to antipeponthos*], as I have already remarked in the *Ethics*, is the salvation of states', (*Pol.* 2, 1261^{a}30–1). A version of it also appears in the *Magna Moralia* (1194^{a}16 f.). Yet the account of fair

[1] D. G. Ritchie, 'Aristotle's Subdivisions of Particular Justice', *Classical Review*, 7 (1894), 185–92.

exchange in *NE* 5. 5 has a reputation for obscurity which ought to seem surprising in view of the importance Aristotle clearly attached to the topic it deals with. A large part of the reason for this is the confusion that has come to surround the formula Aristotle uses to specify it, 'as builder to shoemaker, so many shoes to a house' (ὅπερ οἰκοδόμος πρὸς σκυτοτόμον, τοσαδὶ ὑποδέματα πρὸς οἰκίαν, 1133ᵃ23–5); 'as farmer is to shoemaker, the amount of the shoemaker's product is to that of the farmer's product for which it exchanges' (ὅπερ γεωργὸς πρὸς σκυτοτόμον, τὸ ἔργον τὸ τοῦ σκυτοτόμου πρὸς τὸ τοῦ γεωργοῦ, 1133ᵃ32–3).

Aristotle uses the notion of proportion (*analogia*) in expounding distributive and corrective justice, and he does the same in expounding fairness in exchange. In each case he uses the letters A and B to denote the parties, and C and D to denote what they get. The terms are then arranged in an *analogia* or proportion such as A : B = C : D. In the case of fair exchange the *analogia* is A : B = D : C, as builder to shoemaker, so many shoes to a house. The order of the things which A and B get is reversed in this case, unlike the cases of the two particular justices, so that the second ratio in the proportion is not C : D but D : C. This is simply to mark the fact that in exchange, A, the builder, does not get his own product (houses) back again, but shoes.[2] Commentators have been unable to find an agreed meaning for the formula. This fact, together with the common opinion that chapter 5 is simply about fair exchange (the discussion of economic value usually being overlooked), is enough to explain why the chapter has come to be regarded as something of a failure, and the poor relation in Book 5. Scholars are sceptical about it, apt to

---

[2] In distributive and corrective justice, A is conjoined with C, and B with D, so that in the geometrical figures that are often used to illustrate the proportion or *analogia* in each of these cases, the terms are joined together along the sides of a rectangle. In fair exchange, however, Aristotle says they are joined together along the diagonal (ἡ κατὰ διάμετρον σύζευξις, 1133ᵃ6–7). The point of this is to mark the fact that each party gets the work or product of the other, and not his own product back again. This simple arrangement is often referred to as 'cross-conjunction', and it has often been made to seem mysterious and in need of arcane explanations. But it has none of the mathematical implications that Soudek, Lowry, and others, want to draw from it, as will be seen later in this chapter.

dismiss it as a muddle, and tend to leave it out of selected editions of the *Ethics*. The formula has a simple explanation, however, which has been overlooked because of a persistent and mistaken belief that inequality enters into it.

Modern commentators have often found the idea irresistible that inequality pervades the entire chapter. There has been almost unanimous agreement that the phrase 'as builder to shoemaker' registers some sort of inequality, and that the formula means that the inequality between builder and shoemaker somehow sets the standard for reckoning how many shoes should fairly be given for a house. (I shall call this the standard view.)

There the agreement ends, however, and for the rest, there is a wealth of conjecture about the inequality Aristotle is supposed to have in mind. He does not even hint what it might be, which hardly suggests that he had any sort of inequality in mind, and in the absence of a hint the conjectures are all unsupported, and none has been found convincing. The confusion has blighted the reputation of the chapter, and Finley's conclusion is representative, or even understated: 'that this is not one of Aristotle's more transparent discussions is painfully apparent'.[3] Hardie is inclined to make the commentators share at least some of the responsibility: 'These chapters have been found or made difficult by commentators.'[4] Aristotle is often considered to have been the first to analyse issues in what is now called 'economics'. That view rests partly on this chapter, and if the chapter were as obscure as it is reputed to be, and as it would be if inequality really had the part usually given to it, that claim would be more difficult to sustain.

☞ 2 ☜

'As builder to shoemaker', on the standard view, measures some property in which the two are unequal. Williams thought

---

[3] 'Aristotle and Economic Analysis', 33. See the similar opinions of Bonar and Soudek cited in Ch. 1.

[4] Hardie, *Aristotle's Ethical Theory*, 188.

the property to be 'the worth of the architect as compared with the worth of the cobbler', and Grant the 'quality of the labour'. Rackham considered that 'different kinds of producers have different social values and deserve different rates of reward'. Burnet, following Jackson, thought unequal friendship to be the key, and that the superior party 'is apt to expect to get more services from his friend than he gives in proportion to his own superiority'.[5] Meek suggests that a producer is measured for his status and skill, and Soudek and Spengler that he is measured for his skill alone. [6]

None of these suggestions explains how the ratio 'as builder to shoemaker' might set the standard for a fair exchange. A qualitative comparison will not do. The ratio must be quantitative and precise enough for calculating the number of shoes for a house, because that is supposed to be its purpose. Some of the suggestions are qualitative, others quantifiable only arbitrarily, and others are not independent of the ratio in which the products are exchanged, as they would need to be.

Ritchie, Ross, Hardie, Schumpeter, and Gordon have suggested that the ratio concerns labour time.[7] This has the advantages of being both independent of the ratio of products and quantifiable in principle, but it is a conjecture which attributes to Aristotle an idea he did not have. In our own era,

---

[5] Soudek's use of passages from the beginning of Book 6, continuing the analysis of friendship, is rejected by Finley in 'Aristotle and Economic Analysis', 36, n. 35.

[6] R. Williams, *The Nicomachean Ethics of Aristotle* (London, 1869), 154. Grant, *Ethics of Aristotle*, ii. 118. Rackham, *Nicomachean Ethics*, 283 n. Burnet, *Ethics of Aristotle*, 225 n. R. L. Meek, *Studies in the Labour Theory of Value* (London, 1956), 295 n. Soudek, 'Aristotle's Theory of Exchange', 46, 60. Spengler, 'Aristotle on Economic Imputation', 384, n. 52; 387.

[7] Ritchie suggests 'I feel no doubt . . . that Aristotle *does* think of different kinds of producers having different social values: we can easily give an economic meaning to what he says by understanding the ratio between two producers A and B to mean the ratio between the value of an hour of A's labour and the value of an hour of B's labour', 'Aristotle's Subdivisions of Particular Justice', 186. Ross, *Ethica Nicomachea* (Oxford, 1925), in his note to 1133ª5, produces the same idea more elaborately and confusedly. Hardie, *Aristotle's Ethical Theory*, 196, asserts without argument that 'the comparative values of producers must in Aristotle's view here mean the comparative values of their work done in the same time'. See also Schumpeter, *History of Economic Analysis*, 60-2, and Gordon, 'Aristotle and the Development of Value Theory', 115–28.

political economy developed the notion of labour as an undifferentiated category under which the different natural labours, weaving, building, and farming, fall as qualitatively identical instances differing from each other only as quantities. This abstraction is not to be attributed lightly to any author of the ancient world, and particularly not to Aristotle. When Aristotle has greatest need of that abstraction, he fails to produce it. Most of *NE* 5. 5, as we saw in Chapter 1, is devoted to seeking a property which all products have in common, in order to explain how they are commensurable, as they must be if they are to stand in equations like '5 beds = 1 house' as Aristotle says they do. He tries two properties: that of 'being expressible in money', and that of 'being an object of need'. But he rejects them both and concludes that 'in truth' there can be no such property (1133^{b}18–20). The property of 'being a product of labour' does not occur to him, in spite of the fact that the things in question are artefacts.[8]

Joachim, too, takes the ratio to be one of unequal 'values' of the producers, but he does not care to add to the speculation about its meaning: 'How exactly the values of producers are to be determined, and what the ratio between them can mean, is . . . in the end unintelligible to me.' Finley concurs: 'I must confess that, like Joachim, I do not understand what the ratios between the producers can mean.'[9] A century of speculation has produced little, and in avoiding it, Joachim and Finley produce the least indefensible version of the standard view, but the chapter is none the less left in confusion.

Heath, together with Gauthier and Jolif, departs from the standard view in suggesting that builder and shoemaker are to be considered equal as persons. But Heath is inconsistent in

---

[8] Marx sought to explain why Aristotle, and the Greeks generally, lacked such a notion of labour. He thought the explanation lay in the absence from antiquity of markets in wage-labour, and of the notion of equality which they generate; *Capital*, i. 65–6. Finley accepts the case, 'Aristotle and Economic Analysis', 38. For another account which develops and corrects Marx's suggestion, see F. Rosen, 'The Political Context of Aristotle's Categories of Justice', *Phronesis*, 20 (1975), 228–40. The theme of 'labour' in Aristotle is discussed further in Ch. 9 (1) below.

[9] H. H. Joachim, *The Nicomachean Ethics* (Oxford, 1951), 150. Finley, 'Aristotle and Economic Analysis', 38.

holding also that the ratio compares unequal 'worths'.[10] Gauthier and Jolif offer no argument, and their view is rejected by Finley as an 'ingenious effort'.[11]

☞ 3 ☜

It has been rash to dismiss *NE* 5. 5 as a muddle without examining the assumption which causes all the trouble, that builder and shoemaker are unequal. Yet the assumption has never been examined properly, in spite of the fact that so many commentators have found it irresistibly attractive, or perhaps because of this. Even Finley, while confessing, with Joachim, agnosticism about the meaning of the ratio, still expresses a guarded preference for the assumption of inequality: 'I do not rule out that "as builder to shoemaker" is somehow to be taken literally.'[12] But the assumption is implausible in ways that ought to have been obvious.

[10] T. Heath, *Mathematics in Aristotle* (Oxford, 1949), 275, hits the nail on the head. He suggests that the values exchanged are supposed to be equal, and that this 'is mathematically expressed by saying that $xD = C$ or $xD : C = 1$. Therefore the proportion $A : B = xD : C$ is not true unless the ratio $A : B$ (for the purpose in question at any rate) is equal to 1 or $A = B$. The fact is that the relative "worth" of A and B has really nothing to do with the particular transaction.' Unfortunately, on the previous page, he says that 'A and B represented the "worth" of the two parties [which] might be measured, say, by the value of the work that they could respectively produce in the same time, say an hour' (p. 274), and he returns to this view later with the suggestion that we may equate the values of a pair of shoes and a house 'by considering, for example, the values in relation to the labour and skill required by A and B to produce their unit products respectively' (p. 275).

[11] R. A. Gauthier and J. Y. Jolif, *L'Éthique à Nicomaque* (2 vols.; Paris, 1970), ii 377. Finley, 'Aristotle and Economic Analysis', 34. Finley's reason for rejecting Gauthier and Jolif has to do with the so-called 'cross-conjunction' at 1133ᵃ6–7.

[12] Finley, 'Aristotle and Economic Analysis', 38. Finley thinks that, taken literally, the ratio must represent an inequality, because he cannot imagine that Aristotle could possibly have meant builder and shoemaker to be considered equal (and the ratio A : B to be equal to 1). This would be tantamount, in his view, to treating the ratio as if it did not exist. This is the reason he gives for rejecting the suggestion of Gauthier and Jolif that the parties are equal: 'I cannot believe that Aristotle went out of his way to insist on *proportional* reciprocity as necessary for justice in this one field, only to conclude that one pair of ratios does not in fact exist, and to make that point in the most ambiguous way possible', 'Aristotle and Economic Analysis', 34. Finley is mistaken in thinking that the peculiarity of the formula for fair exchange is that it is proportional. All the formulae Aristotle gives in Book 5 for the different sorts of justice

Justice in Exchange

Honours and other things belonging to the community were distributed unequally, according to the principle of distributive justice, which is

the principle of assignment by desert. All are agreed that justice in distributions must be based on desert of some sort, although they do not all mean the same sort of desert; democrats make the criterion free birth; those of oligarchic sympathies, wealth, or in other cases birth; upholders of aristocracy make it virtue. (1131ᵃ24 ff.)

In the distribution of honours and public property, 'if the people involved are not equal, they will not [justly] receive equal shares; indeed, whenever equals receive unequal shares, or unequals equal shares, in a distribution, that is a source of quarrels and accusations', 1131ᵃ23 ff. Private property could not conceivably be exchanged in anything like this way. If, for reasons of hierarchy, one man could command in the market more for his goods than another, who would choose, without compulsion, to exchange with him, except someone of his own status on whom he could not pull rank? Even this person would try to avoid his equal because exchange with an inferior would be more advantageous. The idea is absurd, and Aristotle understood exchange far too well, as we saw in Chapter 3, ever to have entertained it. Had there been a practice of exchanging private property in such a way, it is certain that we should know about it, because it would have caused monumental trouble, and we might expect to hear as much about it as we do about the cancellation of debts and the redistribution of land. As it is, we do not even hear of dissension between

are proportional in this way, relating two parties A and B, and the things they get C and D. Aristotle says that it is in the nature of justice to have this form. 'Proportion' for Aristotle is a relation not between two terms but between two ratios, and it always means equality of ratios, and it must therefore involve four terms. In the *Magna Moralia* it is said that 'proportion requires at least four terms, being an equality between the two ratios A to B and C to D', *MM* 1093ᵇ37 ff.; see also the confirmation of this view of proportion in Heath, *Mathematics in Aristotle, 272.* The other sorts of justice are 'proportional' in just the same way. What is peculiar to fair exchange is that it is reciprocal, i.e. that its terms are conjoined along the diagonal (ἡ κατὰ διάμετρον σύζευξις, *NE* 1133ᵃ6–7), rather than along the side of the quadrilateral as in the particular justices. Furthermore, making the ratio A : B equal to 1 is not treating it as if it did not exist, and there is nothing odd about its being equal to 1, because that is exactly how Aristotle presents the A : B ratio in corrective justice.

democratic theories of fair exchange and oligarchical and aristocratic ones, which is the least we could expect.

The ratio 'as builder to shoemaker' cannot set the standard of fairness in the way the standard view supposes, because on its own it does not give a way of determining how many of one sort of thing to give for how many of another, which is the point of the exercise. Even if we knew that a builder was 'worth' (leaving aside the problem of what that might conceivably mean) twice a shoemaker, this would tell us only that the ratio of builder to shoemaker was 2 : 1, and the number of shoes to be given for a house would still be unknown, since it clearly is not two shoes for one house. We would know that the number should be twice some other number, but we would not know whether it should be twice half a shoe, twice one shoe, or twice a hundred shoes. To settle this, we would also need to know x in 'x shoes = 1 house' so that, multiplying it by 2, we could arrive at the supposed ratio of inequality 2 : 1.[13] But to do that would contradict Aristotle's theory, because he says that 'If, then, first there is proportionate equality of goods, and then the reciprocal action takes place, the result we mention will be effected', in other words, fairness consists in exchanging equal proportions, that is, according to the equation 'x shoes = 1 house' (1133ª10–12). So multiplying the number of shoes (x) by the supposed inferiority index of the shoemaker (2) would actually be a shift away from the proportions Aristotle requires for fairness. His account is consistent only with the ratio of builder to shoemaker being 1 : 1, and there is simply no room for the introduction of any inequality.

Aristotle says nothing whatever about the exchangers as persons, which itself gives little enough reason to suppose that a

---

[13] It is usually overlooked that even on the standard view it would be necessary to know x in $xD = C$, or x shoes = house. Without it, the calculation of how many Ds should be given for a C would be impossible, because knowing the numbers to be put into the ratio A : B, as builder to shoemaker, is insufficient to yield the number of shoes for a house. Burnet seems to have been the only one to have noticed this, *Ethics of Aristotle*, 226 n; and Heath seems to be the only one to have picked it up from Burnet, *Mathematics in Aristotle*, 275. Spiegel makes the point clearly, *The Growth of Economic Thought* (Englewood Cliffs, NJ, 1971), 31–2.

personal consideration such as inequality has the central place in his theory that the standard view gives it. As we saw in Chapter 1, every step and detail of Aristotle's argument in *NE* 5. 5 bears exclusively on the products and the proportions in which they are exchanged. His argument has four steps: (1) fair exchange is a form of reciprocity (1132^b31–2); (2) reciprocity not of equality but proportion (1132^b33); (3) this is achieved by equalizing proportions of products to be exchanged (1133^a8–12); (4) if proportions of products can be equal, products must be commensurable, and this needs explaining. The inquiry deals only with the ratio in which products are exchanged; persons are irrelevant.[14]

There is a suggestion in the text that before the exchange is transacted, builder and shoemaker are 'unequal and different' (1133^a18). A great deal has been made of this, naturally, by those who see inequality as pervasive in Aristotle's chapter. But there is another suggestion in the text that before the exchange, when they have 'their own', they are equals (1133^b3). These statements cannot be regarded as cancelling each other out, but can they be reconciled? Aristotle thinks it is necessary to establish 'equality of proportion' between the products because 'one product may be too much (*kreîtton*) for the other, so they must be equalized' (1133^a12–14). He means that a house is too much to give for a shoe (a builder can't be expected to hand over two houses if he wants a pair of shoes), so they must be exchanged in proportions, and the proportions should be equal.[15] The difficulty is typical of exchange, he says, because it is not two doctors who exchange, or two farmers, but a doctor and a farmer, and in general people who are different (*heterôn*, 1133^a16–18). So Aristotle does in a way

---

[14] Cf. 1133^a10, 14, 17, 21, 25; 1133^b4, 10, 25, 27. Concern with products rather than producers is evident in the textual detail too. What have to be equalized (*isasthênai*) at 1133^a13–14 are referred to by a neuter plural pronoun (*tauta*). At 1133^b5 it is the *erga* of shoemaker and farmer that have to be equalized. What have to be 'comparable in some way' (*sumbleta pôs*) if they are to be equalized, are *panta*, 1133^a19. What money equalizes are *panta*, 1133^a20. The τὴν ὑπεροχὴν καὶ τὴν ἔλλειψιν in 1133^a21 are the members of *panta* again, and Aristotle instances shoes and houses.

[15] On mistranslations of *kreîtton* as 'better than' or 'superior to', which imply that Aristotle has the quality of products in mind, see Ch. 1.

have in mind an inequality between persons, but persons considered simply as creators of products of different and unequal values, so that the inequality of persons collapses into one of products.

He goes on to say that 'they are equals and associates just because this equality can be effected in their case', and the equality in question is the proportionate equality between their products: 'Let A be a farmer, C food, B a shoemaker, D his product equated to C' (1133^b2–6). In other words, the 'unequal' producers are made equal by establishing proportionate equality between the products, and this could not be true if the inequality were social, as the standard view would have it. The assumption that builder and shoemaker are unequal does not seem so plausible after all.

῾ 4 ῾

There are some remarks scattered about in chapters 1, 2, and 3 of Book 5 of the *Ethics* concerning the nature of justice (*dikaiosunê*) common to all its forms. These remarks reveal assumptions Aristotle makes about fair exchange which do not appear in chapter 5 itself, and they prove that inequality has no part in the chapter.

Justice is a sort of equality (*isotês*). The unjust man (*adikos*) is 'grasping and unfair', and he is 'unequal' (*anison*) and his action is unequal. The just man is an equal man (*isos*, 1129^a32–3, 1131^a1–2). We are speaking of actions which admit of a more or too much (*to pleon*) and a less or too little (*to elatton*), so that there is a mean between too much and too little, and the mean is the equal, 'for in any action which admits of τὸ πλέον and τὸ ἔλαττον, there is also τὸ ἴσον' (1131^a2–3, Jackson). In general, *to dikaion* implies at least four terms, because the persons for whom a distribution is *dikaion* are two, and the things distributed are two (1131^a18–20). The just consists in proper proportion (*analogia*) between these four, and *analogia* means 'equality of ratios', that is, equality between the ratio of persons, A and B, and the ratio of what they get, C and D (1131ª29–32).[16]

There are only two sorts of cases: 'If the persons are *isoi* [equals], then the things will be *isa* [equals], since as one person is to the other, so is the one thing to the other thing, and if the persons are not *isoi* they will not have *isa*' (1131ª20–4, Jackson). (I shall call this Aristotle's general prescription for *dikaiosunê*.) So in general the formula 'as A is to B' (e.g., 'as builder to shoemaker') in Aristotle's mind is as consistent with their being equals as it is with their being unequals, and it carries no suggestion whatever of inequality. Aristotle's contrast between corrective and distributive justice turns precisely on this difference between their respective A : B ratios. Corrective justice is just for cases where A and B are to be considered equals. Fraud is a typical case for corrective justice, and Aristotle says that it makes no difference who defrauds whom, 'for the law looks only at the distinctive character of the injury, and treats the parties as equals', 1132ª21.[17] The formula involves the usual two ratios, but in this case the ratio of persons A : B is formal and equal to 1. Distributive justice, on the other hand, is for the sort of case where it is going to make a difference who the parties are; where it is not fitting to treat them as equals, and where getting back what you gave is not equal, but too much or too little. In this case the ratio A : B is substantial and not equal to 1. If an officer strikes a man, he ought not to be struck back, but if a man strikes an officer, it is not enough that he be struck back, but he ought to be punished as well (1132ᵇ28 ff.).[18]

Fair exchange falls under the general prescription for *dikaio-*

[16] On *analogia* or proportion as equality of ratios, see Heath, *Mathematics in Aristotle*, 272, and n. 12 above.

[17] In this passage it is, admittedly, the goodness or badness of a man that the law is said to ignore. But if the law recognized some other sort of difference as pertinent, inequality especially, we should not expect Aristotle to say that the law 'treats the parties as equals' without mentioning it.

[18] The case is one of corrective justice, but the offence being corrected is one against distributive justice. Aristotle's point is that where an offence under corrective justice (hitting someone) is committed by an inferior on a superior, the simple reciprocity of Rhadamanthys (getting back what you did) is unfitting, though it might be fitting between equals.

sunê, just as corrective and distributive justice do, because, like them, it has to do with unfairness, having your own, and not making gains at the expense of others, or suffering losses at their hands, in things that are desirable or harmful. Aristotle treats it as a distinct sort of justice, rather than as a species of either corrective or distributive justice, and it is clear why it is not a species of corrective justice. Corrective justice corrects bad exchanges (among other things), and its ability to do that depends on there being a procedure for reckoning what a good exchange of shoes and houses should be. This procedure will not itself be part of corrective justice, and it is what chapter 5 is meant to supply.

But if the parties are not to be regarded as *isoi*, as the standard view assumes, can there be as good an explanation of why fair exchange is not treated as a species of distributive justice? No such explanation is possible. If the parties were to be considered unequals in fair exchange, Aristotle would have had to treat it as a species of distributive justice, because, according to his general prescription for *dikaiosunê*, that is what it would have been. The fact that it is a distinct sort of justice, based on the entirely different principle of reciprocity (*antipeponthos*, 1132^{b}23–33), is sufficient to prove that Aristotle does not mean it to satisfy the condition of distributive justice, namely, that the parties are unequal. Since there are only two sorts of case according to the general prescription of *dikaiosunê*, the only remaining possibility is that the parties are *isoi*, and the ratio between them is formal and equal to 1, just as it is in corrective justice.[19]

The same conclusion has to be drawn from his remarks about the use of the terms 'loss' and 'gain', which he uses to define the equality common to all justice. He says that the terms are applied in all cases, but that they may not in every case be applied in their strict senses; he instances assault, where the assailant is not strictly speaking a 'gainer', nor the

---

[19] Aristotle considers buying and selling under corrective justice (1131^{a}2), because it corrects transactions in which parties end up with less or more than 'their own'. Similarly, if he thought fair buying and selling should involve inequality, we should expect them to be considered in the chapter on distributive justice, and they are not.

victim strictly speaking a 'loser': 'For the term "gain" is applied generally to such cases, even if it be not a term appropriate to certain cases, e.g. to the person who inflicts a wound—and "loss" to the sufferer' (1132ª10–14). He explains that these terms are drawn from buying and selling, where they apply in their strict senses; where to have more than one's own is called gaining, and to have less than one's own is called losing; and where, if the exchange results in neither a gain nor a loss, 'they say they have their own': 'These names, both loss and gain, have come from voluntary transactions; for to have more than one's own is called gaining, and to have less than one's original share is called losing, e.g. in buying and selling' (1132ᵇ11–18). This means that an exchange is fair when what A gets back is equal to what he gave, and the same for B; in other words, when the things are *isa*. But according to Aristotle's own general prescription (1131ª20–4), a distribution of things that are *isa* is fair, only if it is fitting to regard the parties as *isoi*. So again the conclusion is that in exchange the parties are equal.

☞ 5 ☜

The upshot is that Aristotle's formula 'as builder to shoemaker, so many shoes to a house' has a perfectly clear meaning. The ratio of builder to shoemaker must equal 1 ($A : B = 1$), and in order to correspond with it, the ratio of shoes to houses must equal 1 also ($xD : C = 1$). So fair exchange is achieved by bringing it about that $xD = C$, or $xD/C = 1$, which is exactly what fair exchange consists in according to Aristotle at 1133ª10–12: 'If, then, first there is proportionate equality of goods, and then reciprocal action takes place, the result we mention will be effected.' His account is incomplete because he does not say how to calculate x, and that is an extension of his deeper problem of being unable to say how Ds and Cs can be commensurable and so equatable in the first place. He does not know what the commensurable feature is in C and D, as we saw in Chapters 1 and 2, so he does not know

142

what it is that has to be equalized, and so he cannot say how *x* is to be calculated. But at least it is clear what he is getting at, and where his real problem lies. It is also clearer how the different strands of his discussion in the chapter are connected, particularly the discussion of fairness and that of commensurability. Since builder and shoemaker are meant to be considered equal, it is also clear that all the invention that has gone into interpreting 'as builder to shoemaker' as registering an inequality can be dispensed with.

Medieval commentators were not so keen as modern ones to read inequality into Aristotle's account. Langholm observes that, according to the Schoolmen, whereas in the distribution of honours men are not considered equal, in the exchange of goods and services 'the parties themselves are considered equal: one should not expect to get a better deal because one is more worthy (or so, at least, did the medieval Aristotelian understand it)'. Nor, incidentally, were medieval commentators as prone to overlook the problem of commensurability. Langholm notes that the Schoolmen were puzzled 'as to what "common substance" (as Marx called it) in the different goods constitutes the principle of equalization'.[20] In the account Aquinas offers, in his *Commentary on the Nicomachean Ethics*, the problem of commensurability is prominent as the main problem of the section.

It is time to raise the vexed question of Aristotle's use of mathematics in the proportion specifying fair exchange, A : B = D : C. On the account given here of this proportion, there is precious little mathematics involved in it, and what there is has been sufficiently dealt with.[21] This in itself might be objected to: if the mathematics is of so little importance, why should Aristotle have introduced it? To get the matter into proportion it should be asked in return 'what mathematics?' All we have is the *analogia* or proportion itself, and the 'geometry' of 'cross-conjunction', which is not geometry at all but merely an

---

[20] Langholm, *Wealth and Money*, 47.
[21] Others have also thought the supposed mathematics to be irrelevant. See Hardie, *Aristotle's Ethical Theory*, 200, and Max Salomon in the appendix to his *Der Begriff der Gerechtigkeit bei Aristoteles* (New York, 1979).

illustrative configuration. There is no serious mathematics involved in these things. Certainly, Aristotle's presentation of fairness in exchange has a mathematical aspect. But so do his presentations of distributive and corrective justice, and no commentator has been tempted to offer a complex mathematical interpretation of them. The mathematics, such as it is, arises from the fact that Aristotle sees all these forms of justice as essentially constituted by a relationship between four terms, designating respectively the two parties (A and B) and the two items they get (C and D). These forms of justice are based on proportions of the form A : B :: C : D, and that is all there is to it. The calculations concerning the adjustments required to get fairness into distributive and corrective justice might appear to be more complicated than they need to be in getting fairness into exchange, and Aristotle might be thought to have had less need to introduce mathematical forms of expression in the latter case than the former. Even so, in whatever way he might have decided to present them, he had good reason for presenting each sort of fairness in the same sort of way, because in each case fairness is a relationship between two people and two lots of something that they are supposed to get, and it is perfectly natural and appropriate that he should represent each sort of fairness as a ratio or *analogia*. In none of these cases are complex mathematical relationships required beyond the *analogia* itself.

If the account given here is right, then the wonderful mathematical stories that have been woven around the proportion are fantasies, and there is nothing constructive to be said about them. The most solidly argued and the most complicated is Soudek's. He interprets the proportion or *analogia* in terms of the harmonic mean, for which there is not the slightest evidence, arriving at the view that Aristotle's proportionate reciprocity is 'a geometric proportion not between four terms but rather between four ratios'. Thus, according to him, Aristotle's A : B = D : C, really means A/B : B/D :: A/D : B/C. He concludes that 'The methodological tool Aristotle has devised for his investigation is a kind of "mathematical model", thus setting a precedent to what has become, among mathematically

oriented economists, a generally accepted practice.'[22] Soudek's
view has been broadly endorsed by Lowry, who claims Heath
as supporting a substantial mathematical analysis, which he
does not,[23] and explains the total absence of any support in
early commentaries for Soudek's interpretation as being due to
the fact that 'the numerous copyists and commentators . . . did
not quite comprehend'.[24] But they appear to have understood
well enough. The first- or second-century periphrasis of
Heliodorus, for example, does not show undue signs of incom-
prehension of anything that is certainly in Aristotle's chapter,
and it even manages to avoid the suggestion that the ratio of
builder to shoemaker registers an inequality.[25] Von Leyden
offers an equally imaginary, but unargued, account of
Aristotle's ratio as involving '(a) the quality of the labour
spent, (b) the quantity, (c) the time expended in the production of the goods, or (d) the productivity', and he adds that 'the
issue is even more complex in that the excellence of work (i.e.
both its quality and its quantity) will have to be measured by
the relation between supply and demand'.[26]

Aristotle's analysis of what today is known as the problem
of exchange value is a great achievement. It is the first conceptual inquiry into the nature of exchange value, and it is still
one of the most lucid and penetrating. Its importance was once
appreciated by economists. Marx's analysis of exchange value
is explicitly based on it, and Böhm-Bawerk, the economist of
the Austrian School and Marx's earliest serious critic, scoffed
at the fact that 'Marx had found in old Aristotle the idea that
"exchange cannot exist without equality, and equality cannot
exist without commensurability" '.[27] Yet Aristotle's discussion of these matters has gone largely unnoticed in the classical and philosophical literature, particularly in the anglophone

---

[22] Soudek, 'Aristotle's Theory of Exchange', 59–60, 45.
[23] *Archaeology of Economic Ideas*, 194. Heath, *Mathematics in Aristotle*, 272–5.
[24] Lowry, *Archaeology of Economic Ideas*, 203 and 209.
[25] G. Heylbut, *Commentaria in Aristotelem Graeca* (Berlin, 1892), xix, pras. 171–6,
pp. 95–8.
[26] Von Leyden, *Aristotle on Equality and Justice*, 16.
[27] Böhm-Bawerk, *Marx and the Close of his System*, 68.

world.[28] One among the many reasons for this has been the belief that Aristotle could not possibly have meant that builder and shoemaker were equal or at least to be regarded as equal. Until fairly recently the preferred translation of *oikodomos* was not 'builder' but 'architect'.

---

[28] A notable exception, not anglophone, is Gianfranco Lotito, 'Aristotele su moneta scambio bisogni (Eth. Nic. v 5)'.

8

The Ancient 'Economy' and its Literature

⌒ 1 ⌒

Near the beginning of *The Ancient Economy*, Finley noted that 'the inapplicability to the ancient world of a market-centred analysis was powerfully argued by Max Weber and by his most important disciple among ancient historians, Johannes Hasebroek; in our own day by Karl Polanyi'. But he added at once that it had all been 'to little avail'.

Finley's own work went far beyond that of Weber, Hasebroek, and Polanyi. He showed with greater clarity, rigour, and detail than ever before, the futility of the modernist case: the persistent reliance on unrepresentative evidence; the misguided application to ancient society of modern theories of investment, banking, and credit; the absence from ancient society of conglomerations of interdependent markets, and of anything like 'economic policy'; and the absence from Greek literature of economics. The case was formidable, and it gave modernist authors so much to chew on that it was reasonable to expect that it would be some time before they were heard from again. Yet modernist retorts to it were quick in coming, and they showed that not a great deal had been learned.

It is not a recent discovery that there is a systematic problem involved in describing antiquity in economic terms. Trever, writing before 1916, was wary of 'an artificial attempt to force the Greek thinkers on the procrustean rack of the concepts of modern economy', though Trever himself found the lure irresistible.[1] Modernism has, it is true, moved from the

---

[1] A. A. Trever, *A History of Greek Economic Thought* (Chicago, 1916), 8. Trever, like Zimmern, however, thought that the Greeks did 'produce economists' and

centre of studies of ancient society to a more marginal position, but the problem it presents has not itself greatly eased. Modernism has shown itself capable of enduring even treatments as potent as Finley's, in spite of its failure to reply adequately to serious empirical and conceptual criticism, or perhaps because of its incapacity to recognize the weight of such criticism. Millett expresses a commonly felt impatience at 'the persistence of the modernist point of view', adding that 'the so-called "primitivist–modernist" controversy ought to have died a natural death long ago, but it still refuses to lie down'.[2] Such impatience is understandable. Scholars have shown empirically, over and over again, that antiquity did not have the institutions, ideas, and practices which modernist claims wittingly or unwittingly attribute to it. This detailed empirical refutation ought to be enough, but it never is, and this suggests that there is an underlying problem which empirical evidence on its own is failing to resolve.

A position which empirical evidence cannot defeat is not an empirical position but an a priori one. Modernism is, indeed, in part an a priori position, so that dealing with it must be partly a conceptual matter. But Finley provided much of the necessary conceptual correction too. He argued that there is a systematic mistake involved in applying modern economic concepts to the ancient world, because that world was predominantly a world of use value, and not a system of market economy, which modern economic concepts were specifically devised to describe and explain. Unfortunately modernist authors have proved pretty thick-skinned to conceptual criticism too, and they have generally shrugged it off without effectively replying to it. Critics of modernism have, therefore, sometimes drawn the conclusion that rational ways of dealing with it seem powerless. In the face of such a degree of perversity, impatience is a natural enough response. None the less,

'economic ideas' (ibid. 14), though he does not explain in which sense of the word 'economic' he intends this. Despite his own warning, he subsequently goes on to endorse Meyer's view that capitalism had dawned in the Greek world.

[2] Millett, *Lending and Borrowing*, 9 and 15.

there must be a reason for the persistence of such perversity, if that is what it is.

Finley's position is that market economy is a recent historical arrival, at most 400 years old, and that the subject of economics is not, and cannot be, any older, if by 'economics' we mean the study of market economy. He concludes that we should not be surprised, therefore, to find that the ancient world produced nothing that we can regard as economics.

The modernist position, in so far as it is inspired by economics, is that economics is the study of laws which hold between humans and economic goods, and laws of such general character must apply in all periods of history, give or take a bit, and to all forms of society. We should, therefore, expect to find some sort of economic writing in antiquity. If what we find is limited and peculiar, this is because ancient economic activity was still too undeveloped to manifest more than a few rather basic economic laws. Since the Greeks had little economic reality to reflect on, it is not surprising that they should have had relatively little to say about it, or that what they did say should be mixed up with other things, like ethics and administration. None the less, if the economic reality of antiquity was too undeveloped to prompt the Greeks themselves to make many discriminations, to form economic concepts, and to find the right relation between ethics and economics, their activity was unavoidably of such a kind that it is properly described in terms of economic concepts, even though these concepts were formed later, when greater insight and discrimination had become possible. The Greeks, after all, did of necessity engage in 'economic activity', and economics merely makes explicit what has always been implicit in economic activity.

There is some truth in this modernist view. The Greeks did develop exchange value, money, and commerce, and even the most resolute primitivist cannot deny it. In the works of Aristotle and Plato, the Greeks also developed systematic thought about matters which today would be called 'economic'. No primitivist can deny this either, even though they may want to insist on the point, which might be thought a quibble, that this work does not constitute 'economic analysis'.

☞ 2 ☜

The core of the controversy is the role that exchange value had in the ancient world, and the terms in which that role is to be described. There has been much exaggeration about this on both sides. In spite of primitivist exaggeration seeking to minimize the role of exchange value, it cannot be seriously contested that money and commodity exchange were vitally important to the polis.

Much of what was produced in the ancient world, it is true, was produced, not for exchange, but for direct consumption by the families of those who made or grew it. The market in textiles, for example, was limited because the work of making textiles was part of the distaff responsibilities in the household, and its product was not generally sold. But not all products were directly consumed. Many kinds of thing were made for exchange, and circulated as commodities against money.

It is possible to argue about the relative scale of production for direct consumption and production for exchange. But whatever the scale of exchange may have been, it was at any rate sufficiently developed to have prompted Aristotle to investigate the conceptual problems that arise in trying to understand exchange value. He inquires into the capacity for being equalized in exchange which products, and some things that are not products, come to acquire, and into the nature of the property by virtue of which things that are incommensurable by nature come to be commensurable and equatable in exchange. If our knowledge of the history of Athens down to Aristotle's time did not tell us that the production and circulation of exchange values, or commodities, had become important elements in polis life, we could in any case infer that they had simply from Aristotle's inquiries, and from his belief that *philia* in buying and selling was the most important form of justice in the polis, 'the salvation of states'.

150

Something further needs to be said about the relations of divided labour between producers which beget the relations between products which Aristotle examines, and about the existence of those relations, alongside others that were quite different, in the historical complexity of fourth-century Athens. Among the conditions of socially divided labour, two are especially important. First, there was a certain level of specialization in production, between agriculture and the crafts, and among the crafts themselves. (This had also been true, to a lesser degree, of the centralized bureaucratic temple- or palace-based cultures of the earlier period in the Near East.) Secondly, each producer produced privately and on his own account, had private property in the product, and marketed it. (This had not been true of the cultures based on palace or temple complexes.) Where some or all of the producers produce their own good, or narrow range of goods, privately, each is more or less in a situation where he has more than he can use of the product of his own specialized labour, and none of all the other goods produced by the specialized labours of others, which, since his needs are manifold, he must acquire. Thus, along with the development of specialization on the one hand, and of privacy in production of the other, there goes a complementary development of private exchange between the private specialists. A point is reached in this development where producers are producing partly or wholly with a view to exchange, and acquire through exchange all the other useful things they need but do not produce themselves.

Under these social relations of privately conducted labour and systematic exchange, the product of labour acquires a particular historical form. It is still a use value, something directly useful, but it is no longer made or grown by the producer only, or predominantly, because of its use value to him, for he produces far more of his item than he can consume. His product is of interest as a use value only to others. To him it is of interest because, as a potential subject of exchange, it represents exchange value, and he makes it in order to realize this value in exchange with others who need its use value, and who produce all the other things he needs. The product of labour has now taken on an independent social identity, as an exchange value, and it enters into social relations with other products which are expressed in relations of equality (1 house = 5 beds, or = so much money).[3] Exchange is the complement of the private form in which labour is socially supplied. The private nature of the producers is complemented by the social relations that come to exist between their products. People make their various contributions to the common effort, but not through direct relations of co-operation as contributors to the common stock. They are private, and produce only on their own account, and their co-operation appears as a social relation between their products: amount x of product A = amount y of product B. This peculiar relation embodies the problem Aristotle confronts in *NE* 5. 5.

Aristotle has been criticized for discussing only the activity of artisans, and not the activities of farmers, gentlemen, traders, and so forth. Artisans, it is said, were only a minor sector of the economy, so that Aristotle's economic coverage is much too restricted. But his discussion concerns exchange value, as we saw earlier in Chapter 4 (2), and artisans merely provide his most prominent examples. It was not only the products of artisans that entered circulation as exchange values, but those of slaves and peasants too, where these were sold rather than directly consumed. However much the primitivist may try to minimize the proportions of exchange value in the society, to maximize the degree of household self-sufficiency, to emphasize the small scale of workshops and so on, it is all in the end beside the point. For the polis in Aristotle's time rested in significant part on exchange value, because it rested on the separation of the crafts from agriculture, and consequently on the relations of exchange that existed between the producers in the countryside and those in the workshops, and between the suppliers of goods and services in the town itself. Aristotle knew it, and knew the importance of it, and that is

[3] Marx terms this the 'elementary form of value', see *Capital*, i, pt. 1, ch. 1, sect. 3a, which includes Marx's analysis of Aristotle's discussion of economic value in *NE* 5. 5.

why he says that fairness in exchange is 'the salvation of states' and holds the polis together (*NE* 1132^{b}34; *Pol.* 1261^{a}30–1).

☞ 3 ☜

There are difficulties in attributing this degree of importance to the market relationships that existed in fourth-century Athens. Market relationships are impersonal and atomized, and the social relationships of ancient Greece generally were not. On the contrary, they embodied the sensibility of *koinô-nia*, or community, to a degree which is quite unfamiliar to denizens of market societies. Finley and Millett have rightly made a lot of this, and so have other anti-modernists. But this is a line of thought which can induce anti-modernists into exaggerating the primitiveness of Athenian commerce, and into portraying the market relationships and institutions of the fourth century as less developed than they were. The work of Karl Polanyi provides ample illustration of the consequences of disregarding the danger.

The spirit of *koinônia* was dear to the Greeks, and it is prominent in Aristotle. Near to the beginning of *NE* 5. 5 Aristotle introduces the spirit of the Graces, and of recipro-city, as important elements in public and private behaviour, including exchange: 'That is why we set up a shrine to the Charites in a public place, since it is a duty not only to return a service done one, but another time to take the initiative in doing a service oneself' (1133^{a}3–5). What significance should be given to this passage?

According to Finley, it should heavily influence the reading of the entire chapter, because it is to be understood as announcing at the outset that the discussion is to be exclusively ethical rather than economic, that exchange is to be seen in the context of the *koinônia*, and that *koinônia* is to be as integral to the chapter as the act of exchange itself. The notion of *koinô-nia* carries elements of fairness, mutuality, and common pur-pose, and these elements, Finley thinks, pervade the chapter. Consequently, Finley concludes that Aristotle's chapter can have little to do with economic matters except under the strict aegis of ethics.[4]

Maybe Aristotle is saying that exchanges should be looked upon in the spirit of the Charites, of gift and counter-gift, and not as occasions for assembling in a public place to 'cheat each other with oaths', which, as Herodotus makes clear, the Greeks had a long-standing reputation for doing.[5] That Aristotle intends something of the sort is more than likely since he thinks there must be *philia* or friendliness in any sort of relationship. But can we conclude that *koinônia* is as integral to the chapter as the act of exchange?

It is obviously integral to Aristotle's conception of fairness in exchange, and we know, because he says it twice, that he was convinced that fairness in exchange was the most important single thing for holding together a polis, many of whose citizens were private producers and exchangers. But, as we have seen, the substance of the chapter is not about any of that. Its greater part is an attempt to analyse a quite distinct problem. The chapter begins with the problem of how to be fair in exchanges, and that passes into the problem of how to bring proportions of different things into the relation of equality required for fairness, so that each 'have their own' after the exchange as well as before it. But it then develops as its major theme the problem of how a relation of equality could conceivably be possible when the things themselves are incommensurable by nature. To this problem, *koinônia* and the spirit of the Graces of gift and counter-gift, have no application. The conclusion must be that *koinônia* is not such an important element in the chapter after all, or at any rate, that it is not important in the way Finley suggests.

Polanyi pursues the *koinônia* line of thought to extremes, and arrives at the view of Aristotle as simply a defender of archaic institutions, 'the philosopher of *Gemeinschaft*'.[6] This is a length to which Finley never went, though at times he may

---

[4] The case is made by Finley, 'Aristotle and Economic Analysis', 32 *et passim*.

[5] Hdt. 1. 152–3.

[6] K. Polanyi, 'Aristotle Discovers the Economy', in G. Dalton (ed.), *Primitive, Archaic and Modern Economies* (New York, 1968), 107.

have exaggerated in the same direction. Polanyi sees Aristotle
as living 'on the borderline of economic ages', and thus finds
'every reason to see in his work far more massive and significant formulations on economic matters than Aristotle has been
credited with'.[7] These massive formulations turn out to be
small beer, however, because Polanyi goes on to interpret
Aristotle as a defender of the archaic institutions of
Gemeinschaft in awkward historical circumstances. Aristotle's
concern with the relation of equality in exchange, he interprets
as an expression of those institutions of archaic societies, or
kinship groups, where ritual gift and counter-gift are made in
order to cement group bonds, and are reckoned on a traditional
and non-quantitative basis of status.[8] This interpretation is
introduced with information about the Arapesh people of
Papua-New Guinea, the reciprocity institutions of the
Trobriand Islanders, and so forth. Aristotle's thoughts about
koinônia, *philia*, and *autarkia*, are all interpreted in this way,
and their importance is attributed to the fact that 'the regulation of mutual services is good since it is required for the con-
tinuance of the group'.[9]

Polanyi observes that in the *Ethics* Aristotle is looking for
the form of *philia* appropriate to exchanges, but he fails to see
that in the search, the character of Athenian society ('on the
borderline of economic ages') led Aristotle into uncovering
'equality of proportion' between goods themselves, and thence
into the problems of exchange value. Having missed that,
Polanyi's own account of the 'massive and significant formulations on economic matters' which he expected from Aristotle
amounts to this: Aristotle was concerned to find ways of determining at what level prices should be set by authority, legally
promulgated and enforced, in order to preserve the social relations of which archaic reciprocal gift-giving on the basis of status was a part.[10] This reading can be sustained only at great
cost, and Polanyi is driven to the ridiculous observation that
'Surprisingly enough, Aristotle seemed to see no other difference between set price and bargained price than a point of

---

[7] Ibid. 95.   [8] Ibid. 109.   [9] Ibid. 96.   [10] Ibid. 97, 106–7, 109.

time, the former being there before the transaction took place, while the latter emerged only afterward.'[11]

Aristotle's concern with holding together the bonds of the polis does not, in the end, take the form of a defence of reciprocity in gift-giving. It takes the form of an attempt to specify reciprocity (*to antipeponthos*) as a relation of equality between proportions of products being exchanged. This means that the problem of holding the polis together in Aristotle's period is no longer a matter of preserving mutual gift-giving on the basis of status. It has become a matter of regulating, or finding some form of *philia* for, buying and selling. Whatever Aristotle may begin with, and he does begin with the spirit of the Charites, he ends with the problems of exchange value. The co-presence of these things in itself suggests that Aristotle's thought is being worked out against the background of a process of change. If mutual cheating and general lack of *philia* in the *agora* had been a joke two centuries earlier in the court of Cyrus the Great, then archaic gift-giving was well on the way out even then. So it is scarcely convincing to read Aristotle, writing two centuries later, as nothing more than an apologist for archaic institutions. If one is determined to see him either in that way, or as no more than a moralist of *koinô-nia*, then one has either to ignore much of the analytical content of his inquiries in the *Ethics* and *Politics*, as Finley does, or to distort it in some way, as Polanyi does in portraying it as prophetic rather than as reflection on (and of) an existing reality.[12]

---

[11] K. Polanyi, 'Aristotle Discovers the Economy', in G. Dalton (ed.), *Primitive, Archaic and Modern economies* (New York, 1968), 108.

[12] Ibid. 53. The heart of Polanyi's chapter is what Finley called his *idée fixe* that the market was a very new, embryonic institution in Aristotle's day. Polanyi was accordingly inclined to interpret any analytical content to do with markets which he might recognize in Aristotle as at least partly prophetic. Ste Croix criticized Polanyi's knowledge and handling of evidence in his review of Polanyi's contribution to *Trade and Market* (K. Polanyi, C. M. Arensberg, and H. W. Pearson (eds.), *Trade and Market in the Early Empires* (Glencoe, Ill., 1957)): 'Polanyi even denies the existence of local food markets in the Peloponnesian War period and in early fourth century Ionia; but the only evidence he cites is sadly misinterpreted. Cities might sometimes set up special markets outside their walls for foreign armies, or generals might create them, but this was simply because the cities did not wish to admit the foreign armies within their gates; there was never any implication that regular markets did not exist inside the cities

The Ancient 'Economy' and its Literature

Exaggerations of this kind in anti-modernist writing have naturally been seized upon by modernists to make their own cause look more defensible. Thompson, in an article entitled 'The Athenian Entrepreneur', concedes that 'the "primitivist" view of the Athenian economy originated as a healthy reaction to the naive presumption of some nineteenth century historians that Athenian business was conducted along the lines of contemporary industry'. But the concession is granted in order to conclude that 'like most reactions it has gone to extremes, both in minimizing the importance of economic activity at Athens and in its denial of enterprise and risk taking on the part of Athenian citizens'.[13] There is something in the claim about the extremity of the reaction, though it is another matter whether this is enough to justify all the baggage of modern business-speak, 'enterprise', 'economic activity', 'risk taking', and the rest, that it is made to bear.

Primitivists often do deny or minimize the importance of 'economic activity' in Athens. But the term 'economic activity' is ambiguous, as many economic terms are, between a use-value meaning and an exchange-value meaning. If the term is used to mean the making and distributing of useful things, then the primitivist would presumably not wish to deny its importance in Athens. But if it means productive and distributive activity systematically regulated by money, as in a market economy, any primitivist worth his or her salt would deny its importance. Economic writers use the term 'economic activity' exclusively in the latter sense; *Financial Times* reports on the market reforms undertaken in Poland in the 1980s and 1990s typically say that 'economic activity' is much better than it used to be; the fact that production is down by 40 per cent on what it used to be does not affect this judgement. It is entirely understandable that primitivists should deny claims about the importance of 'economic activity' in antiquity. Such claims invariably equivocate with the term 'economic activity'.

concerned', (G. E. M. de Ste Croix, review of Polanyi *et al.*, *Economic History Revue*, 2nd ser., 12 (1959–60), 511).

[13] W. E. Thompson, 'The Athenian Entrepreneur', *L'Antiquité classique*, 51 (1982), 53.

~ 4 ~

Rostovtzeff had confidently assumed that 'modern capitalistic development . . . differs from the ancient only in quantity and not in quality'.[14] He went on uninhibitedly to describe the ancient world in terms such as 'bourgeoisie', 'proletariat', 'capitalism', 'mass production', and 'factories'. Some sort of lesson was learned from these excesses, and terms of this kind are avoided today in the description of antiquity. But the measure of convergence between the primitivist and modernist positions represented by this non-use of certain terms is superficial, and it cannot always be taken as a sign of any deeper agreement, either about the nature of ancient society, or about the nature of the difference between ancient and modern society and how it is to be characterized. There is no lack of choice in the terms available for characterizing the difference: 'embedded' and 'disembedded' economies; 'pre-industrial' and 'industrial' societies; 'unspecialized' and 'specialized' societies; 'pre-capitalist' and 'capitalist' societies. The array of terms betrays the political sensitivity of the issue.

Some of the difficulties to be faced in trying to deal with it are illustrated in the account offered by D'Arms. D'Arms agrees that Rostovtzeff's descriptions 'depended too closely on assumptions which are appropriate only to an industrial, highly specialized age', and that Rostovtzeff did not sufficiently emphasize 'the fact that throughout most of antiquity . . . the foundation of economic life for all persons was not commerce and industry but agriculture'. These statements are unexceptionable, and they serve to establish a distance between D'Arms and Rostovtzeff. But they do not help to explain the nature of the difference between ancient and modern society, rather they describe aspects of it. D'Arms expands on the differences:

Commercial shipping and manufacturing ventures were at best ancillary, owing in large part to the smallness of the units of production,

[14] Rostovtzeff, cited by J. H. D'Arms, *Commerce and Social Standing in Ancient Rome* (Cambridge, Mass., 1981), 12.

the tendency for production and distribution to remain nonspecialized and in the same hands, the difficulties, costs, and risks of distant transport, the geographically restricted nature of most markets, and the negligible progress of technological innovation and improvements.[15]

It is difficult to say what this catalogue of differences amounts to. Does it add up to a difference of quality between antiquity and modernity, or only to the difference of quantity which Rostovtzeff had assumed? At any rate, it does little to illuminate the puzzling nature of the primitivist–modernist debate, or to help resolve it. Smallness of scale, lack of specialization and innovation, transport problems, limited markets, and even the predominance of agriculture over commerce and industry, are elements making up the difference between antiquity and modernity which has to be understood and explained; they are not an explanation of the nature of the difference. These are all important elements, but they are important as elements of the problem, not as elements of a solution to it. Even if there is agreement about these elements as a starting-point, as there often is, people still want to move on from them in different directions. Those favouring the sort of view advanced by Finley would tend to want to move towards widening the gap between antiquity and modernity, and others towards narrowing it, as D'Arms himself does.[16]

It is difficult to see, in the tangle of interweaving threads, which thread to pull in order to unravel the tangle. The problem is to decide which is the right question to ask. The decisive question, I believe, concerns the functions of money. Did money function in ancient society in the most important of the ways in which it functions in modern market-economies?

Hoarding was a highly characteristic use of money in Greek

---

[15] Ibid.

[16] Ibid. 13. He writes: 'Granted that the Roman Empire was a preindustrial economy—it nonetheless exhibits signs of complexity, order, and system in its institutions, to an extent which makes labels like "primitive" inappropriate unless they are carefully qualified.' Primitivists might well agree with D'Arms's words, though not with every kind of 'complexity and order' that D'Arms might want to emphasize in antiquity. D'Arms is concerned to argue that expressions of Roman ruling-class contempt for trade and those involved in it might conceal from us the degree to which members of the senatorial order themselves owed their fortunes to trade.

society. Large amounts of gold and silver were buried in the earth over a long period, and archaeologists are still regularly discovering coin-hoards. It needs to be explained why the Greeks preferred to bury their exchange value, rather than to invest it profitably as an 'economically rational' person would do today. We might try to explain it in terms of the attitudes and ethical sensibilities of the Greeks, as Millett has suggested. He rightly puts great stress on the gulf between the Greek sensibility of *koinônia*, and the modern individualist sensibility familiar in the 'first world', and increasingly so in the second and third. Perhaps there is an element of chicken and egg in trying to decide whether attitudes or institutions have explanatory priority, but there is surely more to be learned from such a major feature of ancient society as the predilection for hoarding than can be extracted if it is explained as the result of attitudes. It is fair to ask why the Greeks had the attitudes they did. In any case, there was no productive credit in the ancient world, that is to say, there was no lending or borrowing for establishing or expanding productive enterprises. Whatever the attitudes of the Greeks in the fourth century, none of them could have made a living by trying to lend for that purpose. Furthermore, it may be that both their attitudes, and the absence of productive credit alike, are to be explained in terms of something else.

The development of productive credit is a long process, and it presupposes the prior formation of many other institutions and conditions. One necessary condition is the development of money as a means for the settlement of credit transactions, and the Greeks had nothing like it. There were no credit instruments of any kind, and each individual transaction was settled almost always by physical transfers in person, either by the principal himself or by an accredited agent, even if this involved travelling. There was no double-entry bookkeeping; notions of debit and credit were unknown; there was no accounting of debits and credits through strings of transactions to be settled at the end of a period, and there were no settlement days, quarterly or otherwise.[17]

[17] See Ste Croix, 'Greek and Roman Accounting', 28, 30; see also Millett, *Lending and Borrowing*, 8, 191.

The ancient monetary system provided a medium of circulation, not a means for the settlement of credit transactions. So the Greeks were a very long way from developing productive credit, and the hoarding of exchange value as coin, gold, or silver, was simply the most useful and sensible thing to do with it. This is precisely how Aristotle identifies the usefulness of money: 'it serves as a guarantee of exchange for the future: supposing we need nothing at the moment, it ensures that exchange shall be possible when a need arises, for it meets the requirement of something we can produce in payment so as to obtain the thing we need' (*NE* 5, 1133^{b}10 ff.). Ethical attitudes are not the whole explanation of hoarding but at most a part, and perhaps not a very important part. To explain what opportunities the Greeks lacked for the advantageous use of money in terms of their attitudes, is no more sensible than explaining the opportunities they had in the same way. It would not be very convincing as a first line of explanation to suggest that the lack of 'investment opportunities' open to the Greeks was due to their attitudes, when we have as available explanations the absence of the most essential institutions and social relations.

The fact that money was hoarded is connected with the absence of productive credit. Modernist explanations for the lack of productive credit, such as the high risk of lending, and the supposedly high interest-rates on borrowing, cut little ice, as Millett observes.[18] There simply were no 'investment opportunities', no productive function for money that was a serious alternative to hoarding. There was no market in capital, for the simple reason that there was no market in labour that was anything more than seasonal and casual.[19] Without a significant pool of unattached labour, that is, people needing to work for money-wages as their only way of acquiring use values for living, there cannot be a significant market in capital for establishing productive enterprises. But these were precisely the conditions that prevailed throughout the entire history of the ancient world, and for centuries after it. Money could generally be advanced, in order to grow, only through

[18] Millett, *Lending and Borrowing*, 72.
[19] Ste Croix, *The Class Struggle in the Ancient Greek World*, 179–204.

circulation, or buying and selling, and it was not possible to use production in general as a means to this end, because money did not have the command over labour that is required to achieve that; in other words, money did not function as capital. With the appearance of a credit system, hoarding simply dissappears.

The bulk of production in the Greek world of the classical period was done by free peasant proprietors producing at or near subsistence. The rest was done by a relatively small number of craftsmen producing in workshops of very restricted scale, and by chattel-slaves mainly on the estates of the propertied class. Contracts of wage labour, which become typical with the appearance of market economy, were extremely limited. They were entered into for occasional municipal building programmes like that of Pericles, when local craftsmen were too few to do the job, and others had to be attracted from abroad. They were also sometimes used on agricultural estates, for instance at harvest time, when it was necessary to supplement the normal workforce by the addition of casual labour. But wage-labour was never more than incidental, and there was no large and permanent section of the population which had to rely exclusively on it. In short, the Greeks were hoarders because there was no possibility of the productive investment of money, and consequently there was virtually no lending for that purpose. Millett puts the numbers of instances of lending for such a purpose, for which there is evidence, and on the most liberal definition of that purpose, at eight.[20]

Markets existed in societies of many kinds for millennia without those societies being or becoming market economies. A society can become entirely regulated by exchange value only if there is a market in capital, and that in turn is possible only when there is a serious market in labour, that is, when labour is generally supplied in the form of an exchange value (labour capacity or 'labour power') which capital can buy. These are the defining conditions of a market economy, and neither condition obtained in the ancient world. Virtually all

[20] Millett, *Lending and Borrowing*, 59.

lending was *eranos* lending, and, as Millett notes, 'a survey of the known motives behind *eranos-* or "friendly" loans reveals no instance of a productive use'. The purpose of commercial lending, which in any case was very restricted in scale, was consumption, not productive investment. The main reasons for loans of all kinds 'were almost invariably associated with the unpleasant necessities of life—ransoms, fines, burials, food-shortages, tax-payments and public service'.[21] Wage-labour, where it existed, was entirely seasonal or casual, and free men would do almost anything to avoid it, because they regarded it as a more demeaning condition even than slavery. Hired labourers (*misthôtoi* or *thetes*) were not very numerous or mobile, and many were slaves hired out by their masters.

The propertied class, those who extracted surplus (in the sense defined by Sainte Croix[22]), did so through rent, and through the use of unfree labour in agriculture, first debt-bondage, then chattel-slavery, and, in the Later Roman Empire, serfdom. Society's surplus was not extracted through the employment of wage-labour. D'Arms has suggested that Finley underestimates Roman senatorial involvement in trade in maintaining his view of Roman society as primarily a 'spectrum of statuses'.[23] But whether or not Finley exaggerates, D'Arms himself seems to agree that his own belief that there may well have been Jean Samuel Deponts (rich *arrivistes* who concealed the fact that the origin of their wealth was in trade) in Rome, even if justified, cannot have an impact profound

[21] Ibid. 72, citing Vondeling, *Eranos* (Groningen, 1961). Millett notes that in 'non-capitalist societies non-productive lending is the norm' (*Lending and Borrowing*, 71). He expects the explanation of this in the case of ancient Greece to lie in the attitudes of the Greeks: 'The explanation of so deep seated a phenomenon as non-productive borrowing involves the probing of Athenian mentality', but he does not pursue it on the reasonable ground that this 'is a wide-ranging issue, reaching to the heart of the ancient economy and society', which lies beyond the scope of a study of lending and borrowing (p. 72). The explanation, however, is more likely to lie in the absence of capital and wage-labour; without the possibility of productive investment, there is no reason why there should be productive lending and borrowing. This would also be the most likely direction in which to look for an understanding of the Greek mentality in relation to lending and borrowing, and the 'absence of a productive or entrepreneurial mentality' (p. 73).

[22] Ste Croix, *The Class Struggle in the Ancient Greek World*, 35–7, 43–4, 51, 52–3.

[23] D'Arms, *Commerce and Social Standing in Ancient Rome*, ch. 1.

enough to shift the broad outlines of Finley's position. At any rate, however the evidence is interrogated, it cannot yield the conclusion that there were significant Greek and Roman markets in capital and wage-labour, because we know there were not. Without them it is vain to harp on about the evidence for Athenian 'entrepreneurship', 'risk-taking', and so forth, because, even granting that there were things which can reasonably be described in these terms, they cannot have been anything more than peripheral. Unless there are significant markets in capital and wage-labour, market relationships cannot be the way in which the surplus of society is extracted and appropriated, as they are in market society. In that case, such relationships can have been no more than important marginal aspects of the essential life-processes of that society. To describe the typical productive and distributive activities of antiquity as 'economic activity', in the familiar sense remarked on at the end of the previous section, is unjustified and seriously misleading.

☞ 5 ☜

Schumpeter took the view, as Roll and many others have, that in economics, Aristotle, unlike Plato, had a genuinely analytical intention, for which he deserves to be recognized as the father of economic science.[24] Yet in the accounts given of what is supposed to be Aristotle's outstanding contribution, its substance often appears slight for something thought to deserve such an accreditation, and the evaluations of Aristotle's success in fulfilling his analytical intention are often low. Schumpeter's notoriously low opinion was cited earlier, but it bears repetition: Aristotle offers no more than 'decorous, pedestrian, slightly mediocre, and more than slightly pompous commonsense': not much of an achievement for the 'father of economics'.[25]

Finley rightly sees a paradox here. Why, after all, when

---

[24] Roll, *History of Economic Thought*, 31.
[25] Schumpeter, *History of Economic Analysis*, 57.

Aristotle was capable of 'monumental contributions to physics, metaphysics, logic, meteorology, biology, political science, rhetoric, aesthetics and ethics', should he have been so dismal at economics, once he had set his mind to it?[26] Finley concludes that he did not do dismally, because he never set his mind to it in the first place; he was doing ethics and not attempting any sort of economic analysis. But Schumpeter sees no paradox. Aristotle was simply rotten at economics, and has to be given poor marks because his analysis is restricted to the artisan alone, ignores the 'chiefly agrarian income of the gentleman', disposes perfunctorily of the free labourer, judges the activities of the 'trader (and shipowner), the shopkeeper, the money-lender', only in moral and political terms, and does not subject their gains to an explanatory analysis.[27] Finley concurs. In his opinion, had Aristotle been attempting economic analysis in *NE* 5. 5, Schumpeter's low marks would have been perfectly justified, because 'an analysis that focuses so exclusively on a minor sector of the economy [sc. artisans] deserves no more complimentary evaluation'.[28]

Aristotle is not discussing artisans at all, as we have seen; he is using them as examples in the discussion of something else altogether. The problem of commensurability which he examines in *NE* 5. 5 is at a high level of generality, and in going about his examination, Aristotle needs as an example only the simplest case. He does not need to catalogue every associated phenomenon, every derivative form of exchange, every occupation, form of revenue, and so forth. That would have got him no nearer solving his problem. To say that Aristotle was discussing only artisans, is to mistake the examples he uses for the subject under discussion. Schumpeter's listing all the items Aristotle does not discuss, and his propaedeutic admonition of Aristotle's lack of professional accomplishment in not discussing them, reveals less about Aristotle than it does about Schumpeter.

Schumpeter draws a distinction between common-sense

---

[26] Finley, 'Aristotle and Economic Analysis', 28.
[27] Schumpeter, *History of Economic Analysis*, 64–5.
[28] Finley, 'Aristotle and Economic Analysis', 37–8.

knowledge about economic matters, and economic analysis. He identifies economic analysis as 'intellectual efforts ... to understand economic phenomena', by which he means the workings of the market mechanism. It consists, not in recording common-sense observations, but in constructing an analytical superstructure on them: 'most statements of fundamental facts acquire importance only by the superstructures they are made to bear and are commonplace in the absence of such superstructures'.[29] His excuse for Aristotle's bad showing in economics is that 'in the beginning of scientific analysis, the mass of phenomena is left undisturbed in the compound of commonsense knowledge'. Finley retorts: 'the mass of what phenomena?'[30] He cites Roll: 'If, then, we regard the economic system as an enormous conglomeration of interdependent markets, the central problem of economic enquiry becomes ... '.[31] Finley justly replies again that antiquity knew no such enormous conglomerations of markets. How, then, so the logic of the argument runs, can we expect to find in Aristotle a scientific study of such 'masses' and 'conglomerations' when none existed? Without them it would 'not be possible to discover or formulate laws ... of economic behaviour, without which a concept of "the economy" is unlikely to develop, economic analysis impossible'.[32]

Schumpeter's definition of economics as the study of 'actual market mechanisms' is unobjectionable. But its corollary is that the phenomena studied by that subject, to the extent that they existed at all in antiquity, existed on the margin of society and not at its centre. There were no 'masses' of market phenomena, and consequently they could not have been studied by any Greek. To complain, as Schumpeter does, that Aristotle did not do the study well is simply a confusion, and Finley is right to conclude that Aristotle not only did not do economics, but could not have done it, and could not even have conceived of it.

How did Schumpeter come to be so confused? The less

---

[29] Schumpeter, *History of Economic Analysis*, 54.
[30] Finley, 'Aristotle and Economic Analysis', 44–5.
[31] Ibid. 22.   [32] Ibid.

interesting part of the answer is that the economic historians of the ancient world, on whom Schumpeter had to rely, had themselves been confused over the same issues at the time when Schumpeter was writing. Schumpeter believed there had been a 'rising merchant-class', with all the social and economic implications hinted at in such a phrase. In this he was doing no more than reiterating what many classical scholars of the time were saying. Even later, Barker, in a passage cited earlier, was prepared to write that 'deposit banks, which made loans to merchants from their funds, were coming into existence; and Athenian banks were making Athens the principal money-market of Greece'.

The more interesting part of the answer has to do with a curious conception of what economics is. A definition of the kind offered by Schumpeter himself succeeds in making it more or less clear that the objects of study are the relationships and behaviour characteristic of market economy. It carries no strong implication that market relationships are central defining features of societies of all kinds, and for that reason it does not implicitly threaten confusion if it is carried into historical studies.[33] It does imply, however, that economics is not a universal science, but one whose object, market economy, since it is a historical object, has a beginning, a middle, and presumably an end. It would follow from this that economics, as the science of such an object, must also have a beginning, a middle, and presumably an end too, coextensively with its object. It is not particularly surprising that a definition of economics with that kind of implication has not commanded the general assent of economists.

Lionel Robbins's definition, however, casts economics as a universal science, which is applicable to all periods of history, because it deals with 'relationships between men and economic goods' in a tenseless way.[34] This definition has been more

---

[33] Schumpeter's definition was crucial to Finley's argument and conclusion in 'Aristotle and Economic Analysis', and later in *The Ancient Economy*. Without a definition having the strengths that Schumpeter's has, Finley could not have constructed his case at all.

[34] Robbins, *Nature and Significance of Economic Science*, 69.

popular. The conceptual apparatus of economic theory corresponding to this definition is constructed in a way that is intended to transcend any particular set of social relations. In order to achieve this, economic terms are so defined as to be independent of any specific social content, so that they may apply to any period of history. Consider the term 'wages' for instance. In its modern use the term means the sums of money paid at short intervals by an employer to an employee. In economic theory, however, wages are defined as the product, whether expressed in value or in physical terms, which is imputable to human activity engaged in production. Robinson Crusoe, slaves, and small peasant-proprietors all earn wages in this sense, as well as the modern wage-employee.[35] Such definitions are not conducive to clear thinking about historical matters, whatever might be their other advantages.

Market economy is a fairly recent historical arrival, and so, since the study of a thing can hardly precede the existence of the thing to be studied, the study of market economy is a fairly recent arrival too. On Robbins's definition of that study, however, economics deals tenselessly with 'relationships between men and economic goods', as if these were as general and unchanging as the relationships studied in chemistry or mathematics. Such a view is a standing invitation to anachronism, and a sizeable part of the literature on the economic history of the ancient world, of which Finley has been such a rewarding critic, is testimony to the fact. This confusion may not matter much so long as the object of study is some aspect of a society based on market economy, because in that case an accompanying false belief that the relationships involved are general and non-historical might be irrelevant. But the position is quite different if the object of study is some aspect of a pre-capitalist society, because market relations, though they often existed, were peripheral to the life of those societies. Much of the literature on Aristotle's 'economic' thought in the *Ethics* and *Politics* is unsatisfactory, and mainly because of this confusion. If there were not this confusion to explain the fact, it might

[35] The example is Sweezey's, *The Theory of Capitalist Development* (Oxford, 1942), 5–6.

otherwise beggar the imagination how anyone could have read *NE* 5. 5 and got the idea that Aristotle was looking for a theory of price-formation, or laying down markers in mathematical economics.

🙓 6 🙓

Primitivist work often seems to equivocate over what an 'economy' is, and it does this in a way that affects the main thesis of primitivism. Finley holds that Greek society had no masses of market phenomena embodying economic laws, and that the Greeks accordingly had no occasion to engage in economic policy. He cites Schumpeter as his authority for the view that economics is the science of the masses of such phenomena, and he concludes that the absence of such phenomena from the Greek world explains why the Greeks did no economics. But if they had not the phenomena, or the study of the phenomena, or the need to contend with the phenomena by means of policy, it would seem that, in the sense that matters most, the Greeks did not have what we normally mean by an 'economy'.

On the other hand, Finley is prepared to speak of 'the ancient economy'. He concedes that the Greeks and other 'non-capitalist or pre-capitalist societies have economies, with rules and regularities . . . whether they can conceptualise them or not', and that these can be studied. But the study of these 'economies', he seems to be suggesting, can be a matter only for us in the present, not for the contemporaries of those 'economies' who were incapable of conceptualizing them.[36]

Did Greek society have a lawlike economy, or didn't it? And if it did, why should it have been impossible for the Greeks to make some sort of attempt to study those laws, rules, and regularities? The position looks contradictory, and Finley makes no attempt at reconciliation—for instance, by arguing that these are regularities or laws of different kinds. It remains a puzzle why, if the Greek had an 'economy' with regularities

---

[36] Finley, *Ancient Economy*, 23.

169

which made a difference to their lives, we should be able to think about them but the Greeks were not. There is a related contradiction over whether or not the Greeks wrote anything that could count as economics. Finley holds that they did not, and that it is a mistake to think that even Aristotle did economics rather than ethics. But he also holds that they did write economics, though it was excessively banal economics.[37] So what do Aristotle's inquiries amount to—banal economics, or nothing that could be called economics at all, banal or otherwise? There is evidently a confusion somewhere.

The confusion was already present earlier, in the work of Polanyi. He had concluded that the source of the persistent anachronism in modern attempts to interpret ancient economic life lay in a failure to appreciate the nature of the difference between modern capitalist market-economy, and all precapitalist 'economies'. He sought to register the difference by distinguishing between the 'embedded economy', one which is integral to the whole social fabric and does not stand above it, and the 'disembedded economy', one which is torn out of the social fabric to become an independent entity that dominates social decision-making.[38] Pre-capitalist societies had embedded economies, and only capitalist society has a disembedded one.

The difference was real enough, but the terms of the distinction Polanyi drew in order to mark it were ambiguous between two quite different conceptions of how to resolve the problem he faced. The ambiguity is in the term 'economy'. The 'economy' could be conceived as a single species of thing,

---

[37] See Finley, 'Aristotle and Economic Analysis', *passim*, and *Ancient Economy*, 22, for the first view. For the second view see *Ancient Economy* 19–20: 'The Roman agricultural manuals (and no doubt their lost Greek forerunners) do occasionally consider marketing and soil conditions and the like, but they never rise above rudimentary common-sense observations (when they do not simply blunder or mislead). Varro's advice (*De re rustica* I. 16. 3) to cultivate roses and violets on a farm near a city but not if the estate is too far from an urban market, is a fair sample of common-sense . . . The one Greek attempt at a general statement is the opening of the second book of the pseudo-Aristotelian *Oikonomikos*, and what is noteworthy about these half a dozen paragraphs is not only their crashing banality but also their isolation in the whole of surviving ancient writing'.

[38] Polanyi, 'Aristotle Discovers the Economy', 81.

with 'embedded' and 'disembedded' variants. As members of a single species, these variants, though they might differ from each other in accidental features, would share their essential features and have a common nature. Alternatively, the 'disembedded' economy might be a thing of quite a different kind from the 'embedded' economy, rather than both being variants of a single kind. In this case, they would not share a common nature, though they might share a common appearance in features that are accidental rather than essential. To call them both by the same name of 'economy', in this case, would invite puns on the word. The puns would be serious, because they would tend to defeat the very purpose for which the distinction between 'embedded' and 'disembedded' was introduced in the first place, which was to correct the source of the persistent anachronism.

The main difference between non-market societies and market ones lies in the fact that human decisions take effect in quite different ways in each case. In non-market societies, decisions operate directly over the realm of natural kinds, and the main constraints are natural necessities and social mores. Under market economy, decisions operate primarily over exchange values, and the most imperative constraints, overriding even custom and ethics, are laws and cycles arising largely from the system of exchange value itself. A market economy, or 'disembedded economy', has a nature of its own, which expresses itself in laws that we have to discover by scientific inquiry, in something like the way in which we have to discover the laws of physical nature, and which are inflexible constraints on our decision-making in much the way that laws of nature are. A market society is predominantly a system of exchange value, and exchange value is the regulator of its production and distribution. Economics is the study of the developed forms of exchange value, of the regularities in its movement, and of its interaction with use value. The science of economics came into being historically, only with the appearance of market economy, that is, with the appearance of markets in labour and capital. Antiquity was predominantly a system of use value, not of exchange value, and if it had regularities in its nature, these were not the laws and cycles which characterize a system of exchange value, which economics studies, and which economic policy tries to contend with.

These are the differences that Polanyi and Finley had in mind in emphasizing the world of difference between the ancient 'economy' and the modern one. In order to capture those differences, the distinction that seems to be required is that between use value and exchange value. Pre-capitalist societies are systems in which use value is predominant, and capitalist society is a system in which exchange value is predominant.

The fact that both sorts of system are, by established usage, called 'economies' need not in itself be a cause of confusion. But it is usual to think that the object of the study of economics is the 'economy', and since ancient society is said to have had an economy, it is tempting to suppose that ancient society is a suitable object for study in terms of economics. But this would be to suppose that a use-value economy can be described and explained in the terms in which an exchange-value economy is described and explained, and this has effectively been shown to be false.

Within ancient society, there were early forms of exchange value. There was money, for instance, and money became sufficiently developed to be the subject of debasement and inflation. These things did not always escape ancient writers, and Aristotle notes that money is not always worth the same though it tends to be more stable than other things (*NE* 5, 1133^{b}13–14). In studying these specific aspects of antiquity today, we may at times need to use economics, because economics is the science of that kind of thing. But in doing this we will not be studying relations and institutions that were central and defining features of ancient society. The institutions and relations of exchange value were peripheral to ancient society, not central and dominating as they have become in modernity. The nub of the objection to modernism is that it fails to take sufficient account of this. In insisting on trying to describe and explain ancient social behaviour in modern eco-

172

nomic terms, modernism implicitly and constantly insinuates a view of the nature of ancient society which is known to be false.

Modernists might want to reply that they accept that this view of antiquity is false, and that the modernist position of Meyer, Rostovtzeff, and their descendants, who wrote of ancient society as if it had been a market economy, was an extreme modernism which they do not endorse. With such a moderate modernism it might seem reasonable to continue to describe at least some ancient behaviour in modern economic terms, provided it were made clear, with suitable qualifications, that only marginal aspects of the society were being so described, and that the wider historical implication that antiquity had been an exchange-value economy, with its associated institutions, behaviour, values, and attitudes, was not intended. But there are problems with this more moderate line too.

Even the attempt to use economic terms judiciously, confining them strictly to the description of ancient practices to which they genuinely apply, carries risks, because of the ambiguity that many economic terms have between use-value and exchange-value applications. A term like 'productivity', for example, may be used in evaluations of exchange-value phenomena, but it has a purely use-value application as well. If we consider the method that was used in the ancient world to produce some good, we may try to work out the number of people who would have been needed to produce a unit of it, and how long they would have taken, on average, using that method. This is a use-value calculation, and there is no reason in principle why we should not speak of 'productivity' in this sense in relation to the ancient world. But in practice, the use of the term carries a heavy burden of exchange-value connotations which it can be difficult to set to one side. Its use would be misleading, for instance, if it induced the supposition that productivity was a systematic concern in the ancient world as it is today. In fact, there is little or no evidence that the Greeks bothered much about yields per acre and so forth, and throughout antiquity there was relatively little innovation in methods of production.[39] A term like 'investment' is even more difficult to detach from its modern associations with capital. As a result of the pretensions of economics to be a universal science of use value as well as exchange value, the temptation has proved too great for some writers to describe even the ploughing of manure into the soil as 'investment', so that the manure itself becomes 'capital'.[40] The use of economic terms, even in their use-value senses when they have them, constantly invites the assimilation of ancient behaviour and mentality to modern market behaviour and mentality. This mentality is second nature to us, and it is all too easy for us to transfer it to the Greeks, and for that reason the greatest caution is needed if ancient behaviour is to be described in the market terms of 'risk-taking', 'enterprise', 'entrepreneur', and the rest, even when those terms might in some ways fit.

If the modernist accepts neo-classical economics, as experience suggests is likely to be the case, adopting the more moderate modernist line is not as straightforward as it might appear. According to the neo-classical economic view, there is no categorical distinction to be drawn between use-value and exchange-value, and it is not easy to see that a subscriber to neo-classical economics could, or should want to, allow a distinction between a use value economy and an exchange value economy. It would be a fairly natural extension of the economic view of the world to hold that 'economies' constitute a single species with a common nature, and that may be why many modern historians of economic thought, and ancient economic historians, have in practice taken that view. According to neo-classical principles, there should be no objection in principle to describing the ancient economy in general in terms of modern economic theory, and not merely marginal aspects of it.

[39] See H. W. Pleket, 'Technology in the Greco-Roman World: A General Report', *Talanta*, 5 (1973), 6–47.

[40] On the uses of economic terms to describe pre-capitalist societies, see C. Meillassoux, 'From Reproduction to Production: A Marxist Approach to Economic Anthropology', *Economy and Society*, 1 (1972), 93–105; and 'Essai d'interprétation du phénomène économique dans les sociétés traditionnelles d'auto-subsistance', *Cahiers d'études africaines*, 4 (1972), 38–67.

Classical scholars have sometimes found the modernist debate tiresome and unduly political. The modernist position has seemed tiresome at times because of the apparent imperviousness to argument and evidence of its adherents, though this criticism has to be qualified in view of the interesting reasons behind this apparent imperviousness. The complaint that the debate is unduly political, however, is too fastidious. The use of classical studies as a terrain on which to fight modern battles is not only a fact of life, but a hallowed tradition too. Ellen Meiksens Wood has written revealingly of the slur, beloved of eighteenth- and nineteenth-century anti-democrats, Mitford, Boeckh, Burckhardt, and Fustel among them, that the Athenians were able to exercise citizen rights to the detriment of the rich and virtuous, only because they were an idle mob living on the labour of slaves.[41] She showed these authors projecting into their work on antiquity the fears and values of the well-to-do in Europe in the aftermath of the French Revolution. This use of antiquity is a valuable tradition, because in modern times classical studies at their best have also served a serious purpose as a mirror in which to examine what we have made of ourselves; and at their worst too, because modernist writing in its own way shows that only too clearly. The suggestion that classical studies should be pursued only for their own sake is a council not of perfection, but of imperfection.

☞ 7 ☜

Punning on the word 'economy', as Polanyi and Finley did, created problems for them, and opportunities for their modernist opponents which have been ingeniously expoited by Lowry. Polanyi and Finley allow that the Greek world did have an 'economy', and consequently they faced the problem of explaining why, in that case, the Greeks should have been unable to think and write systematically about it. The

---

[41] E. M. Wood, *Peasant-Citizen and Slave: The Foundations of Athenian Democracy* (London, 1988), ch. 1.

improbable conjunction of having an economy but being unable to think about it can be dealt with in one of two ways. One can tighten the notion of an 'economy' in such a way that it becomes clearer why the Greeks should have done no economics. The previous section followed this course, in arguing that the Greeks did not have an economy of the kind that would have made it possible for them to engage in economic thinking. Alternatively, one can loosen the notion of 'economic thought' in such a way that some Greek literature may be described as 'economic' in the loosened sense of the term. This is the course followed by Lowry.

Lowry builds a modernist case which is unique in taking serious account of the work of Polanyi, Finley, and other primitivists. He concedes that it is anachronistic and unprofitable to try to understand antiquity 'in terms of modern market theory';[42] that 'Xenophon's view of the world was . . . essentially one in which individuals deal acquisitively or manipulatively, not with the forces of an economy, but directly with the open book of nature';[43] and that the nearest Xenophon came to 'developing a theory of exchange-value was the recognition of a social context for use value' in which a thing might be sold.[44]

These are big concessions in the context. Finley's case rested in part on the argument that the mass of exchange value phenomena characteristic of a market economy is what economic theory theorizes, and that the absence of such a mass of phenomena from the Greek world made it impossible for the Greeks to embark on economic thought. Finley agreed with Schumpeter that commonplace observations with an economic flavour do not amount to economics, and that economics consists in the analytical structures that are developed out of those commonplaces to explain market phenomena. Lowry appears to be attempting the impossible in conceding on the one hand the absence from the Greek world of the phenomena studied in economics, and in affirming on the other hand that the Greeks did do economics in spite of this. He pulls the rabbit out of the hat in an ingenious way.

---

[42] Lowry, *Archaeology of Economic Ideas*, 10.   [43] Ibid. 74.   [44] Ibid. 80.

The economics the Greeks wrote, he argues, does not look like economics as we usually understand it because it is not cast in market terms. Ancient society, he agrees, was not a market society, and it was regulated not by exchange value, or price, but by administration. He concludes from this, not that the Greek world was one of administered use-value, but that it was in terms of administration that the Greeks did their economics: 'What both Finley and Schumpeter fail to see is that, since the mechanism of control of ancient economies was not the market but administrative procedures, ancient writings framed in administrative terms *do* bear an appropriate analytical superstr1cture. Indeed, the administrative superstructure is the *only* context in which ancient economic statements could be expected to be framed.'[45]

Lowry is using two definitions of 'economics'. The first connects it with exchange value and market economy, and the second connects it with 'the efficiency concept' and administrative procedures.[46] He wants to keep the two apart because he agrees with the primitivists in doubting the usefulness of 'attempting to explain primitive economic activities with modern market theory'.[47] He believes that anachronism arises only from using the first definition, and that it may be avoided by using only the second: the crucial distinction, in his view, and 'one of the major contributions of this work is the separation of the administrative perspective from exchange and market analysis as a basis for studying ancient . . . decision making and efficiency criteria'.[48]

There is an obvious danger in pursuing this line of thought. The modern economic notion of 'efficiency' is so closely tied to exchange value and money, to economic theory, to market conceptions of economic rationality, and to essentially economic theories like the utilitarian theory of action, that it cannot easily be pulled away from them. Unless a determined and clear-headed effort is made to demarcate means–end rationality in general from the particularities of the modern economic notion of efficiency, there is a danger that the two will be run

---

[45] Ibid. 69–70.   [46] Ibid. 70.   [47] Ibid. 10.   [48] Ibid.

together, with the consequence that any ancient writing which concerns means–end rationality might be mistaken for evidence of economic thinking. Lowry reviews likely parts of the ancient literature in search of such evidence, and in the process the two definitions of economics, which he had tried to separate, constantly rejoin to produce supposed evidence that is mistaken in just this way.

Often the evidence is conjured up simply by redescribing events, actions, or debates, in terms of the current argot of economics. Hesiod's account of Prometheus' dealings with Zeus, for instance, are said to provide 'an example of a pure isolated distribution where two parties meet on an equal footing and negotiate the division of a joint asset', so that we can speak of the 'Promethean transaction'.[49] The motivation of the characters in the *Iliad* 'is unmistakably a concern for gain, a kind of entrepreneurship', and Achilles and Agamemnon disagree over the 'distribution of the returns to warfare', 'coloured though it may be with shadings of status and honor'.[50] Glaucon's views on justice (*Rep.* 358e–359a) are redescribed in the language of cost–benefit analysis, and the reader is pointed in the right direction for drawing his own conclusions: 'Glaucon even uses economic terms later in the discussion in describing the unprofitability of being just without appearing so: "The consequences", he asserts, are "not assets . . . but liabilities, labor, and total loss" '.[51]

In the confusion, things which, according to Lowry's programme, should have been examples of ancient economic thought cast in terms of administration, become instead precursors of economic thought cast in market terms. Thus, the views of Protagoras are 'an embryonic expression of the utilitarian calculus upon which modern economic theory is based. Moreover, the adversary system in the law courts . . . was a prototype for bargaining in exchange and price-forming processes.'[52] 'The public assemblies in ancient Greece where the citizens gathered to exchange opinions . . . served, in effect,

---

[49] Lowry, *Archaeology of Economic Ideas*, 126.   [50] Ibid. 131.
[51] Ibid. 97–8.   [52] Ibid. 159.

as an ancient prototype of the market.'[53] Plato's discussion of
the division of labour 'has the elements of a simple matrix and
could be presented in a Leontief-style input–output table'.[54]
The discussion of pleasure in the *Protagoras* is so close 'to the
hedonic calculus which Bentham elaborated that it might be
assumed that [it] must have been an adaptation of a perspective learned from the marketplace. So far as we know, however,
this value system was applied only to a sort of microeconomics of moral conduct.'[55]

Lowry's inability to avoid thinking in market terms in spite
of his best intentions, and contrary to the obvious requirements of his own thesis, are nice illustrations of the nature of
economics as a closed system of thought with bogus pretensions to universality. Modernism in the study of ancient society is evidently a product of economic thinking and of the
economic view of the world, which are recent things. Ever
since it first appeared late in the last century, it has repeatedly
shown itself to be indefeasible by evidence and argument.
Students of antiquity will probably just have to learn to live
with it, because it seems that the spring of its eternal youth lies
outside the intellectual realm.

---

[53] Ibid. 158.   [54] Ibid. 104.   [55] Ibid. 40.

9

Nature and Commensurability

It is difficult to imagine that the economic view of the world, when it came to be formed, could in the end have found an Aristotelian foundation, or even an expression that would have been consistent with the Aristotelian view of the world. Applying Aristotelian metaphysics to the analysis of the chief economic notions—use value, exchange value, wealth, money, and exchange—does not seem capable of yielding any very more favourable judgements on the worth of commercial values and behaviour than those Aristotle himself arrived at.

Within the later scholastic tradition, attempts were made at finding a compromise, but none was found. The scholastics of eighteenth-century Spain concluded, from an examination of Smith's *Wealth of Nations*, that economics and ethics were incompatible. Smith's book was found in French translation in a bookshop in Pamplona in 1791, and it was referred to the Madrid Inquisition. Fray Antonio de la Santisima Trinidad, one of the three *calificadores* to whom it was sent for report, wrote to the Inquisition that the book was about how to get rich, but contained no advice on the moral pitfalls to be avoided in the pursuit of wealth. This was bad enough, but Fray Antonio noted that it is 'in the nature of his system', that is, in the nature of political economy, that there is no room for such advice.[1] The scholastics were fighting a losing battle against the *Sociedades Económicas de los Amigos del País* and

---

[1] Fray Antonio also reports that Smith 'is not just a mere Protestant, but a man of no religion, good or bad'. For the text of Fray Antonio's report, see Javier Lasarte, 'Adam Smith ante la Inquisición y la Academia de la Historia', *Hacienda pública española*, 33–4 (1975), 201–42. Traditional Catholic social teaching still holds Fray Antonio's view. The historian Menendez-Pelayo writes that Adam Smith's 'so-called science of wealth ... came forth contaminated with a utilitarian and basely practical spirit, as though it aspired to be an independent science and not a branch and end of morality', *Historia de los heterodoxos españoles* (2 vols.; Madrid, 1932), ii. 381.

against liberal statesmen like Jovellanos and Campomanes, whose main concern was that Spain might lose heavily if she were too slow getting into the new international market-economy.[2]

For a century and a half before this, early modern anglophone authors had been developing a style of thought more accommodating to the new market-society, and they probably had no alternative but to do what they did: to rip up 2,000 years of European Aristotelianism. A Whig philosophy was developed, by the school known as the 'British Moralists', which provided the doctrines needed to give the economic view of the world something like a coherent philosophical basis. Hume brought together the most workable and the most radical, deepened them, and gave them a sophisticated expression: the fact–value gap, the elimination of metaphysics, the separation of ethics from reason and its attachment exclusively to sentiment, the dissolution of the notions of substance and nature, and with them any notion of real and incommensurable thinghood. These have since become standard positions or assumptions in economic thought, and in the philosophical thought which expresses the economic view of the world. Not all of them caught on straight away, but they did eventually, especially after the rediscovery of Hume by the Viennese positivists of the late nineteenth and early twentieth centuries.

Aristotelianism was torn up with vigour. Hobbes, in a section of *Leviathan* entitled 'The Schoole of the Græcians unprofitable', gave Aristotle short shrift: 'I believe that scarce anything could be more absurdly said in Natural Philosophy, than that which is now called Aristotle's *Metaphysiques*; nor more repugnant to Government than much of what he hath said in his *Politiques*; nor more ignorantly than a great part of

---

[2] Jovellanos, typically, wrote in 1785: 'The greatness of nations will no longer rest, as in other times, on the splendours of its triumphs, on the martial spirit of its sons . . . Commerce, industry, and the wealth which springs from both, are, and probably will be for a long time to come, the only foundations of the preponderance of a nation; and it is necessary to make these the objects of our attentions or condemn ourselves to an eternal and shameful dependency, while our neighbours speed their prosperity upon our neglect', *Informe dado a la Junta General de Comercio y Moneda sobre el libre ejercicio de las artes*, cited in Robert Sidney Smith, 'The *Wealth of Nations* in Spain and Hispanic America, 1780–1830', *Journal of Political Economy*, 65 (1957), 107.

his *Ethiques.*' Aristotelianism was inseparably connected with the Catholic Church, and the two would not have been easy to distinguish as targets, even if there had been a desire to distinguish them. The university attracted Hobbes's ire because 'for the study of Philosophy it hath no otherwise place, than as a handmaid to the Romane Religion: And since the Authority of Aristotle is onely current there, that study is not properly Philosophy, (the nature whereof dependeth not on Authors,) but Aristotelity'.[3] Hume called it, as Hobbes sometimes had, 'school metaphysics', a term of contempt with harsh associations in England, Ireland, and Scotland, and he recommended readers of his *Enquiry* to 'commit it then to the flames', because, in failing to conform to empiricist legislation defining true knowledge, 'it can contain nothing but sophistry and illusion'.[4]

Enlightenment writers usually understood the term 'metaphysics' to mean a science which purported to prove the existence of things in the supernatural world, and that was primarily how their opponents in the declining scholastic tradition understood it too. Neither side distinguished between this sense of the term, and the primary sense in which metaphysics, together with logic, is the most fundamental area of philosophical inquiry, and one which informs all other areas of thought, since thought of any kind works to one metaphysics or another. When Hume and others 'eliminated' metaphysics, they eliminated it in both senses at once. Logic and metaphysics largely disappeared from native anglophone philosophy for the best part of 300 years.[5]

---

[3] *Leviathan*, 461–2. Furthermore, 'the Metaphysiques, Ethiques, and Politiques of Aristotle, the frivolous distinctions, barbarous Terms, and obscure Language of the Schoolmen, taught in the Universities, (which have been all erected and regulated by the Popes Authority)' serve to keep the ill deeds of Popery from being detected (p. 477). This is to be found in pt. 4, entitled 'Of the Kingdome of Darknesse', ch. 46, entitled 'Of Darknesse from Vain Philosophy, and Fabulous Traditions'.

[4] D. Hume, *An Enquiry Concerning Human Understanding*, ed. L. A. Selby-Bigge (Oxford, 1894), 165.

[5] British undergraduates studying philosophy are still mostly trained in a curriculum which covers a little of the Pre-Socratics, Plato and Aristotle, 'the Rationalists and Empiricists', Descartes, Locke, Berkeley and Hume (perhaps with a little Leibniz), J. S. Mill, Moore, Russell and Wittgenstein, with the addition nowadays of some

◈ 1 *◈*

Yet, in spite of the incompatibility of the Aristotelian and the economic views of the world, attempts have repeatedly been made to show that Aristotle's thought prefigures economic thinking of one kind or another. It has sometimes been suggested, for instance, that he held, or got near to holding, a labour theory of value.[6] This is impossible in virtue of quite general features of his thought, and the failure of anglophone scholars to notice this, even scholars who knew Aristotle's writings well, is an indication of how de-Aristotelianized mainstream English-speaking culture had become.

In the classical political economy of Smith and Ricardo, the notions of use value and exchange value are not examined conceptually with any care, the expression of value '5 beds = 1 house' or 'x of commodity $A = y$ of commodity B' is not analysed, and the distinction between *nomos* and *phusis* does not seriously impinge on the discussion. The apparatus of logic and metaphysics, required for the task, was no longer available to them. Furthermore, they both held the views, characteristic of classical political economy, that exchange value is a property intrinsic to products, and that its content is human labour, and since they considered labour as a natural thing belonging to *phusis*, exchange value itself confusedly appeared natural. This route was not open to Aristotle.

According to Aristotle's theory of action, labours are natural activities which differ from each other in each having a different

Modern Continental philosophy. The gap between Aristotle and Descartes has customarily been passed over in silence, a matter of 2,000 years, and teachers and students alike are scarcely aware of it. This practice continues with an agenda set in the seventeenth and eighteenth centuries. When Aristotelian studies returned, they showed the marks of this history. Sir David Ross, the leading anglophone Aristotelian scholar of his generation, was capable of insensitivity to Aristotle's metaphysics, and he sometimes misconstrued aspects of the scientific theories for that reason. Until recently it was fairly commonly thought that in order to rehabilitate Aristotle it was necessary to detach him from 'the Schoolmen', and to show instead how Humean he could be. When category distinctions were reintroduced by Gilbert Ryle, a student of 'school metaphysics', this was widely regarded as originality—as in the context, it was.

[6] Authors attributing a notion of labour to Aristotle are noted in Ch. 7, n. 7.

aim, end, or *telos*. His general principle is that an action 'is defined by its end'.[7] This holds for the Aristotelian tradition as a whole, and when Aquinas asks 'do human acts receive their species from their end?' he answers that they do.[8] Labours or actions cannot therefore be added up or aggregated, and so they could not constitute the uniform substance of something so clearly non-natural, conventional, and undifferentiated as exchange value. The feature that makes beds and houses commensurable could not, for Aristotle, have been labour, because the labours that produced these things were no more commensurable by nature than the things themselves. An attempt to solve the problem of the commensurability of products by having recourse to the notion of the labours that produced them would, for Aristotle, give rise to a logically similar problem about the commensurability of labours. An hour of weaving is not an hour of the same thing as an hour of digging potato-drills. They share duration and perhaps a few accidental features, but that is all, and it isn't much, because actions are defined by their ends.

Marx, adhering to an Aristotelian theory of action, holds actions to be identified and discriminated by their ends, so that kinds of labours are distinct and incommensurable because they have different ends.[9] This is what leads him to distinguish the labour embodied in commodities into two kinds. There are, first, what he calls 'useful labours' (perhaps 'natural labours' would be more appropriate in the context) which produce natural things, or use values. These are discriminated into kinds or species, just as their products are. And, secondly,

---

[7] *NE* 3, 1115ᵇ22. See also *Met. Θ*, 1050ᵃ22–4, where Aristotle says 'the action is the end'.

[8] Aquinas, *Summa Theologiae*, I-II q. 1 a. 3.

[9] The common judgement that Marx is to be reckoned an Enlightenment author needs considerable qualification. He certainly shared many Enlightenment values, and in *The German Ideology* and elsewhere he appears as the enemy of superstition, obscurantism, dogmatism, religion, and authority. But he did not suppose all those things to be summed up in the word 'Aristotelianism', as many of his followers, especially the early ones, did. Marx's relation to the Enlightenment was ambiguous, and analytically he was far removed from the Enlightenment ideal of science associated with the name of La Mettrie, and much closer to Aristotle. See my 'Marx and the Stalinist History Textbook', *Critique*, 27 (1995).

there is what he calls 'abstract labour', which is non-natural (*übernatürlich* is the word he uses), which produces exchange value, and this is all of one kind. Being merely a quantity, it lacks any attribute other than magnitude, and any part of it is commensurable with any other.[10] — Example :

This metaphysical distinction is not one that has to be imaginatively coaxed out of the text. Marx is perfectly explicit about it. He writes in the *Contribution*, which was the dry run for *Capital* written some eight years earlier: 'Let us suppose that one ounce of gold, one ton of iron, one quarter of wheat and twenty yards of silk are exchange values of equal magnitude ... But digging gold, mining iron, cultivating wheat and weaving silk are qualitatively different kinds of labour. In fact, what appears objectively as diversity of the use values, appears, when looked at dynamically, as diversities of the activities which produce those use values.'[11] Since Marx is so explicit, it needs explaining why so many of his expositors, friendly or otherwise, should have missed his main point, as they have in seeing little difference between his theory of value and that of Smith and Ricardo.[12]

The likeliest explanation seems to be a lack of familiarity among Marx's readers with the Aristotelian theory he was working from. This shows partly in a pervasive metaphysical insensitivity to the logic of categories, particularly those of quantity, quality, and relation, which are as crucial to Marx's argument about value as they were to Aristotle's, and partly to a lack of familiarity with the Aristotelian theory of action. The

---

[10] This is in essential respects the modern economic conception of labour, though curiously Marx himself never seems to have drawn attention to its proximity to his own notion of abstract labour.

[11] Marx, *Contribution to a Critique of Political Economy*, 29.

[12] Samuelson quipped that Marx is best seen as 'a minor post-Ricardian', and the quip has often been repeated. The view goes back at least to G. D. H. Cole, who wrote that 'not one single idea in this theory of value was invented by Marx, or would have been regarded by him as an original contribution of his own to economic science. Marx merely took over this conception from the classical economists ... broadly repeating what they had said, and what most economists of the earlier nineteenth century implicitly believed. There is nothing specifically Marxian about Marx's theory of value; what is novel is the use to which he puts the theory, and not the theory itself.' (Introduction to the Everyman edn. of *Capital* (London, 1930), p. xxi.

utilitarian theory of action has had great influence among economically literate readers of all shades of opinion. Utilitarianism recognizes only one end, pleasure or utility, and all actions are means to it. They differ, not by end, but only in their efficacy in promoting the single end they are all supposed to share. This conception of action harmonizes well with the economic concept of 'labour', which aggregates activities without regard to differences of end. Marx found the economic concept of 'labour' peculiar for recognizably Aristotelian reasons, though his expositors seldom have because they seldom grasped those reasons.

If it is supposed, as it was by Marx, that labour is the matter of exchange value (or its 'substance' as Marx was apt to put it), then it cannot have this role in the form of the natural or useful labour which produces use values, as Smith and Ricardo had believed. Such a role can be played only by a metaphysically peculiar kind of labour, one which is homogeneous, uniform, and without quality, or as Marx put it, 'equal human labour, and consequently labour of equal quality [*als gleiche menschliche Arbeit und daher als gleichgeltend ausgedrückt sind*]'.[13] If natural labours were somehow to be at the bottom of this, then they would have to have undergone a metaphysical tranformation into an abstract sort of labour with the same properties as exchange value itself; a transformation from

---

[13] Marx, *Capital*, i. 152. Marx was proud of this distinction because he considered that it overturned Smith and Ricardo, who had held the theory, often mistakenly attributed to Marx himself, that (natural) labour is the substance of value. He writes: 'I was the first to point out and to examine critically this twofold nature of the labour contained in commodities' (*Capital*, i, ch. 1, sect. 2). He only ever claimed to have been original in the discovery of three things, and this distinction is one of them, so it is strange that the precise distinction he had in mind should have been so generally overlooked by his expositors. To suggest, as it sometimes has been, that machinery and de-skilling can by a sociological process turn useful labour into abstract labour is a category mistake, because natural labour cannot be the substance of exchange value, not at any rate without some modulation into a non-natural and quantitative property. Rosdolsky, who is aware of the importance of the distinction, none the less commits the category mistake; *The Making of Marx's Capital*, trans. P. Burgess (London, 1977), 510–12. See also Cohen, who can be at least construed as suggesting the same idea in writing that 'labour becomes abstract under capitalism in a further sense', since the considerations he goes on to offer describe changes in natural labour, *History, Labour, and Freedom* (Oxford, 1988), 194.

something qualitative, which is discriminated into species, into a quantity without species. According to Marx, this transformation is brought about by the process of systematic exchange; it is through the adjustments of prices that labour is allocated in a market economy.[14]

The same problem of the incommensurability of labours faced Smith and Ricardo, but they did not see it. In their day, the word 'labour' had become ambiguous, as it still is. In its first sense, it refers to types of activity, each qualitatively different from the others in requiring different sorts of movements, instruments, and blends of human capacities, and each aiming at its own specific end by which above all it is identified and discriminated from the others. The second sense is the modern economic notion of labour, which is conceived of as a quantity, indifferent to ends and to the distinctions between different types of activity, regarding them all alike as undifferentiated expenditures of a single undifferentiated capacity (which Marx called 'labour-capacity' or 'labour-power'). In this economic sense, labours are discriminated only under the headings of intensity, skill, and duration, which happen to be the very ways in which expenditures of human capacities differ in respect of their productiveness of greater or lesser amounts of exchange value.

Smith and Ricardo failed to distinguish the two senses, and this allowed them to think it was possible to build a bridge, illicit according to Aristotelian metaphysics, across the *nomos–phusis* gap which divides use value and exchange value, a gap of whose existence they appear to have been unaware. Without a clear idea either of substance and its differentiae, or of actions and of ends as their differentiae, and without sensitivity to the *nomos–phusis* gap, Smith and Ricardo cannot keep a firm enough grip on reality to separate what is natural and what is non-natural in labour, and for that reason they cannot formulate clearly the problem of commensurability.[15]

[14] See I. I. Rubin, *Essays on Marx's Theory of Value*, chs. 13–15, for the best available discussion of the transformation and how it is effected by exchange.

[15] Marx's conclusion that products and the labours that produce them are by nature incommensurable follows from the Aristotelian metaphysics and theory of action that

Ricardo, for instance, at the beginning of chapter 1, section 2 of the *Principles*, seems about to recognize the problem of the incommensurability of labours: 'In speaking, however, of labour, as being the foundation of all value, and the relative quantity of labour as almost exclusively determining the relative value of commodities, I must not be supposed to be inattentive to the different qualities of labour, and the difficulty of comparing an hour's or a day's labour, in one employment, with the same duration of labour in another.' Ricardo appears to be about to address matters of quality, intention, and end, which might lead into consideration of the problem of commensurability. But in the next sentence he changes direction: 'The estimation in which different qualities of labour are held, comes soon to be adjusted in the market with sufficient precision for practical purposes, and depends much on the comparative skill of the labourer, and the intensity of the labour performed.'[16] If he had at first got the matters of quality, end, and commensurability in his sights, which is at best doubtful, he veers away from it in his second sentence in order to consider the market estimation of the qualities, not the qualities themselves. In any case, the qualities he has in mind are not those by which activities are identified and discriminated, but only those of skill and intensity, which are more quantitative in nature, and which any execution of any activity has in one degree or another.

Finley remarks that the Greeks had no conception of labour, and that ancient Greek and Latin had no word for it. The ancient world also had no labour markets, and as Finley observes, Marx thought the absence of the concept to be

---

he holds, and it follows from that position that the operations of the market effect a commensuration in each case that can only be artificial and conventional. This commensurated 'labour' is therefore of a single kind, since it is not distinguished by ends. This view has usually been misunderstood in a curious way. It has come to be a standard objection to Marx that he postulates, but cannot prove, a 'reduction' of all labours to a single labour. See e.g. Schumpeter, *Capitalism, Socialism and Democracy*, 24; M. C. Howard and J. E. King, *The Political Economy of Marx*[2] (London, 1985), 123–6.

[16] Ricardo, *Principles of Political Economy and Taxation*, 20.

connected with the absence of labour markets.[17] A collective term for activities would be understood to collect things that have ends, even though it would generalize over them. The term 'labour', however, collects activities as commensurable items, and therefore does so without regard to ends in principle. On Aristotle's theory, this is impossible in principle. A labour theory of value is, for that reason, even more remote from Aristotle's thought than the utility theory of value was seen to be in Chapter 2. When Aristotle himself seems to have most need of the concept of labour, when he is looking for something common to all artefacts or products, he fails to come up with it (see Chapter 7 (2)). The idea of abstract activity, to which ends are simply irrelevant rather than generalized over, can make no sense in Aristotelian philosophy, any more than the idea of an abstract usefulness to which the qualities of useful things are irrelevant rather than just generalized over. Marx thought those ideas made no philosophical sense. He regarded them as conceptual nonsenses which have to be taken seriously because the operations of the market beget them and make them realities of a kind, economic realities. They were, in his view, instances of the perversity and unnaturalness of market society, where 'all that is solid melts into air, all that is holy is profaned', and the natural thing, activity, or person, is

[17] Finley writes that 'Marx believed that there was "an important fact which prevented Aristotle from seeing that, to attribute value to commodities, is merely a mode of expressing all labour as equal human labour, and consequently as labour of equal quality. Greek Society was founded upon slavery, and had, therefore, for its natural basis, the inequality of men and of their labour power." That natural inequality is fundamental to Aristotle's thinking is beyond argument: it permeates his analysis of friendship in the *Ethics* and of slavery in the *Politics*. True, his builder and shoemaker in the exchange paradigm are free men, not slaves, but the concurrent existence of slave labour would still bar his way to a conception of "equal human labour" ', 'Aristotle and Economic Analysis', 38. Finley notes earlier (p. 35) that 'Aristotle does not once refer to labour costs or costs of production. The medieval theologians were the first to introduce this consideration into the discussion, as the foundation of *their* doctrine of just price, and their alleged Aristotelianism in this respect rested on the ambiguity of the Latin translations of Aristotle made available to them in the middle of the thirteenth century.' Finley does not note, and neither explicitly does Marx, the difference regarding ends between the Aristotelian theory of action and the utilitarian one, and the difficulty this would constitute for Aristotle in arriving at such a notion of labour.

supplanted by the economic abstraction, the utility, the service, or the human resource.[18]

Aristotle has no labour theory of value. He simply has no theory of value at all. His contribution is not to have offered such a theory, but to have given a precise formulation of the problem which a theory of value has to solve. Roll seems perfectly justified in concluding that 'While Aristotle is thus responsible for the beginning of a real analysis of the problem of exchange-value, it was not until the rise of the classical political economy of the eighteenth century that a positive theory of value was first developed.'[19] Aristotle's metaphysics was a metaphysics of the solid world of use value, and because of that he was able to frame the problem of exchange value. But he was unable to solve it for the same reason. On his metaphysics, the concepts needed for the solution are conceptual impossibilities.

2

In Aristotelian theory, actions are heterogeneous in virtue of the heterogeneity of their ends, and use value is heterogeneous both in itself and as the end-product of heterogeneous actions. Economics has appeared to overcome the heterogeneity of actions by holding that there is only a single end, 'utility', and it has appeared to overcome the heterogeneity of use value by holding that there is only a single usefulness, utility, in relation to which all things are commensurable. This enforced homogeneity is bought at a price.

Economic theory has ridden roughshod over the category distinction between quality and quantity which holds between use value and exchange value. In the course of its development, economic thought has increasingly suppressed use value as an

---

[18] Marx, *The Communist Manifesto*, in Marx and Engels, *Collected Works* (50 vols.; Moscow, 1975–), vi. 487. For commentary on Marx's phrase, and on his criticism of modernity, see M. Berman, *All that is Solid Melts into Air* (New York, 1982), esp. ch. 2.

[19] Roll, *History of Economic Thought*, 37.

independent category. Smith and Ricardo had distinguished between use value and exchange value, even though they did not probe the distinction with any metaphysical care. Marx, too, recognized the distinction, but unlike Smith and Ricardo he worked painstakingly through the metaphysics of economic value in chapter 1 of *Capital*, although he seems not to have been entirely satisfied with the inquiry, because he took several shots at it and returned to it repeatedly until very late in his life, notably in the *Notes on Wagner*. The conclusion he reached was that use value and exchange value are distinct and largely incompatible ends, which in their natures cannot both be pursued satisfactorily in a society at the same time. The remainder of *Capital*, after chapter 1 is devoted to showing the lawlike nature of market economy as a system organized by, and for, the pursuit primarily of exchange value, and to showing how this entails the systematic subordination of use value and human good. Gudeman and Rivera observe that 'the analytical division between use value and exchange value has remained a central theme only in Marxist economics'.[20]

The distinction between use value and exchange value comes to be progressively elided in the nineteenth and twentieth centuries. In Mill's definition, wealth is 'all useful or agreeable things, which possess exchangeable value'. The elision goes still further with the subsequent appearance of neoclassical economics. Jevons's overriding concern was to replace qualitative economic concepts with quantitative versions of them, and utility was at the top of his list. In the preface to *The Theory of Political Economy* he writes of economics:

I have long thought that it deals throughout with quantities ... I have endeavoured to arrive at accurate quantitative notions concerning Utility, Value, Labour, Capital, &c ... Mathematical readers may think that I have explained some elementary notions, that of degree of utility, for instance, with unnecessary prolixity. But it is to the neglect of economists to obtain clear and accurate notions of

---

[20] S. Gudeman and A. Rivera, *Conversations in Colombia* (Cambridge, 1990), 49. The authors draw interesting and pertinent connections between Aristotle's way of looking at economic matters and Marx's.

quantity and degree of utility that I venture to attribute the present difficulties and imperfections of the science.[21]

By the time Alfred Marshall wrote, some twenty years later, the distinction is mentioned, in the familiar citation from Smith, only to be rejected without argument, and use value itself is dismissed out of hand:

'The word value' says Adam Smith 'has two different meanings, and sometimes expresses the utility of some particular object and sometimes the power of purchasing other goods which the possession of that object conveys.' But experience has shown that it is not well to use the word in the former sense. The value, that is the exchange value, of one thing in terms of another at any time and place, is the amount of that second thing which can be got there and then in exchange for the first. Thus the term value is relative, and expresses the relation between two things at a particular time and place.[22]

One of the advantages that the neo-classical notion of utility seems to have over the classical notion of use value is a practical one: it seems to make possible the aggregation of use values which is needed for purposes of economic calculation. But this aggregation of use values results in practice in ever recurrent problems such as those of national-income accounting. These problems centre on the category difference between quality and quantity. Expressions such as 'output of consumer goods' and 'average price-level of agricultural goods' are inherently problematical, as Wassily Leontief has pointed out:

The operation of determining the magnitude of such artificial aggregative objects—the economic statistician calls them index numbers—involves, in other words, adding pounds or tons of steel and yards or meters of cloth . . . the reduction in qualitative variety

---

[21] W. S. Jevons, *The Theory of Political Economy*[2] (London, 1879), pp. vii–viii. Jevons returned to the question, and he begins the preface to the second edn. of the work by explaining that 'certain new sections have been added, the most important of which are those treating of the *dimensions of economic quantities*. The subject, of course, is one which lies at the basis of all clear thought about the basis of economic science. It cannot be surprising that many debates end in logomachy, when it is still uncertain how many meanings the word value has, or what kind of quantity *utility* itself is.'

[22] Marshall, *Principles of Economics*, 8.

is attained at the cost of ever increasing quantitative indeterminacy.[23]

In tackling what Leontief calls 'the essentially unsolvable problems of so-called index-number theory', the economist 'winds up either with a system of quantitatively well-defined relationships between qualitatively ill-defined variables or with a set of quantitatively indeterminate—or at least loosely described—relationships between sharply defined variables'.[24] If problems of such a kind arise systematically, and if they resist every attempt to resolve them, as these have, it is reasonable to look for a systematic cause. The homogenization of use values, apparently made possible by replacing the notion of use value by that of utility, was desirable for the sake of economic calculation, but the calculations it yields are imperfect because they require the homogenization of use values.

If the economic activities dealt with in economic theory are M–C–M′ in nature, as Smith, Marx, and Keynes thought them to be (see Chapter 5 (5) above), then there is a problem to be faced about how well, or whether, these activities serve human well-being or use value, when they primarily serve another end altogether, exchange value. Smith, Marx, and Keynes each face up to this problem and answer it in their different ways. This is a problem about ends, and it can be formulated at all only if use value (C) and exchange value (M) are distinguished. But if an independent concept of use value is removed from economics, then the distinction is removed, with the consequence that the question of ends cannot be formulated within economics. It is perhaps the most important question that can be asked in respect of economic matters, and whatever answer may be favoured, it does not reflect well on a theory if that theory is incapable even of formulating the question.

---

[23] W. Leontief, 'The Problem of Quality and Quantity in Economics', in his *Essays in Economics: Theories and Theorizing* (Oxford, 1966), 55–6. See also his remarks about the 'production function' in the same essay, 46 ff.

[24] Ibid. 46 ff.

☞ 3 ☜

The notion of utility seemed to promise the fulfilment of an ancient hope. Plato, in his investigation of practical reason in the *Protagoras*, had considered the idea of finding a way of making things that are different in kind commensurable, by reducing qualitative differences to quantitative ones. If that could be done, as Nussbaum notes, the trouble that the diversity of ends causes in life could be overcome, because all ethical and political ends, however they may appear to conflict, could be reduced to a single end. This would allow decision and choice to become clear, uncontentious, and simple. Disputes over values would be resolved without confusion and conflict by having resort to an objective procedure of measurement in a hedonist calculus.[25] Bentham, 'the Newton of the moral sciences', laid the foundation of the claim made on behalf of modern economics to have realized this dream.[26] That foundation was extended by others, including Edgeworth, who, in a work entitled *Mathematical Psychics*, pressed further with the Newtonian ambition:

'Méchanique sociale' may one day take her place along with 'méchanique céleste' throned each upon the double sided height of one maximum principle, the supreme pinacle of moral as of physical science. As the movements of each particle, constrained or loose, in a material cosmos are continually subordinated to one maximum sum total of accumulated energy, so the movements of each soul, whether selfishly isolated or linked sympathetically, may continually be realising the maximum energy of pleasure, the divine love of the universe.[27]

Such intellectual ambition and enthusiasm of expression is not in vogue in economic writing at present. Economics now represents itself as a common-sense and mundane science,

[25] For a discussion of the idea among the Greeks, with parallels to Bentham and Sidgwick, see M. C. Nussbaum, *The Fragility of Goodness* (Cambridge, 1986), 94–117, and for Aristotle's criticism of it, see 294–8.

[26] A classic treatment of the Newtonian ambitions is given in chs. 1 and 2 of Halévy's, *The Growth of Philosophic Radicalism*, trans. Mary Morris (London, 1928).

[27] F. Y. Edgeworth, *Mathematical Psychics* (London, 1881), 12.

modest in its claims and not given to extravagance. Protecting scientific credentials has required for a long time that any connection with Benthamite utilitarianism be denied.[28] Yet plausible deniability is not so easily achieved when it is standard practice to teach that all things are commensurable with one another, even those that are different in kind, that qualitative differences are reducible to quantitative ones, that there exists a single end, utility, and that all rational human behaviour is aimed at maximizing it. These are the most extravagant philosophical claims imaginable, which few philosophers today would take seriously if they thought about them. So it would appear that the modesty and common sense of current economics is a matter of style rather than substance. These grandiose philosophical claims are presented as assumptions which reasonable people can be expected to grant without much in the way of support.

The widespread modern acceptance of the utilitarian conviction that the ancient will-o'-the-wisp of universal commensurability, floated by Plato, had at last been realized, is only partly to be explained by the conceptual penetration of Bentham, Mill, Jevons, Edgeworth, and Wicksteed. Such a grand conclusion would require a grand philosophical infrastructure of proofs to support it, and this has not been supplied by economists any more than it was by Plato. The proofs are still missing. All that has changed is that people generally are now more ready to overlook the omission. The commensurability which the market has established in the exchange of products has come to be extended to everything as a matter of routine. If a market in orphans were to be permitted, it would

---

[28] Such protestations are constantly repeated by Schumpeter in his *History of Economic Thought*. He says of Edgeworth, for example, that he 'did much to keep alive—quite unnecessarily—the unholy alliance between economics and Benthamite philosophy on which I have commented repeatedly. But let me also repeat that in this case, as in that of Jevons, we can leave out the utilitarianism from any of his economic writings without affecting their scientific contents' (pp. 830–1). Economists may have become squeamish about these utilitarian commitments, but there is some recent moral philosophy which might give some comfort; for a discussion and criticism of it, see D. Wiggins, 'Weakness of Will, Commensurability, and the Objects of Deliberation and Desire', in A. Rorty (ed.), *Essays on Aristotle's Ethics* (Berkeley, 1980), 241–65.

produce the exchange value of an orphan.[29] Where there is no market to beget an exchange value for something, special officers make one up. Insurers, actuaries, accountants, and economists have come to be expected to give the exchange value of a kidney, an education, or a life.

☞ 4 ☜

It is quite natural to refer to *NE* 5. 5, and *Pol.* 1. 8–10, as 'Aristotle's economic thought', yet the upshot of the foregoing chapters is that Aristotle did not do any economics, and that no ancient author could have done any. Something needs to be said about this appearance of paradox.

Finley had argued that Aristotle did no economics of any kind, but only ethics. His case was in the main well made and his conclusion seemed inescapable, but it also seemed incredible. Finley had almost entirely missed the inquiry into the nature of exchange value in *NE* 5. 5, and so he was unable to appreciate the value of the contribution Aristotle had made to what later became known as economics. But if Finley's conclusion seemed inescapable that Aristotle did no economics, as I have argued it is, it seems equally inescapable that Aristotle made a contribution to economics, and I have argued for this too. The same considerations apply to the chapters of the *Politics*, since they continue with further aspects of the analysis of exchange value, its development, its forms, and its effects on human behaviour.

The paradoxical appearance lies in the idea that an analysis might be a contribution to economics without itself being economics. But it is not good enough to identify an inquiry as an economic one, just because it is an inquiry into a topic that is classed as 'economic'.[30] The nature of an inquiry is not

---

[29] See R. T. Byrne and J. W. Stone, *Microeconomics*[4] (Glenview, Ill., 1989), 77–8. The authors see the establishment of a market in orphans as a rational procedure for dealing with problems of fostering, not as an abomination.

[30] This is commonly done, as it is, for example, by Langholm, *Wealth and Money*, 48.

decided simply by the subject-matter inquired into. Suicide, for instance, may be the subject of treatments that are legal, anthropological, ethical, or economic. Differences of aim can be decisive in identifying the nature of an inquiry.

Aristotle's aim in *NE* 5. 5 is to elucidate the nature of exchange value, that is, to identify what kind of property it is. It is clearly a property that things acquire in virtue of becoming objects of systematic exchange, but it is not clear exactly what it is, or even to which order of being it belongs. An inquiry aiming to answer questions of this kind is a metaphysical inquiry. It is true that exchange value is a fundamental concept of economics, but it does not follow from this that an inquiry into its nature is itself an economic inquiry. It does follow, however, that economics presupposes the results of metaphysical inquiry into the nature of exchange value. Bailey's account of exchange value as a relation rather than a property, primitive though it may be, is none the less a piece of metaphysics in just this way, and not a piece of economics. So there is no paradox in saying both that Aristotle's analysis in *NE* 5. 5 is a contribution to economics, and that it is not itself economics.[31]

Pol. 1. 8–10, however, is clearly not metaphysics, and it looks a lot more like economics. Its character, however,

[31] In an earlier article, 'Aristotle and the Political Economy of the Polis', *Journal of Hellenic Studies*, 99 (1979), 57–73, I criticized Finley for having overlooked Aristotle's penetrating investigation of the nature of what is now called exchange value, and argued that because of this he had been wrong to conclude that Aristotle did no economics but only ethics. In subsequent correspondence Finley agreed that he had not discussed value, but, unreasonably as it seemed then, he did not budge on his conclusion that Aristotle had done no economic analysis. He was right not to budge; my mistake in that article had been to think that an analysis of exchange value must itself of necessity be a piece of economic analysis. I went on to argue that the kind of economics Aristotle had been doing belonged generically with Marxian political economy. This later prompted Millett to observe that, despite my own pointed criticisms of Lowry's attempts to find prefigurings of economics in ancient authors, I was myself not 'averse to identifying an ancient thinker with a nineteenth century economist' (Millett, *Lending and Borrowing*, 249, n. 31). The point is a good one; the closeness of Marx and Aristotle in their respective analyses of exchange value is best expressed by saying that Marx, like Aristotle, did the metaphysics of exchange value; not that Aristotle, like Marx, did Marxian political economy. The title of the present book, *Aristotle's Economic Thought*, is admittedly an odd one for a book which argues that Aristotle did no economic thought, but it is handy.

depends on its relation to *NE* 5. 5. In the latter discussion Aristotle establishes a category distinction between use value and exchange value, and in the *Politics* he considers the differences between them as ends of action that must flow from this difference of category. He pays particular attention to exchange value as an end of action, and he contrasts the pursuit of it as an end with the pursuit of use value as an end. The controlling principle of the discussion is the good for man, and the judgements he arrives at about exchange value as an end of action are determined in relation to that principle. It is therefore an inquiry about ends: the nature of exchange value as an end, what is involved in pursuing it, the consequences of pursuing it, and its compatibility or otherwise with the overriding end of *politikê*, the good for man. An inquiry about ends of this kind is part of the art of *politikê*, or, in the nearest modern equivalent term, ethics. This was Finley's conclusion, and though he did not draw it for exactly these reasons, the difference of reasons is secondary. Aristotle's discussion is ethical not economic. Economics itself does not consider ends, and indeed it makes a virtue of this.[32] Aristotle's inquiries are therefore ethical and metaphysical, not economic.

☞ 5 ☜

Marx's analysis of exchange value follows out the logic of Aristotle's, and it is worked out on the basis of Aristotelian metaphysics. Yet most of the common arguments usually regarded as fatal to it rest on principles of Humean metaphysics, so that it is fair to say that the case against Marx's theory largely depends on a decision to favour Humean rather than Aristotelian metaphysics. It cannot be claimed that the metaphysical underpinning of the neo-classical theory of value has been well done, or that the Aristotelian metaphysical

---

[32] For an amusing and telling onslaught by an economist on the instrumental view of reason adopted in contemporary economics in preference to a substantive one, see W. F. Campbell, 'Pericles and the Sophistication of Economics', *History of Political Economy*, 15/1 (1983), 122–35.

underpinning of Marx's theory has been adequately evaluated and criticized, yet in spite of all the unanswered questions, the flow of literature on the theory of economic value has almost dried up, and the topic is scarcely considered any longer.

The analysis of exchange value, or economic value, tends to be regarded as properly belonging to economics rather than to philosophy. I have argued that this is a mistake, and that such an analysis must of its nature be metaphysical. But the mistake is not simply one affecting the rights of this or that discipline to handle the question. It is a mistake which affects the capacity of philosophy to discharge what has traditionally been one of its responsibilities. Philosophy has generally been understood to be concerned with coming to understand the world and our place in it; and from the beginning, in the work of Plato and Aristotle, part of the task was seen to be the attempt to understand human social existence. The task facing Plato and Aristotle, however, was different from the task facing philosophers in the modern world, because we have an economic system of exchange value and they did not. Theirs was a world of use value, and they dealt directly, as Lowry puts it, with 'the open book of nature'. Our social world is first and foremost a vast conglomeration of interdependent markets, and we deal with the realm of real natures indirectly through exchange value and markets.

Exchange value does not rest content with becoming the form taken by the products of labour. It is a form that can take as its matter almost anything that humans do and esteem. When exchange value latches onto other activities in this way, as Aristotle was aware, its own peculiar aim is transferred to them. The trouble is that each of those activities, from sport to education, already has an aim or point of its own. Every activity has a point for the sake of which it is pursued, and almost all of them can be pursued for the sake of exchange value as well, or instead. Each can have this nature imposed on it; each can become 'a business'. When exchange value enters an activity, the real end of that activity becomes a means to the end of exchange value, so that the real end is compromised or destroyed. In this way exchange value enters thought, culture, and morals. The nature of everything tends to become secondary to this universal form, and all capacities become particular applications of a single general capacity: 'enterprise'. In this world of parodies, 'everything is another thing, and not what it is', to parody Bishop Butler.

If we are to make as good a job of our task as Plato and Aristotle made of theirs, we need to understand this difference between their world and ours, and that is not possible if exchange value is taken for granted, or consigned to the 'dismal science' of economics. Looked at in this light, the analysis of exchange value is the main problem in modern social philosophy.

BIBLIOGRAPHY

ARISTOTLE: EDITIONS AND TRANSLATIONS

BARKER, E., *The Politics of Aristotle* (Oxford, 1946).
BURNET, J., *The Ethics of Aristotle* (London, 1900).
DIRLMEIER, F., *Aristoteles Nikomachische Ethik* (Berlin, 1966).
GAUTHIER, R. A., and JOLIF, J. Y., *L'Éthique à Nicomaque²* (2 vols.; Paris, 1970).
GRANT, A., *The Ethics of Aristotle* (2 vols.; London, 1874).
IRWIN, T. H., *Aristotle: Nicomachean Ethics* (Indianapolis, 1985).
JACKSON, H., *The Fifth Book of the Nicomachean Ethics of Aristotle* (Cambridge, 1879).
JOACHIM, H. H., *The Nicomachean Ethics* (Oxford, 1951).
JOWETT, B., *The Politics of Aristotle* (Oxford, 1885).
KIRWAN, C., *Metaphyiscs: Books Γ, Δ, and E* (Oxford, 1993).
LORD, C., *Aristotle: The Politics* (Chicago, 1984).
NEWMAN, W. L., *The Politics of Aristotle* (4 vols.; Oxford, 1887–1902).
RACKHAM, H., *The Nicomachean Ethics* (London, 1926).
—— *The Politics* (London, 1932).
ROBINSON, R., *Aristotle's Politics: Books III and IV* (Oxford, 1962).
ROSS, W. D., *Ethica Nicomachea* (Oxford, 1925).
SUSEMIHL, F., and HICKS, D. R., *The Politics of Aristotle* (New York, 1976).
WILLIAMS, R., *The Nicomachean Ethics of Aristotle* (London, 1869).

OTHER WORKS

ACKRILL, J. L. (ed.), *A New Aristotle Reader* (Oxford, 1987).
AMBLER, W., 'Aristotle on Acquisition', *Canadian Journal of Political Science*, 17 (1984), 487–502.
ANSCOMBE, G. E. M., 'Modern Moral Philosophy', *Philosophy*, 33 (1958), 1–19.
AQUINAS, T., *Commentary on the Nicomachean Ethics*, trans. C. I. Litzinger (Chicago, 1964).

Bibliography

ASHLEY, W. J., 'Aristotle's Doctrine of Barter', *Quarterly Journal of Economics*, 9 (1895), 333–41.

AUSTIN, M. M., and VIDAL-NAQUET, P., *Economic and Social History of Ancient Greece: An Introduction* (London, 1977).

AYER, A. J., *Language, Truth and Logic* (London, 1936).

AYERS, M., *The Refutation of Determinism* (London, 1968).

BAILEY, S., *A Critical Dissertation on the Nature, Measures, and Causes of Value* (London, 1825).

BARKER, E., *The Political Thought of Plato and Aristotle* (London, 1906).

BARNES, J., SCHOFIELD, M., and SORABJI, R. (eds.), *Articles on Aristotle* (4 vols.; London, 1975–9).

BASAÑEZ, F., 'El Lugar epistemológico de "lo económico" en Aristóteles', *Thémata*. *Revista de Filosofía*, 12 (1994), 133–70.

BERMAN, M., *All that is Solid Melts into Air* (New York, 1982).

BIEN, G., *Die Grundlegung der politischen Philosophie bei Aristoteles* (Freiburg, 1985).

—— 'Die aktuelle Bedeutung der ökonomischen Theorie des Aristoteles', in B. Biervert, K. Held, and J. Wieland (eds.), *Sozialphilosophische Grundlagen ökonomischen Handelns* (Frankfurt am Main, 1990).

BLAUG, M. (ed.), *Aristotle (384–322 BC)* (Aldershot, 1991).

BÖHM-BAWERK, E. VON., *Karl Marx and the Close of his System*, ed. P. M. Sweezey (London, 1975).

BOLKESTEIN, H., *Economic Life in Greece's Golden Age*, ed. E. J. Jonkers (Leiden, 1958).

BONAR, J., *Philosophy and Political Economy* (London, 1909).

BOOTH, W. J., *Households: On the Moral Architecture of the Economy* (New York, 1993).

BORTKIEWICZ, L. VON, 'War Aristoteles Malthusianer?', *Zeitschrift für die gesamte Staatswissenschaft*, 62 (June 1906), 383–406.

BRAUN, E., 'Zum Aufbau der ökonomik (Aristoteles, *Politik* Buch I), in *Jahreshefte des Österreichischen Archäologischen Institutes*, 42 (1955), 117–35.

BURY, J. B., *The Idea of Progress* (London, 1920).

BYRNE, R. T., and STONE, J. W., *Microeconomics*[4] (Glenview, Ill., 1989).

CAIRNCROSS, A., *Introduction to Economics*[3] (London, 1960).

CALDWELL, B. (ed.), *Carl Menger and his Legacy in Economics* (Durham, 1990).

CALVEZ, J.-Y., and PERRIN, J., *The Church and Social Justice* (London, 1961).

Bibliography

CAMPBELL, W. F., 'Pericles and the Sophistication of Economics', *History of Political Economy*, 15/1 (1983), 122–35.

CANNAN, E., ROSS, W. D., BONAR, J., and WICKSTEED, P. H., 'Who said "Barren Metal"?', *Economica*, 5 (June 1922), 105–11.

CARTLEDGE, P. A., and HARVEY, F. D., *Crux: Essays Presented to G. E. M. de Ste. Croix on his 75th Birthday, History of Political Thought*, 7/1–2 (1985).

CARVER, T., *Marx's Social Theory* (Oxford, 1982).

CASHDOLLAR, S., 'Aristotle's Politics of Morals', *Journal of the History of Philosophy*, 11 (1973), 145–60.

CASTORIADIS, C., 'From Marx to Aristotle, from Aristotle to Us', *Social Research*, 45 (1978), 667–738.

CHANTRAINE, P., *La Formation des noms en grec ancien* (Paris, 1933).

CLARK, S. R. L., *Aristotle's Man: Speculations upon Aristotelian Anthropology* (Oxford, 1975).

COHEN, G. A., *History, Labour, and Freedom* (Oxford, 1988).

COLE, G. D. H., introduction to the Everyman edition of Marx's *Capital* (London, 1930).

COOK WILSON, J., 'Aristotle's Classification of the Arts of Acquisition', *Classical Review*, 10 (1896), 184–9.

COOPER, J. M., 'Aristotle on the Goods of Fortune', *Philosophical Review*, 94/2 (1985), 173–96.

D'ARMS, J. H., *Commerce and Social Standing in Ancient Rome* (Cambridge, Mass., 1981).

DAY, J., and CHAMBERS, M., *Aristotle's History of Athenian Democracy* (Berkeley, 1962).

DEFOURNEY, M., 'Aristote: Théorie économique et politique sociale', *Annales de l'Institut supérieure de philosophie*, 3 (1914), 1–34.

—— *Aristote: Études sur la 'Politique'* (Paris, 1932).

DENZINGER, H., *Enchiridion Symbolorum* (Rome, 1976).

DUNLEAVY, P., and STANYER, J. (eds.), *Contemporary Political Studies 1994* (Proceedings of the Political Studies Annual Conference; Belfast, 1994).

EDELSTEIN, L., *The Idea of Progress in Classical Antiquity* (Baltimore, 1967).

EDGEWORTH, F. Y., *Mathematical Psychics* (London, 1881).

FERGUSON, J., 'Teleology in Aristotle's *Politics*', in A. Gotthelf (ed.), *Aristotle on Nature and Living Things* (Bristol, 1985), 259–73.

FINLEY, M. I., review of Aristotle, *Économique*, ed. B. A. van Groningen and A. Wartelle (1968), *Classical Review*, 20 (1970), 315–19.

—— 'Aristotle and Economic Analysis', *Past & Present*, 47 (1970),

Bibliography

3–25 (reprinted in M. I. Finley (ed.), *Studies in Ancient Society* (London, 1974), 26–52, also in M. Blaug (ed.), *Aristotle (384–322 BC)* (Aldershot, 1991), 150–72, and in J. Barnes, M. Schofield, and R. Sorabji (eds.), *Articles on Aristotle* (4 vols.; London, 1975–9)), ii. 140–58.

—— *The Ancient Economy* (Berkeley, 1973).

FITZGIBBONS, A., *Keynes's Vision: A New Political Economy* (Oxford, 1988).

FLASHAR, H., 'Ethik und Politik in der Philosophie des Aristoteles', *Gymnasium*, 78 (1971), 283–5.

FREDE, M., *Essays in Ancient Philosophy* (Oxford, 1987).

FRITZ, K. VON, and KAPP, E., 'The Development of Aristotle's Political Philosophy and the Concept of Nature', in J. Barnes, M. Schofield, and R. Sorabji (eds.), *Articles on Aristotle* (4 vols.; London, 1975–9), ii.

GARNSEY, P., and SALLER, R., *The Roman Empire* (London, 1990).

GEACH, P. T., 'Aquinas', in G. E. M. Anscombe and P. T. Geach, *Three Philosophers* (Oxford, 1963).

GELESNOFF, W., 'Die ökonomische Gedankwelt des Aristoteles', *Archiv für sozialwissenschaft und sozialpolitik*, 50 (1923), 1–33.

GORDON, B. J., 'Aristotle, Schumpeter and the Metalist Tradition', *Quarterly Journal of Economics*, 75 (1961), 608–14.

—— 'Aristotle and Hesiod: The Economic Problem in Greek Thought', *Review of Social Economy*, 21 (1963), 147–56 (reprinted in M. Blaug (ed.), *Aristotle (384–322 BC)* (Aldershot, 1991), 103–12).

—— 'Aristotle and the Development of Value Theory', *Quarterly Journal of Economics* 78 (1964), 115–28 (reprinted in M. Blaug (ed.), *Aristotle (384–322 BC)* (Aldershot, 1991), 113–26).

—— *Economic Analysis before Adam Smith: Hesiod to Lessius* (London, 1975).

GOTTHELF, A. (ed.), *Aristotle on Nature and Living Things* (Bristol, 1985).

GUDEMAN, S., and RIVERA, A., *Conversations in Colombia* (Cambridge, 1990).

HALÉVY, E., *The Growth of Philosophic Radicalism*, trans. Mary Morris (London, 1928).

HARDIE, W. F. R., *Aristotle's Ethical Theory* (Oxford, 1968).

HARRÉ, R., and MADDEN, E. H., *Causal Powers* (Oxford, 1975).

HEATH, T., *Mathematics in Aristotle* (Oxford, 1949).

Bibliography

HEYLBUT, G., *Commentaria in Aristotelem Graeca* (Berlin, 1892).

HINTIKKA, J., 'Some Conceptual Presuppositions of Greek Political Theory', *Scandanavian Political Studies*, 2 (1967), 11–25.

HOBBES, T., *Leviathan*, ed. R. Tuck (Cambridge, 1991).

HOWARD, M. C., and KING, J. E., *The Political Economy of Marx*[2] (London, 1985).

HUME, D., *An Enquiry Concerning Human Understanding*, ed. L. A. Selby-Bigge (Oxford, 1894).

—— *A Treatise of Human Nature*, ed. L. A. Selby-Bigge (Oxford, 1946).

HUMPHREYS, S. C., 'History, Economics and Anthropology: The Work of Karl Polanyi', *History and Theory*, 8 (1969), 165–212.

IRWIN, T. H., 'Moral Science and Political Theory in Aristotle', in P. A. Cartledge and F. P. Harvey (eds.), *Crux: Essays Presented to G. E. M. de Ste. Croix on his 75th Birthday, History of Political Thought*, 7/1–2 (1985).

—— 'Generosity and Property in Aristotle's Politics', *Social Philosophy and Policy*, 4 (1987).

—— *Aristotle's First Principles* (Oxford, 1988).

JEVONS, W. S., *The Theory of Political Economy*[2] (London, 1879).

—— *Money and the Mechanism of Exchange* (London, 1910).

JOHN PAUL II, Pope, *Veritatis Splendor*, English trans., Catholic Truth Society (London, 1993).

JOHNSON, V., 'Aristotle's Theory of Value', *American Journal of Philology*, 60 (1939), 445–51.

JOSEPH, H. W. B., *The Labour Theory of Value in Karl Marx* (Oxford, 1923).

JUDSON, L., 'Aristotle on Fair Exchange', forthcoming.

KAUDER, E., 'Genesis of the Marginal Utility Theory from Aristotle to the End of the Eighteenth Century', *Economic Journal*, 63 (1953), 638–50 (reprinted in M. Blaug (ed.), *Aristotle (384–322 BC)* (Aldershot, 1991), 42–54).

KAULLA, R., *Die geschichtliche Entwicklung der modernen Werttheorien* (Tübingen, 1906).

KENNY, A. J. P., *Will, Freedom and Power* (Oxford, 1975).

—— *The Aristotelian Ethics: A Study of the Relationship between the Eudemian and Nicomachean Ethics of Aristotle* (Oxford, 1978).

KEYNES, J. M., *Essays in Persuasion* (London, 1931).

—— *The Collected Works of John Maynard Keynes*, xxix (London, 1971).

Bibliography

KEYT, D., 'Three Fundamental Theorems in Aristotle's Politics', *Phronesis*, 32 (1987), 54–75 (reprinted as 'Three Basic Theorems in Aristotle's *Politics*' in id. and F. D. Miller, jun. (eds.), *A Companion to Aristotle's Politics* (Oxford, 1991), 118–41).

—— 'Aristotle's Theory of Distributive Justice', in id. and F. D. Miller, jun. (eds.), *A Companion to Aristotle's Politics* (Oxford, 1991), 238–78.

—— and MILLER, jun., F. D. (eds.), *A Companion to Aristotle's Politics* (Oxford, 1991).

KRAUS, O., 'Die aristotelische Werttheorie in ihren Beziehungen zu den Lehren der modernen Psychologenschule', *Zeitschrift für die gesamte Staatswissenschaft*, 61 (1905), 573–92.

—— *Die Werttheorien* (Brünn, 1937).

LAISTNER, M. L. W., *Greek Economics* (London, 1923).

LANGHOLM, O., *Wealth and Money in the Aristotelian Tradition: A Study in Scholastic Economic Sources* (Oslo, 1983).

—— *The Aristotelian Analysis of Usury* (Oslo, 1984).

LASARTE, J., 'Adam Smith ante la Inquisición y la Academia de la Historia', *Hacienda pública española*, 33–4 (1975), 201–42.

LEONTIEF, W., *Essays in Economics: Theories and Theorizing* (Oxford, 1966).

LEWIS, T. J., 'Acquisition and Anxiety: Aristotle's Case against the Market', *Canadian Journal of Economics* 11 (1978), 69–90 (reprinted in M. Blaug, (ed.), *Aristotle (384–322 BC)* (Aldershot, 1991), 173–94).

LEYDEN, W. VON., *Aristotle on Equality and Justice* (London, 1985).

LOTITO, G., 'Aristotele su moneta scambio bisogni (Eth. Nic. v 5)', *Materiali e discussioni per l'analisi dei testi classici*, 4–6 (Pisa, 1978).

LOWRY, S. T., 'Aristotle's Mathematical Analysis of Exchange', *History of Political Economy*, 1 (1969) 44–66 (reprinted in M. Blaug (ed.), *Aristotle (384–322 BC)* (Aldershot, 1991), 127–45).

—— 'Aristotle's "Natural Limit" and the Economics of Price Regulation", *Greek, Roman, and Byzantine Studies* 15 (1974), 57–63.

—— *The Archaeology of Economic Ideas* (Durham, 1987).

MCCARTHY, G. E., *Marx and the Ancients: Classical Ethics, Social Justice and Nineteenth Century Political Economy* (Savage, Md., 1990).

—— (ed.), *Marx and Aristotle: Nineteenth-Century German Social Theory and Classical Antiquity* (Savage, Md., 1992).

MACINTYRE, A., *After Virtue* (London, 1981).

Bibliography

McMYLOR, P., *Alasdair MacIntyre: A Critic of Modernity* (London, 1994).

McNEILL, D., 'Alternative Interpretations of Aristotle on Exchange and Reciprocity', *Public Affairs Quarterly*, (1990), 55–68.

MACPHERSON, C. B., *Democratic Theory: Essays in Retrieval* (Oxford, 1973).

—— *The Rise and Fall of Economic Justice* (Oxford, 1985).

MARSHALL, A., *Principles of Economics*[4] (London, 1898).

MARX, K., *Theories of Surplus Value* ii (Moscow, 1968).

—— *A Contribution to the Critique of Political Economy* (London, 1971).

—— 'Marginal Notes on Adolph Wagner', in T. Carver (trans. and ed.), *Karl Marx: Texts on Method* (Oxford, 1975).

—— *Capital*, i. (London, 1976).

—— and ENGELS, F., *Collected Works* (50 vols.; Moscow, 1975–).

MEEK, R. L., *Studies in the Labour Theory of Value* (London, 1956).

MEIKLE, S., 'Aristotle and the Political Economy of the Polis', *Journal of Hellenic Studies*, 99 (1979), 57–73.

—— 'Et in Arcadia Chicago', a review article of S. T. Lowry, *The Archaeology of Economic Ideas*, *Polis*, 8/1 (1989), 25–34.

—— 'Aristotle on Equality and Market Exchange', *Journal of Hellenic Studies*, 111 (1991), 193–6.

—— 'The Metaphysics of Substance in Marx', in T. Carver (ed.), *The Cambridge Companion to Marx* (Cambridge, 1991).

—— review of P. Millett, *Lending and Borrowing in Ancient Athens*, *Polis*, 10/1 and 2 (1991), 187–90.

—— 'Aristotle and Exchange Value', in D. Keyt and F. D. Miller, jun. (eds.), *A Companion to Aristotle's Politics* (Oxford, 1991), 156–81 (reprinted in M. Blaug (ed.), *Aristotle (384–322 BC)* (Aldershot, 1991), 195–220).

—— review of Salkever, *Finding the Mean: Theory and Practice in Aristotelian Political Philosophy*, *Philosophical Books*, 32/3 (1991), 144–5.

—— 'Aristotle on Money', *Phronesis*, 39/1 (1994), 26–44.

—— 'Was Marx an Economist?', in P. Dunleavy and J. Stanyer (eds.), *Contemporary Political Studies 1994* (Proceedings of the Political Studies Annual Conference; Belfast, 1994).

—— 'Marx and the Stalinist History Textbook', *Critique*, 27 (1995).

—— 'Aristotle on Business', *Classical Quarterly*, NS 46 (1996), 138–51.

Bibliography

MEILLASSOUX, C., 'Essai d'interprétation du phénomène économique dans les sociétés traditionnelles d'auto-subsistance', *Cahiers d'études africaines*, 4 (1972), 38–67.

MEILLASSOUX, C., 'From Reproduction to Production: A Marxist Approach to Economic Anthropology', *Economy and Society*, 1 (1972), 93–105.

MENENDEZ-PELAYO, M., *Historia de los heterodoxos españoles* (2 vols.; Madrid, 1932).

MILL, J. S., *Principles of Political Economy* (New York, 1969).

MILLETT, P., *Lending and Borrowing in Ancient Athens* (Cambridge, 1991).

MITCHELL, H., *The Economics of Ancient Greece*[2] (Cambridge, 1957).

MOREAU, J., 'Aristote et la monnaie', *Revue des études grecques*, 82 (1969), 349–64.

MULGAN, R. G., *Aristotle's Political Theory* (Oxford, 1977).

NICHOLS, M. P., *Citizens and Statesmen: A Study of Aristotle's Politics* (Savage, Maryland, 1992).

NUSSBAUM, M. C., *The Fragility of Goodness* (Cambridge, 1986).

—— 'Nature, Function and Capability: Aristotle on Political Distribution', *Oxford Studies in Ancient Philosophy*, suppl. vol. (1988), 145–84.

O'MEARA, D. (ed.), *Studies in Aristotle* (Washington, 1981).

PARETO, V., *Manual of Political Economy*, trans. A. Schwier, ed. A. Schwier and A. Page (London, 1971).

PLEKET, H. W., 'Technology in the Greco-Roman World: A General Report', *Talanta*, 5 (1973), 6–47.

PÖHLMANN, R. VON, *Geschichte des antiken Sozialismus und Kommunismus* (2 vols.; 1893 and 1901; 3rd. edn. entitled *Geschichte der Sozialen Frage und des Sozialismus in der antiken Welt*, 1925).

POLANYI, K., 'Aristotle Discovers the Economy', in G. Dalton (ed.), *Primitive, Archaic and Modern Economies* (New York, 1968).

—— ARENSBERG, C. M., and PEARSON, H. W. (eds.), *Trade and Market in the Early Empires* (Glencoe, Ill., 1957).

RAPHAEL, D. D., *British Moralists: 1650–1800* (2 vols.; Oxford, 1969).

RICARDO, D., *The Principles of Political Economy and Taxation*, ed. P. Sraffa (Cambridge, 1986).

RITCHIE, D. G., 'Aristotle's Subdivisions of Particular Justice', *Classical Review*, 7 (1894), 185–92.

ROBBINS, L., *The Nature and Significance of Economic Science* (London, 1932).

Bibliography

ROBIN, L., *Greek Thought* (London, 1928).

ROBINSON, J., *Economic Philosophy* (London, 1964).

ROLL, E., *A History of Economic Thought* (London, [1938] 1961).

ROSDOLSKY, R., *The Making of Marx's Capital*, trans. P. Burgess (London, 1977).

ROSEN, F., 'The Political Context of Aristotle's Categories of Justice', *Phronesis*, 20 (1975), 228–40.

ROSS, W. D., *Aristotle*, rev. edn. (London, 1949).

ROWE, C. J., *The Eudemian and Nicomachean Ethics: A Study in the Development of Aristotle's Thought* (Proceedings of the Cambridge Philological Society, supp. 3; Cambridge, 1971).

RUBIN, I. I., *Essays on Marx's Theory of Value* (Detroit, 1972).

RUSSELL, B., *The Principles of Mathematics*[2] (London, 1903).

STE CROIX, G. E. M. DE, 'Greek and Roman Accounting', in A. C. Littleton and B. S. Yamey (eds.), *Studies in the History of Accounting* (London, 1956), 14–74.

—— review of K. Polanyi, C. M. Arensberg, and H. W. Pearson, *Trade and Market in the Early Empires*, *Economic History Revue*, 2nd. ser., 12 (1959–60), 510–12.

—— 'Ancient Greek and Roman Maritime Loans', in H. Edey and B. S. Yamey (eds.), *Debits, Credits, Finance and Profits*, (London, 1974).

—— *The Class Struggle in the Ancient Greek World* (London, 1981).

SALOMON, M., *Der Begriff der Gerechtigkeit bei Aristoteles* (New York, 1979).

SAMUELSON, P., *Economics*[8] (New York, 1970).

SCHUMPETER, J., *Capitalism, Socialism and Democracy*[4] (London, 1952).

—— *Economic Doctrine and Method*, trans. R. Aris (London, 1954).

—— *History of Economic Analysis* (Oxford, 1954).

SELBY-BIGGE, L. A. (ed.), *British Moralists* (Oxford, 1897).

SEN, A., *On Ethics and Economics* (Oxford, 1987).

SINGER, K., 'Oikonomia: An Inquiry into the Beginnings of Economic Thought and Language', *Kyklos*, 11 (1958).

SMITH, A., *The Wealth of Nations*, ed. Edwin Cannan (2 vols.; London, 1904).

SMITH, B., 'Aristotle, Menger, Mises: An Essay in the Metaphysics of Economics', *History of Political Economy*, suppl. to vol. 22 (1990), 263–88 (reprinted in B. Caldwell (ed.), *Carl Menger and his Legacy in Economics* (Durham, 1990), 263–88).

SMITH, R. S., 'The *Wealth of Nations* in Spain and Hispanic America, 1780–1830', *Journal of Political Economy*, 65 (1957), 104–25.

Bibliography

SOUDEK, J., 'Aristotle's Theory of Exchange: An Inquiry into the Origin of Economic Analysis', *Proceedings of the American Philosophical Society*, 96 (1952), 45–75 (reprinted in M. Blaug (ed.), *Aristotle (384–322 BC)* (Aldershot, 1991), 11–41).

SPENGLER, J. J., 'Aristotle on Economic Imputation and Related Matters', *Southern Economic Journal* (1955), 371–89.

SPIEGEL, H. W., *The Growth of Economic Thought* (Englewood Cliffs, NJ, 1971).

SPRINGBORG, P., 'Aristotle and the Problem of Needs', *History of Political Thought*, 5 (1984), 393–424.

SWEEZEY, P. M., *The Theory of Capitalist Development* (Oxford, 1942).

TAWNEY, R. H., *Religion and the Rise of Capitalism* (London, 1926).

THOMPSON, W. E., 'The Athenian Entrepreneur', *L'Antiquité classique*, 51 (1982), 53–85.

TREVER, A. A., *A History of Greek Economic Thought* (Chicago, 1916).

URBAIN, Y., 'Les Idées économiques d'Aristophane', *L'Antiquité classique*, 8 (1939), 183–200.

VONDELING, J., *Eranos* (Groningen, 1961).

WEIL, R., *La Politique d'Aristote* (Entretiens sur l'antiquité classique; Geneva, 1965).

—— 'Aristotle's View of History', in J. Barnes, M. Schofield, and R. Sorabji (eds.), *Articles on Aristotle* (4 vols.; London, 1975–9), ii. 202–17.

WELSKOPF, E. C., 'Marx und Aristoteles', in J. Burian and L. Vidman (eds.), *Antiquitas Graecoromana et Tempora Nostra* (Prague, 1968).

WIGGINS, D., *Sameness and Substance* (Oxford, 1980).

—— 'Weakness of Will, Commensurability, and the Objects of Deliberation and Desire', in A. Rorty (ed.), *Essays on Aristotle's Ethics* (Berkeley, 1980), 241–65.

—— *Needs, Values, Truth* (Oxford, 1987).

WILL, É., 'De l'aspect éthique des origines grecques de la monnaie', *Revue historique*, 212 (1954), 209–31.

—— 'Trois quarts de siècle de recherches sur l'économie grecque antique', *Annales*, 9 (1954), 7–22.

WILLIAMS, B., *Morality* (Cambridge, 1972).

WOOD, E. M., *Peasant-Citizen and Slave: The Foundations of Athenian Democracy* (London, 1988).

WORLAND, S. T., 'Aristotle and the Neoclassical Tradition: The Shifting Ground of Complementarity', *History of Political*

Bibliography

Economy, 16 (1984), 107–34 (reprinted in M. Blaug (ed.), *Aristotle (384–322 BC)* (Aldershot, 1991)).

ZIMMERN, A. E., 'Suggestions towards a Political Economy of the Greek City State', in his *Solon and Croesus* (Oxford, 1928), 165–99.

—— *The Greek Commonwealth*[5] (Oxford, 1931).

ZMAVC, J., 'Die Geldtheorie und ihre Stellung innerhalb der wirtschafts- und sozialwissenschaftlichen Anschauungen des Aristoteles', *Zeitschrift für die gesamte Staatswissenschaft*, 58 (1902), 48–79.

—— 'Die Werttheorie bei Aristoteles und Thomas von Aquino', *Archiv für die Geschichte der Philosophie*, 12 (1899), 407–33.

INDEX

Index

Index

Index